Time Out
ADVENTURE!

Time Out Guides Ltd
Universal House
251 Tottenham Court Road
London W1T 7AB
United Kingdom
Tel: +44 (0)20 7813 3000
Fax:+44 (0)20 7813 6001
Email:guides@timeout.com
www.timeout.com

Published by Time Out Guides Ltd, a wholly owned subsidiary of Time Out Group Ltd.
Time Out and the Time Out logo are trademarks of Time Out Group Ltd.

© **Time Out Group Ltd 2009**

10 9 8 7 6 5 4 3 2 1

This edition first published in Great Britain in 2009 by Ebury Publishing.
A Random House Group Company
20 Vauxhall Bridge Road, London SW1V 2SA

Random House Australia Pty Ltd 20 Alfred Street, Milsons Point, Sydney, New South Wales 2061, Australia
Random House New Zealand Ltd 18 Poland Road, Glenfield, Auckland 10, New Zealand
Random House South Africa (Pty) Ltd Isle of Houghton, Corner Boundary Road & Carse O'Gowrie, Houghton 2198, South Africa

Random House UK Limited Reg. No. 954009

For further distribution details, see www.timeout.com.

ISBN: 978-1-84670-140-5

A CIP catalogue record for this book is available from the British Library.

Printed and bound by Firmengruppe APPL, aprinta druck, Wemding, Germany.

The Random House Group Limited supports The Forest Stewardship Council (FSC), the leading
international forest certification organisation. All our titles that are printed on Greenpeace approved
FSC certified paper carry the FSC logo. Our paper procurement policy can be found at
http://www.rbooks.co.uk/environment.

Time Out carbon-offsets its flights with Trees for Cities (www.treesforcities.org).

'WE LIVE IN A WONDERFUL WORLD THAT IS
FULL OF BEAUTY, CHARM AND ADVENTURE.
THERE IS NO END TO THE ADVENTURES
THAT WE CAN HAVE IF ONLY WE SEEK THEM
WITH OUR EYES OPEN.'

JAWAHARLAL NEHRU

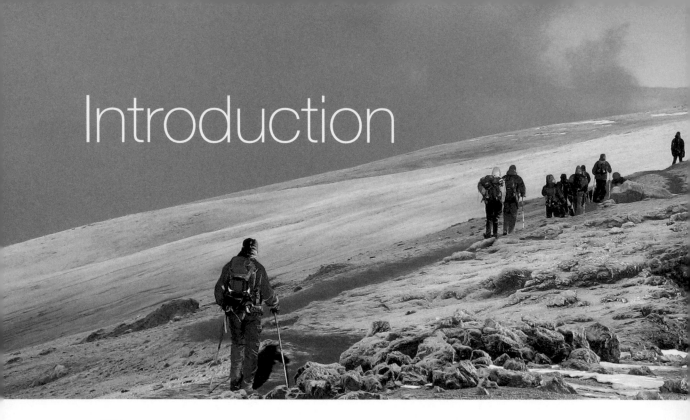

Introduction

Since Victorian men and women started to collect bugs, gallop across the plains and row up uncharted rivers for the sheer joy of getting their frocks and frock coats dirty, there has been adventure travel. It's a back-to-nature thing, a tiredness with tourism's more mainstream offerings. Your average mid-rank 1850s toff probably thought the prospect of a Grand Tour a bind and a bore, and Florence – for all its domes – was just another city, another queue and another supper with Aunt Matilda.

It's the same today. In increasing numbers, we are using travel as an opportunity to move, exercise, refresh and reboot – more, that is, than a consumer fix. And the range of countries and trails and experiences on offer today means we can all be a Charles Darwin or an Isabella Bird, at least for 14 nights a year. Nowadays, it's probably airless offices, commuting, round-the-clock news and wall-to-wall carpeting that hem in the human spirit, but the urge to travel adventurously is much the same: if we can't be Spanish conquistadores in our working life, we're going to make up for it in our leisure time.

Even so-called 'soft' adventures – sweat-free activities such as rambling, riverboat trips and hot-air ballooning – will open up new vistas, and introduce the mind to new flora, fauna and weather systems. Tougher adventurers get kitted out in fluorescent Lycra, neoprene and Gore-Tex linings to do all sorts of impractical activities (kitesurfing, snowboarding, rafting) – and, suspended over an abyss, or bouncing around on white water, we get a healthy adrenalin boost, and a sense of well-being.

Adventure tourism is booming. It sits neatly with a general desire to be greener and leaner. If you travel independently, you'll meet likeminded people and deal directly with informed local guides, drivers and cooks – not to mention lions, caimans and rhinos. But sometimes it's wise, necessary or more relaxing to book ahead and go with a group. The best tour operators take small groups, and make use of local skills, hotels and cuisine – and invest in local businesses.

An adventure also sets you up for life's other challenges – work, study, family, routine, relationships. Think of it like therapy without the

clock and couch, or a spa without all the daft ointments. When we get back from adventure travels, we have some colour in our cheeks, a new muscle or two, and some annoyingly (for friends and colleagues) out-there photographs to remind us of our great escape, and prompt us to plan the next one as soon as time and money allow.

ABOUT THE BOOK

Attempting to steer clear of adventure clichés, we have cherry-picked dozens of diverse and exciting experiences from all corners of the world – from wilderness wanderings, volcano climbs and canoe expeditions to snow safaris, epic rail journeys and foodie explorations.

Adventure! has been compiled with achievability in mind, and is packed with accessible challenges that don't demand decades of training, or prohibitively expensive equipment – and can comfortably be squeezed into your annual leave. Which isn't to say you won't sometimes need time to mentally prepare – or that you will always be in your comfort zone – but you won't need to give up your day job. Unless, that is, you get hooked…

Turn to page 254 for a world map; page 246 for essential information and advice on tour operators and travel; and page 12 for our author credentials. Now, go forth and adventure!

Ismay Atkins
Editor
Time Out Adventure!

Chris Moss
Travel editor
Time Out magazine

All information was correct as we went to press, but prices, itineraries and conditions can change, so we advise you check all details carefully before booking a trip. Many of these adventures can be tackled by anyone with good all-round physical fitness and an adventurous outlook. Others are very demanding and may require an intermediate level in the sport (for example, surfing, kiteboarding, diving). In all cases, plan ahead and assess your fitness before taking on a challenge – if in doubt consult your tour operator.

Contents

114

42

18 WILD HORSES
Horseride along the old Silk Road through the Tian Shan mountains of Kyrgyzstan

24 THE OTHER INCA TRAIL
High-altitude **Inca trail** from the Sacred Valley to the citadels of Choquequirao and Machu Picchu

29 WALKING WITH WARRIORS
Foot safari with Samburu tribesmen in the Leroghi Mountains of northern Kenya

37 WILD LIFE
Bear-watching and volcano ascent in the wilds of the Kamchatka Peninsula, Eastern Siberia

42 CASTLES IN THE SAND
Walk across the **Libyan Sahara**

48 TOP OF THE WORLD
Climb Iran's **Mount Damavand** in the Alborz Mountains

58 PLEASURE AND PAINE
Wilderness trek in Torres del Paine, southern Patagonia

66 SNOW MOTION
Dog-sledding expedition in the Arctic Circle, northern Norway

74 DIVING INTO THE ABYSS
Scuba-dive the Silfra crack between two continents in Thingvellir Lake, Iceland

74

108

66

182

142

132

Make the most of London life

Who we are

EDITORIAL

Editor Ismay Atkins
Deputy Editor Edoardo Albert
Copyeditors Matt Chesterton, Janice Fuscoe, Phil Harriss
Consultant Editor Chris Moss
Proofreader Tamsin Shelton

Managing Director Peter Fiennes
Editorial Director Ruth Jarvis
Series Editor Will Fulford-Jones
Business Manager Dan Allen
Editorial Manager Holly Pick
Assistant Management Accountant Ija Krasnikova

DESIGN

Art Director Scott Moore
Art Editor Pinelope Kourmouzoglou
Senior Designer Henry Elphick
Graphic Designers Kei Ishimaru, Nicola Wilson
Advertising Designer Jodi Sher

PICTURE DESK

Picture Editor Jael Marschner
Deputy Picture Editor Lynn Chambers
Picture Researcher Gemma Walters
Picture Desk Assistant Marzena Zoladz
Picture Librarian Christina Theisen

ADVERTISING

Commercial Director Mark Phillips
International Advertising Manager Kasimir Berger
International Sales Executive Charlie Sokol
Advertising Sales (Mallorca) Margarita Calderón Blanco

MARKETING

Marketing Manager Yvonne Poon
**Sales & Marketing Director, North America
 & Latin America** Lisa Levinson
Senior Publishing Brand Manager Luthfa Begum
Marketing Designer Anthony Huggins

PRODUCTION

Group Production Director Mark Lamond
Production Manager Brendan McKeown
Production Controller Damian Bennett
Production Coordinator Julie Pallot

TIME OUT GROUP

Chairman Tony Elliott
Chief Executive Officer David King
Group General Manager/Director Nichola Coulthard
Time Out Communications Ltd MD David Pepper
Time Out International Ltd MD Cathy Runciman
**Time Out Magazine Ltd Publisher/
 Managing Director** Mark Elliott
Group IT Director Simon Chappell
Marketing & Circulation Director Catherine Demajo

MAPS

Pinelope Kourmouzoglou

PHOTOGRAPHY

Front cover Fox Glacier, New Zealand © StockShot/Alamy.
Back cover Top left: courtesy of Explore; top right Steve Bly/Alamy; middle Henry Wismayer; bottom Buzz Pictures/Alamy.
Photography Alamy Images except; pages 3, 43, 44 (left), 46 courtesy of www.walksworldwide.com; pages 4, 5 Alex Ekins; 6 (left), 94, 95, 116, 117, 118 Alf Anderson; pages 6 (right), 8 (right), 31 (top), 32, 38 (top), 39, 40, 44 (bottom), 80, 112 (top), 136 (left), 148, 149, 151, 192, 193, 195 (right), 196 (left), 220, 224, 225, 226 courtesy of Explore; pages 7 (left), 13, 76, 78 James Burns; pages 7 (middle), 108, 110, 111, 112 (bottom) Helen Gilchrist; pages 9 (middle), 232, 233 Courtesy of Utah Olympic Park; page 9 (right), 162, 163, 177, 178 (left & bottom), 180 courtesy of the Des Moines Register; pages 16, 17, 19, 20 (top), 22 (left) courtesy of Wild Frontiers; pages 20 (bottom), 21, 22 (right) Kathryn Miller; pages 24, 26, 38 (left), 40 (left), 190, 195 (left), 196 (bottom) Chris Moss; pages 31 (bottom), 33, 34, 35, 103, 104 courtesy of Wilderness Scotland; pages 45, 46 (left) J R Lickiss; pages 48, 50, 51, 52, 53, 54 Henry Wismayer; pages 59 (bottom), 60, 62 Ismay Atkins; page 63 Courtesy Indigo Hotel; page 70 Courtesy of The Border Inn; pages 96, 99, 100 James Mutter; page 120, 122, 123, 124 (left) Daniel Nielson; page 130 Diego M. Loiacono; pages 132, 134, 135, 136 (right), 138 Claire Boobyer; page 141 Karl Baz; page 145, 146 Jeffrey Chock; page 150 www.monkeyshrine.com; pages 154, 155 Guy Dimond; page 160 (left) Amar Grover; page 165 Jubilee Sailing Trust; page 166, 167 M.S. Stonehouse; page 170, 171, 172, 173 Simon Richmond; page 174 courtesy of the South Africa Tourist Board; page 175 Cape Town Time Out; page 178-179 Alan Whitaker; page 184 (right), 185 (bottom) Damian Hall; page 186 Jason Friend; page 204 (top right) Ben Rosenzweig; page 214 (bottom & top right) McCoy-Wynne/Natural England; page 218, 219 (top & right) Chris Pierre; pages 235, 238 (left) Tania Richards; page 236 Donald Bremner; page 237, 238 Cyrus Shahrad; pages 242, 244 (top) Water by Nature UK.

Special thanks to: Nick King and all at Alamy, Karl Baz, Jeffrey Chock, Stevie Christie, Corinne Hitching, J R Lickiss, Diego Loiacono, Maureen Stonehouse, Chloe Watson, Alan Whitaker, Mike Wynne.

Contributors

ISMAY ATKINS

Ismay Atkins, the Editor of this book, has lived in Buenos Aires, Havana and Mexico – and recently moved to the wild west of Cornwall. For *Adventure!*, she acquainted herself with the complex world of thermal base layers for a first foray into the world of super-sub-zero temperatures: to Arctic Norway to see what minus 25 feels like (see page 66). She has edited *Time Out* guides to Stockholm, Shanghai and Havana.

RUTH JARVIS

Time Out Guides Editorial Director Ruth Jarvis is a former editor of *Cycing Today* magazine and has crossed not only Iowa on her bike but also France, Spain, England and the Chilean Andes, none of them very quickly. She has travelled widely in the US, particularly in the Southwestern deserts, racking up around 25,000 miles of road trips.

CHRIS MOSS

Time Out London magazine Travel editor Chris Moss got roped into adventure tourism because other journalists had bagged all the boutique hotels, luxury weekend breaks and posh pith-helmetted safaris. His most recent big adventures were in the Mongolian Altai, Patagonia and Antarctica – and Wales. 'You don't have to go very far to find adventure,' he says. 'Hopefully, the credit crisis will draw people away from treks to the high street and get them back into the hills.' Chris is the author of *Patagonia: A Cultural History*.

JOE MACKIE

edits the Adventure section of *Men's Health* magazine, which has taken him quad biking the sand dunes of the Namib desert and snowboarding down a volcano in Chile. His Silfra scuba dive (page 74) is the closest he's come to the centre of the earth.

YOLANDA ZAPPATERRA

lives in London but would like to live in Trinidad, where she could practise chippin' and whinin' so that next time she covers carnival (see page 142), she'll be up for doing it in a bikini. She is a regular contributor to *Time Out London*.

DANIEL NEILSON

is a freelance journalist with a long-standing passion for football – and a new passion for paddling (see pages 120 & 102). He has written about derbies and interviewed fans and hooligans in Siberia, Paraguay, Chile, Colombia and Argentina.

ALF ALDERSON

is an award-winning travel and adventure sports journalist and photographer whose work appears regularly in various UK newspapers and magazines. He is based in Pembrokeshire but spends much of the year travelling in search of perfect surf and snow.

LIBBY PURVES

has been sailing small boats for 36 years but in 1999 discovered the buzz of square-riggers. She has crewed in six Tall Ships' Races in the North Sea, Baltic and Atlantic and still sails a humbler boat with her husband Paul Heiney. In the remaining time she is a novelist, broadcaster and *Times* columnist. She has given up climbing the rigging due to cowardice and a bad knee. Her new book is *Shadow Child*.

MATT CHESTERTON

is a confirmed landlubber who gets queasy on a pedalo; but even he was excited at the prospect of an Antarctic cruise. This was his first real adventure and, perhaps uniquely for a tourist to Antarctica, only his third continent. When not snacking on krill, Matt works for a new media start-up.

Get the local experience

Over 50 of the world's top destinations available.

GUY DIMOND

Guy Dimond has been the Food & Drink Editor of *Time Out London* since 1998. A former travel writer, he has eaten fugu (poisonous puffer fish) in Japan, fermented shark in Iceland, and – worst of all - deep-fried pizza in Scotland.

HENRY WISMAYER

divides his time between working for the man in the civil service, and working for himself as a freelance adventure travel writer. He scaled the heights of Mount Damavand for this book (see page 48).

CLAIRE BOOBBYER

is a London-based writer and photographer. She has been fascinated with wildlife ever since a piranha in Bolivia bit her and she caught a flesh-eating tropical disease through a sandfly in the Peruvian jungle.

WILL FULFORD-JONES

Since writing his undergraduate thesis on Jack Kerouac, *Time Out* City Guides Series Editor Will has logged innumerable miles behind the wheel in America. His favourite drive is along the Blue Ridge Parkway; his least favourite is anywhere in LA during rush hour.

JULIE DAVIDSON

is an award-winning writer with a special interest in African travel – she is currently working on a book on the life and journeys of Mary Livingstone, wife of David Livingstone. The walking safari in the remote Leroghi Mountains of northern Kenya (see page 29) was one of her most exciting to date.

CYRUS SHAHRAD

dreams about the perfect powder at least once a week – dreams now set entirely in Japan (see page 96). The former editor of a snowboard magazine, he has – in 17 years of riding – started one avalanche, concussed himself twice and broken several fingers, but no limbs.

'DO NOT GO WHERE THE PATH MAY
LEAD, GO INSTEAD WHERE THERE IS
NO PATH AND LEAVE A TRAIL.'

RALPH WALDO EMERSON

The road less travelled

Wild horses

Horseriding the old Silk Road through Kyrgyzstan, **Kathryn Miller** discovers a land of celestial mountains, empty plateaux and lonely yurts.

WHAT	**HOW LONG**
Mountain trek on horseback	Eight days
WHERE	**THRILL FACTOR**
Tian Shan mountain range, Kyrgyzstan	● ● ● ● ○

On a quest for the ultimate odyssey on horseback, thoughts turn naturally to the American West: big skies, wide open prairies, cowboys and hearty camp food. But I wound up tapping into a far older equestrian culture: my bracing excursion was to cross the remote Tian Shan ('Mountains of Heaven'), a 930-mile range stretching from Kazakhstan through Kyrgyzstan into China, on horseback.

Few people can spell the name of this young nation, let alone pronounce it (it's 'Kir-gih-stan'), plot it on a map (between China and Kazakhstan) or choose it as a holiday destination. Yet Kyrgyzstan is a land of startlingly raw beauty, its wild, untouched plains and rugged mountain ranges (over 80 in total) offering an enormous blank canvas for adventure – landscapes, steeped in nomadic tradition, just made for horses.

BEGINNING IN BISHKEK

When I stepped off the plane in Bishkek, the capital of Kyrgyzstan, the air was dry and hot, even at two in the morning. At the foot of the steps stood a handful of policemen in Soviet-era visor caps holding big guns. I met my group – ten UK vacationers and our hosts Dom, an Italian now living in Kyrgyzstan, and Essex-born farrier Jonathan – and after a quick round of the sights of leafy Bishkek (a city whose Soviet legacy is still palpable in its austere architecture and wide boulevards), we set off on the two-day jeep ride to the remote mountain lake of Son Kul to pick up our horses.

Son Kul provided the first real insight into the isolation, tranquillity and unspoiled beauty of this little-explored country: there were no tarmac ribbons bisecting the landscape, no pylons, no aeroplanes and no brick buildings. Just a few yurts and grazing livestock, and a sweeping mountain backdrop.

RIDING THE SILK ROAD

As we drove, we planned our route. From Son Kul we'd ride to Sari Tash in the south-west of the country, via Kashka Suu, over the Dawan Pass and along the Kek Suu River and the Chinese border. It was a route that would cover 180 miles

'NO TARMAC RIBBONS BISECTING THE LANDSCAPE, NO PYLONS, NO AEROPLANES, NO BRICK BUILDINGS. JUST A FEW YURTS AND GRAZING LIVESTOCK, AND A SWEEPING MOUNTAIN BACKDROP.'

– as the crow would never fly – and take eight days, with six hours in the saddle each day.

We'd be riding part of the legendary Silk Road, the network of ancient trade routes that, for some 2,000 years, linked China with Europe. This was also the country where the Great Game was played out, the landscape across which gung-ho young Victorian officers took on Tsarist Russia in a surreptitious war to control the area between the Caucasus and China.

As we rode we passed remote farms and villages where residents waved while staring in bemusement at our cowboy hats. The wildlife added to a sense of the mysterious East colliding with the Wild West – vultures, a lone Bactrian camel and herds of wild horses – and the terrain was just as diverse: we enjoyed long gallops across grassy plateaux and entrusted our lives to our surefooted mounts to traverse razor-like ridges and ride up deep gorges.

When not in the saddle, we indulged in Lilia's sensational stir-fries and thigh-soothing dips in freshwater rivers. I learned to remove saddlebags at lunchtime (the horses had a tendency to roll), and that a traditional *shyrdak* (felt rug) is a much more effective barrier against the cold than any self-inflating camping mat.

The riding was hard but rewarding. The landscape was epic and timeless – and that's not mere hyperbole; if Genghis Khan galloped into

Kyrgyzstan today he'd doubtless feel completely at home. The nights were as thrilling as the days – I spent hours gazing up at the night sky, unpolluted by light and smog.

LONE ON THE RANGE

By late afternoon on Sunday, a week after we had started out, we pitched our tents by a babbling brook at Arpa, a remote flat expanse of grassland with a 360-degree mountain panorama as a backdrop; the snowcapped peaks of the Chinese border could be seen in the distance. It was our first camp without back-up crew – and we were alone, miles from civilisation. Without proper lamps to provide light we ate long before dusk, took photos of the setting sun and, as the last rays of light faded, shared out the beer ration.

Saddling up at 9am the following day, we planned to cross the Ferghana Range and meet Lilia for supper. The sun shone all morning as the horses headed west across lush pasture punctuated by marmot holes. We covered around 40 miles – the terrain was filled with valleys, which slowed progress and involved crossing several full-flowing rivers. Riding along tracks that probably hadn't been used by humans since the end of the USSR and co-operative farming, we didn't see another soul.

Realising we weren't going to cross the pass before dusk, we decided to stop and set up camp, pitching the tents on a steep slope. At an altitude of 10,498 feet, it was going to be a cold night. We were on to emergency rations: dinner was chicken noodle soup and, as we'd finished the beer, we left off socialising and retreated to our cosy two-man tents. The roar of a nearby waterfall was the only sound.

The following morning, the clear blue skies had been replaced with some menacing clouds

and glacial winds. Dressed in waterproofs, we saddled up and, at 9.30am, headed up and up, towards where we hoped to locate the pass. An hour later we were immersed in cloud, visibility was low, the air temperature had plummeted and it started to snow.

GETTING HIGH

While negotiating the second high-altitude pass that day I was convinced we'd be camping wild again and began to give serious thought to catching a marmot for supper. It was a relief when, from the top of the pass, we established the exact whereabouts of the valley we needed and were able to plot our descent. We were 4,000 metres above sea level and the only way down was to walk along a narrow scree ridge. Hungry and in air short of oxygen, we were all shattered. Ali, an Army officer and one of the most practical members of the group, was battling vertigo.

'I can't think of anything I'd rather be doing right now… except pushing pins underneath my fingernails,' she complained.

Two and a half hours later, I was sitting on my horse staring down at two mouthwatering rounds of freshly baked bread. The lady proffering the plate was smiling. 'Rahmat, rahmat, rahmat,' I grinned ravenously, and tore off a chunk to dip in a dish of fresh cream. The Kyrgyz custom is to remain mounted on your horse if your visit is brief; if you dismount and are invited to drink tea it's rude to refuse. So we stayed in our saddles, grateful to this family who'd given away their day's bread to a group of strangers. A few hours later, we were reunited with the ground crew, hot water, cold beer and Lilia's fabulous feasts.

Riding under searing sun across dusty landscapes, wild camping on the side of a mountain and not seeing a soul for days had given me a taste of just how solitary life can get

'THE NIGHTS WERE AS THRILLING AS THE DAYS – I SPENT HOURS GAZING UP AT THE NIGHT SKY, UNPOLLUTED BY LIGHT AND SMOG.'

on the steppes. Riding across Kyrgyzstan might be easier now than in the past, but it's still adventurous – and full of pitfalls. It's also the only way to feel a connection with the nomads who've roamed across this region for millennia.

Despite the Soviet hiatus, we're not the first generation of British tourists to explore the Wild East. There was, unsurprisingly, a coterie of intrepid Victorian explorers who came to map this uncharted territory. But Kyrgyzstan still feels new and exciting and epic, perhaps because its mythologies remain unmapped – and you certainly can't say that about Montana. ●

WHEN TO GO
The summer months are the best time to visit Kyrgyszstan; winters on the treeless steppes bring a whole new meaning to the word 'bitter', with temperatures frequently dipping below minus 20°C in the mountains.

GETTING THERE
International flights take you to Bishkek, the capital of Kyrgyszstan; from there it's a dusty few days by 4X4 to the Son Kul Lake, where the trek begins.

ORGANISING YOUR TRIP
Wild Frontiers (www.wildfrontiers.co.uk) and Ride Worldwide (www.rideworldwide.com) organise horseback safaris in the 'Mountains of Heaven' in summer months.

COST
Around £2,400, excluding flights to Bishkek; includes food, accommodation and transfers.

AM I UP TO IT?
Intermediate horseriding skills are required, plus a sense of adventure, but no specific fitness training.

MORE LIKE THIS
Cross the Andes from Chile to Argentina on horseback via the Puelo Valley with Ride Worldwide (www.rideworldwide.com).

FOR REFERENCE
The Great Game: The Struggle for Empire in Central Asia by Peter Hopkirk; and Colin Thubron's poetic Shadow of the Silk Road.

The other Inca trail

Chris Moss beats a path through the Sacred Valley to the Inca citadels of Choquequirao and Machu Picchu.

WHAT	HOW LONG
High-altitude trek in the Andes	12 days
WHERE	**THRILL FACTOR**
Vilcabamba, Peru	● ● ● ● ○

How do you get a mule up a mountain? Try shouting, 'Mula, carajo, mula!' No English expression quite captures the fricative force of 'carajo', but 'damn you, mule' is about right.

This became just about all I heard as I climbed and descended the steep slopes of the 75-mile Inca road from the village of Cachora to Aguas Calientes in the Andean mountains of the Vilcabamba region. The purpose of my pains: to visit the Inca ruins of Choquequirao, a site rivalling Machu Picchu for size and significance, and far more remote and tourist-free.

THE JUNGLE'S EYEBROWS

I was joining a recce for a tour company so it felt more like an expedition. We all met up in Cachora, a hamlet a couple of hours outside Cuzco. There were 24 mules, three horses, five guides, four cooks, 12 tents and an oxygen tank – and me.

The first two days were spent setting a pattern for the rest of the walk: a descent of more than 1,000 metres to a narrow valley – in the first instance, the canyon riven by the fast-flowing Apurimac, one of the great rivers in the Americas – and then an even greater distance up a mountain slope, trudging, scrambling and sometimes hacking through thick woods, before coming into the relative calm of open grasslands and, near the summit, entering the dense, humid *ceja de selva* (literally, 'the jungle's eyebrows').

Throughout the Vilcabamba there are settlements of Quechua Indians who farm terraces of maize, papaya, coca and potatoes – many of these high up and crazily inclined – as well as arable land for pigs and lambs. But this is primarily the habitat of condors and spectacled bears (indigenous, rather than short-sighted) – which we weren't lucky enough to see – as well as eagles, hawks, parrots and butterflies galore (which we did see). I also saw, and slept with, long-legged biting insects called *zancudos* and was physically assaulted by a mosquito known in Quechua as *pumahuacachi* ('the one that makes the puma cry').

By the afternoon of day two, we were within sight of Choquequirao. High on the adrenaline of seeing the ashlar terraces and the vague outline

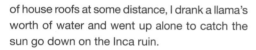

of house roofs at some distance, I drank a llama's worth of water and went up alone to catch the sun go down on the Inca ruin.

BETWEEN PEAKS

The main building sits, as at Machu Picchu, in a saddle at a natural high pass between two peaks. There are well-preserved irrigation channels, small ceremonial chambers and long halls that seem to have been used for hanging adornments, as well as storage rooms for the produce that the Inca emperor's minions would have heaved up from the farming areas.

Paths advance up both extremes of the saddle to vantage points, the lower of the two appearing to be some kind of altar or sanctuary.

Inside the rooms and covering the terraces is a carpet of neat lawn, giving the ruin a dignified air, rather like a cemetery. When the fortress was 'discovered' in 1834 by a French count, Eugène de Sartige (who called the approach trail 'détestable'), and when it was visited by the American explorer Hiram Bingham in 1909, the site was completely overgrown.

Digs over the past 15 years have uncovered terraces all over the mountain and no one is yet sure just how vast the complex is.

From the main site, nothing clutters the panoramic views of the neighbouring higher mountains, many of which are laden with snow and glaciers – in *The White Rock*, Hugh Thomson's book about the dozens of unexplored ruins dotted round the Vilcabamba, the site is described as 'romantically isolated'.

CRADLE OF GOLD

As I was alone, there was also a slightly eerie quality as the wind came in gusts over the walls and the dying light danced through the clouds on to the stonework. Choquequirao means

'THE YAMANA VALLEY BEGAN AS A PASTORAL IDYLL OF GREEN FIELDS, PLUMP COWS AND HUMMINGBIRDS'

'cradle of gold': this could well refer to the light – I revisited the site with the rest of the group in the morning and this time the eastern walls were shrouded in orange, before a mist obscured any view of the site.

Many theories have been ventured as to the purpose of high-altitude Incaic sites, from sacrificing virgins (as repeated by scores of Machu Picchu guides every day), to the new-millennial notions of hunting follies and summer retreats suggested in Thomson's book. All no doubt contain some truth, but for the walker, the lofty citadels appeal as airy gestures of contempt for the hot, sweaty jungle below.

WHITE-WATER CROSSINGS

Relief while on the slopes was provided by the sudden appearance of Inca paths in good condition, and even of unnamed sites and ancient mortars and pestles left lying around in grassy meadows. Orchids were good reasons to stop and catch our breath, as were the perfumed scents of peppermint and *muña*, a wild oregano that is supposed to keep flies away, stop vomiting and ease menstruation pains.

River crossings were fun, especially when the currents were whitewater standard by virtue of the melting glaciers, or when bridges were dilapidated and unstable; only a couple of campsites had access to rudimentary showers and in the Río Blanco we all bathed and half-swam in the ice-cold water. Also diverting – and equally refreshing – were the pauses to eat foodstuffs that we found growing wild in the valleys: we picked peaches, Cape gooseberries, prickly pears and blackcurrants.

The cooks made us Neo (or even Nouvelle) Andean cuisine: lamb in wine sauce, sweet and sour chicken, fig tart, *arepas* (maize muffins) and *sopa criolla* (the national noodle soup). Local ingredients such as quinoa, yucca, lupins, maize in all its forms, alpaca meat and hot chilli pickles were everyday delicacies.

UP THE INCA STAIR

Sometimes, though, I couldn't eat at all. Above 3,350 metres, I hyperventilated and could only chew coca leaves. The Yamana Valley began as a pastoral idyll of green fields, plump cows and hummingbirds, but then rose to its namesake pass, which, at nearly 4,900 metres, almost killed me. I have a photograph of myself at the cairns on the summit: a dense grey mist obscures a view I know to be wonderful from a picture book, but the onset of *soroche* (altitude sickness) obscures my own sense of satisfaction and turns my attempted smile into a grimace. My pulse and head thumping, I just wanted to get off the hill.

Up and down, up and down, the Choquequirao–Machu Picchu trail is a natty combination of Inca staircases that attack the slopes frontally, and less aggressive, but more tedious zig-zags designed for mules, goats and such. Occasionally, valley dwellers passed by and I would ask, '*Cuánto falta para...?*' ('How far to...?'). The only rule I could deduce was: whatever a local says, double it and then some.

But passers-by were few and far between. As the group spread out over the trail, I felt as if I were alone in one of Peru's most inaccessible corners – little wonder that the Incas retreated up these valleys in the 1560s when Spain had taken Cuzco.

ANYONE FOR GUINEA PIG?

We spent the last night in a small village called La Playa, camping on a football pitch. Wilbur hooked up with one of his cousins, whose name was Bill Clinton. No joke: Peruvians often give their children celebrity forenames, a recent TV survey unearthing hundreds of global personalities living in far-flung hamlets, including a 'Garfield', a 'Michael Jackson' and a 'Hulk'.

I was presented with a barbecued guinea pig: it was sweet, peppery, somewhat bony. I preferred the other regional speciality, alpaca, which is surprisingly tender and subtle-tasting for a relative of the camel.

From La Playa it was a one-day dash to Machu Picchu, by way of an ascent of Llactapata, a small mountain made to seem very big by its exuberant undergrowth – that is why the rainy season is only for recces. A previous walker had macheted the head off a red-and-black adder we found beside the main trail, and we could have done with the same weapon to beat aside the bamboo and knots of creepers, especially on the descent. I literally fell down the last few stretches and it was a joy to see people again, and cars, and soft-drink advertisements on the metalled road to Machu Picchu's hydroelectric power station.

MISTS OF MACHU PICCHU

The finale is, of course, the famed ruin itself. With its steep, jungle-clad mountains, swirling mists and huge, partially hewn boulders, Machu Picchu remains an awesome experience and is still very much the must-see ending to any trek in the Vilcabamba. For all that, its 2,000-plus daily visitors make for a lot of human traffic; and constant chatter and the increasingly musical clicks of digital camera shutters do detract from the splendour of the temples and residences.

For these reasons, and because of new restrictions for entry to the established Inca Trail, both British and Peruvian tour operators would like to see Choquequirao begin to compete with Machu Picchu, at least for intrepid walkers.

But until an easier trail is built, the site will stay off the beaten track. But if you have good legs and lungs (or are at least, like me, as obstinate as a *mula*) and want to walk like a warrior to two of the greatest sites on the planet, the Choquequirao trail is waiting, quietly, for your visit. ●

WHEN TO GO

The weather in Vilcabamba is mild. Days are warm and sunny with an average high of 22°C; nights are cooler with an average low of 5°C. The rainy season runs from November to March and the dry season April to October.

GETTING THERE

Fly to Lima and then take a bus or plane to Cuzco, 350 miles to the south-east.

ORGANISING YOUR TRIP

This trek should only be attempted as part of a group. There are long stretches through unpopulated areas and carrying a heavy pack for the duration would be a military feat. Explore (www.explore.co.uk) organises an 18-day tour, which includes four days of acclimatising in Cuzco.

COST

Around £1,300-£1,500 (without international flights) for guides, mules, cooks/food and local transfers.

AM I UP TO IT?

This is harder and longer than the classic Inca Trail so you should be a reasonably fit hiker who enjoys camping.

MORE LIKE THIS

Peru's Huayhuash (featured in the film *Touching the Void*) and the Cordillera Blanca ranges are becoming popular alternatives to Machu Picchu-bound walks.

FOR REFERENCE

Hugh Thomson's *The White Rock: An Exploration of the Inca Heartland*.

Walking with warriors

Following in the tracks of early explorers, **Julie Davidson** goes on a Kenyan foot safari with Samburu tribesmen.

WHAT	HOW LONG
Trekking safari with the Samburu tribe	One week

WHERE	THRILL FACTOR
Leroghi Mountains, northern Kenya	● ● ● ● ●

It was my first night in the Leroghi Mountains and the noises of the forest were alarming: the wail of a tree hyrax sounded like a soul in torment, the bark of baboons signalled danger and – lifting the hairs on my scalp – I heard the rasping call of a leopard. Eventually I succumbed to sleep thanks only to the exertions of our first climb, several glasses of wine and a delicious dinner (pumpkin soup, red snapper casserole and tree tomato tart, all cooked over a campfire).

By contrast, my wake-up call the next morning was sweet. Birdsong encouraged me to unzip the tent flap and smell the air: rich, pungent yet peculiarly homely – a blend of wood smoke and donkey. The elusive predators of the Leroghi Mountains love the smell of donkey, we were told, but our caravan of baggage carriers had survived the hours of darkness thanks to our 'guards': 12 Samburu warriors – all lean as knife blades, wearing brilliantly coloured robes, and armed with fearsome-looking spears and machetes – and trek leader John Faull, who shouldered a game rifle (between safaris, John is a career soldier in the British Army). Men at arms, indeed.

SAMBURULAND

We were in Samburuland, home of the handsome Nilotic people who share with their kin, the Maasai, a taste for braided hair, elaborate beadwork, ochre face paint and striking scarlet or plaid shukas – voluminous cotton cloths worn like togas and wraparound skirts. Like the Maasai, the Samburu are semi-nomadic pastoralists with a warrior caste, and count their wealth in cattle. Between the 17th and 19th centuries, they migrated from the Nile basin down the Rift Valley to colonise what is now Samburuland, where they have largely absorbed the existing hunter-gatherers, the Ndorobo.

GET SET...

Adventure travel is exciting and life enhancing, and the better prepared you are the more rewarding it will be. Explore has been leading tours worldwide for over two decades, getting closer to the cultures, people and environments that make our world such an amazing place. With our professional planning, foresight and expertise, you can feel the adventure, every step of the way.

EXPLORE!
WORLDWIDE ADVENTURES

CALL 0844 499 0901
VISIT EXPLORE.CO.UK

Still deciding where to go? See the inside front cover for some ideas and inspiration.
Like some action with your adventure? See the inside back cover to see all the activities we can cram into an Explore trip!

>> choose your trip
OK. So do you want to be active every day, or stick to sightseeing? Do you prefer culture or wildlife? Can you rough it, or do like your home comforts? Be honest, choose wisely and you'll have the time of your life.

>> before you go
Plan carefully. Active holidays can be arduous or gentle (15k uphill feels very different to 15k flat!) so consider the season, think about terrain, wear-in those walking shoes and enjoy the build up to your big adventure!

>> don't forget!
You get a full trip dossier when you book with Explore. This includes a comprehensive list of things to take, some obvious: insect repellant, sun screen, water bottle; and some less so: head-torch (campsite toilets, 3am?)!

'WE RETRACED THE STEPS OF LEGENDARY VICTORIAN HUNTER-EXPLORER, ARTHUR HENRY NEUMANN WHO CAME HERE IN THE 1890S TO PLUNDER THE ELEPHANT POPULATION FOR IVORY.'

Walking safaris are nothing unusual in northern Kenya, but John Faull's company, Samburu Trails, is the only one operating in the isolated Leroghi Mountains. Unlike many Kenyan ranges that have lost their indigenous woodland to tree-felling for fuel, agriculture and grazing, the Leroghi are thickly covered in pristine forest from their 1,828-metre base to the 2,440-metre summit ridge.

INTO THE FOREST

On this trip, our party of eight retraced the steps of legendary Victorian hunter-explorer Arthur Henry Neumann, who spent three years in the area in the 1890s, plundering the elephant population

for ivory. The trek takes you to the site of his old camp – through bewitching woods, where shy populations of elephant, buffalo, big cats and wild dogs hide themselves away, and the only humans you might meet are Samburu cattle herders.

The Leroghi forest is a dense mix of African olive, cedar, Cape chestnut and towering podocarpus trees, each occupying its own zonal niche in the ecological mosaic of the mountains that lie between the eastern edge of the Great Rift Valley and the wild Mathews Range. Until recently, they had rarely been visited by Europeans since the days of Neumann.

Over 100 years later, our route to his main camp was researched by another veteran white hunter: the late Peter Faull, John's brother, who settled in the area and became a safari operator. Inspired by Neumann's memoirs and the ancestral memories of the locals, he and a village elder, Lekermogo, explored the forest with two donkeys and a mule, using elephant and cattle tracks to

'THERE WERE TWELVE SAMBURU WARRIORS – ALL LEAN AS KNIFE BLADES, WEARING BRILLIANTLY COLOURED ROBES, AND CARRYING SPEARS AND MACHETES.'

reach the El Bogoi Valley and the base camp from which Neumann had dispatched donkey caravans loaded with tusks to the Indian Ocean coast.

'Peter had studied Neumann's account of his adventures, which contained detailed descriptions of the camp and its location,' explained his widow, Rosalie. 'When he and Lekermogo unearthed the makings of cooking fires and the near-calcified bones of giraffe and hippo, they were confident they had found the right spot.'

By the time Peter died three years ago, Samburu Trails was up and running. Peter's son John now takes trekkers into the Leroghi with Rosalie, and the venerable Lekermogo remains chief guide. There are 20 donkeys and a support team of a dozen warriors, including Lekermogo's elegant young lieutenant Lentaiya, who speaks valiant English, translates for Lekermogo and is something of a bird expert. In this distinguished company, over the six-day trek to El Bogoi we rediscovered the true meaning of the word 'safari', which in Swahili simply means 'journey on foot'.

PROCEED WITH CAUTION

Our trek began gently, from the base camp near the valley home of our Samburu escorts, but when we reached the edge of the forest Lekermogo made a short but solemn speech: 'We are going where there are risky animals. We must always be wary. So tighten your hearts and ask God's blessing.'

Tight hearts and trembling knees began to relax as we climbed through the giant trees, noisy with birdsong and the scrambling of vervet monkeys and baboons. We saw plenty of evidence of 'risky' animals – buffalo spoor and elephant dung – and in the thickets caught the flash of several bushbuck (among the shyest of antelope). But our seductive surroundings and the expert forest craft of the Samburu, who caught sight of movements and heard noises lost to my dull urban senses, soon built confidence.

Our guides remained vigilant. It was Lentaiya who first heard the rumbling of elephant in the trees, and took us on a side-trip to find them. We saw what resembled a colossal boulder as a huge bull rolled away from us; excitement enough. Trekkers are schooled to do exactly as they're told if an elephant or buffalo crosses their path – keep still, keep quiet and let the guides deal with the 'obstacle'. (In most situations big game will back off.)

'SHY POPULATIONS OF ELEPHANT, BUFFALO, BIG CATS AND WILD DOGS HIDE AWAY, AND THE ONLY HUMANS YOU MIGHT MEET ARE SAMBURU CATTLE HERDERS.'

No daily trek takes more than four or five hours; you may reach camp in time for lunch and always well before dark, leaving time to spot a few red-fronted parrots and silver-cheeked hornbills, hang out with the four-legged porters that roll on the grass as soon as they are unloaded, and enjoy the locations (five of them, all very different). There is space for grazing the animals at every site, and only one is deep in the forest: Upper Bawa, the second camp, where a bucket shower in the trees outside the circle of firelight adds to the sense of adventure.

In general, though, this is exploration of a comfortable, not to say civilised, kind, and the only sweat you're likely to break on the trek is induced by climbing or spotting wildlife. All the donkey work is in fact done by the donkeys, while the Samburu guides raise and break camp, build fires, light paraffin lamps, heat water and even bring mugs of smoky tea to your dome tent, where you sleep on mattresses.

SPECTACULAR SUNRISE

Up with first light, we watched sunrise from the giddy heights of the Tilia Rock camp, where, emerging suddenly from the green glow of the forest, we found ourselves on an open clifftop at the highest point of the climb. An immense view stretched out, at eye level, to the Mathews Range in the distance, and 600 metres below were the El Bogoi Valley and the thin coils of a stream.

Fan-tailed ravens cruised the thermals, and the only human imprint on this stupendous landscape was the tiny circle of a *manyatta*, a Samburu tribal homestead. Manyattas are always built in the round within a high thorn fence, which protects not only the mud and thatch homes of the pastoralists but also their livestock.

We spent two days exploring the El Bogoi Valley, where there's a good chance of seeing elephant in the more open acacia woodland, or even the rare greater kudu, among the largest and most dramatic of African antelope. (The bulls are easily identified by their great corkscrew horns.) Some time was spent inspecting the site of Neumann's hunting camp and visiting the *manyatta*, then we started the climb back to the Leroghi ridge with its monumental forest and the camp at Naibolo Rock. This second viewpoint afforded a vista across the Laikipia plain to Lake Kisimi, where we witnessed lightning pyrotechnics and cluster bombs of rain explode on the strange pyramid-shaped Naibor Keju hill.

That night, our last, the Samburu danced in the firelight, leaping high into the air like spring-loaded athletes, singing of women and cattle and cattle and women, and battles for both.

The long but easy descent into the Bawa Valley was the last lap and it was impossible not to feel sad as we watched our guides load up the caravan and whoop the troop on its way. We had grown accustomed to the calm presence of the donkeys and mules, John's hunting anecdotes and Lekermogo's forest wisdom, but at least the old man had a final prayer for us: 'Now we say goodbye to the people of the cars and planes. May the metal of your cars and planes be strong and keep you from harm.' ●

WHEN TO GO
Despite the equator's proximity, trekkers needn't fear excessive heat as walking is mainly in shade. Avoid the wet months (April and May).

GETTING THERE
The Leroghi Mountains lie 400 miles north of Nairobi's Jomo Kenyatta Airport. Onward journey by road (about seven hours) or light aircraft to Kisima airstrip (one hour).

ORGANISING YOUR TRIP
Julie went with www.wildernessjourneys.com.

COST
Seven days on the El Bogoi Valley route costs £1,128 per person (excluding international flights and transfers).

AM I UP TO IT?
The route can be managed by anyone who takes regular exercise and is comfortable walking up and down hills.

MORE LIKE THIS
Gorilla trekking in Rwanda's Virunga Mountains (www.volcanoessafaris.com) is the ultimate walk on the wild side. Or take a bush walk in Zambia's South Luangwa National Park, where there is every chance of meeting elephant, buffalo and big cats on foot (www.robinpopesafaris.net).

FOR REFERENCE
The work that inspired Peter Faull to develop Samburu Trails Trekking Safaris is Arthur H Neumann's *Elephant Hunting in East Equatorial Africa*, first published in 1898.

Wild life

Chris Moss choppers into the remote Kamchatka peninsula, one of the earth's last untamed wildernesses..

WHAT	**HOW LONG**
Bear-watching and volcano ascent	One week
WHERE	**THRILL FACTOR**
Kamchatka, Eastern Siberia, Russia	● ● ● ● ●

Dusk had fallen and brought with it a mist-like drizzle. The light was fading fast. We'd become a drawn-out straggle of weary hikers, walking along with our heads only just above the long, thick grass, panning the horizon. In front was Victor the Hunter, with his thigh-high waders, camouflage and big knife (but no gun).

We rounded a final clump of trees, finding ourselves on the bank of a sharp bend in a wide, fast-flowing river. My concentration was broken for a moment by flashes of crimson and gold, and a series of sudden, violent splashes – thousands of male sockeye salmon, spawning their way to oblivion.

Then to the right, a rustle of leaves announced the arrival of a brown bear – perhaps nine or ten metres away and, more importantly, on the same side of the river. Victor shouted something in Russian but no one paid attention as the bear lolloped down the riverbank and waded into the shallows to leap upon a doomed salmon. He was young, but he was huge, and he used all his heft to stun the salmon before thrashing it with his paws. It was all over in a few thrilling seconds, and the hairy, chocolate-coloured bear shuffled off nonchalantly into the undergrowth with his supper.

NO ROADS LEAD TO KAMCHATKA

I'd come to Two Yurts Camp in central Kamchatka by way of 12 time zones – by aeroplane, ten hours on a gravel road by bus, and one hour on a noisy helicopter flight over mountains cloaked in virgin forests of birch, alder and spruce. Already, our first encounter with the peninsula's most famous resident had been more than sufficient reward for the epic journey. For a few minutes at least, I'd communed with nature, and been reminded by this powerful mammal, totally at home in the dank Eden of the Russian forest, that I was a privileged visitor to his realm, but also that there were food chains that I was completely excluded from – and that it would be wise to keep it this way.

Kamchatka is one of the planet's few remaining wildernesses where 'unspoiled' isn't an overstatement. The 140,000-square-mile peninsula, roughly the size of Montana, is best

known for its string of 160 volcanoes (29 of which are active) that form part of the Pacific 'Ring of Fire'. Yet between the steamy calderas and smoking craters are carpets of virgin forest, some 14,000 rivers and streams and a long, pristine coastline. Cut off from the rest of the world – neither road nor rail links Kamchatka to Russia – it's little wonder that this antediluvian place should harbour arctic foxes, Steller's sea eagles, northern seals, rare snow sheep and millions of salmon. But ursus arctos, the brown bear to you and me, is the king of this cold jungle, and the reason it is beginning to draw a few tourists.

WILD BEAR CHASE

The next morning we went bear-scouting again. On our way through the grassy area, a second guide, also named Victor, pointed out some flattened areas and said, 'this is where the bears sleep during the afternoon.' 'Although these animals are very unlikely to attack a human – they are too busy killing salmon – you certainly wouldn't like to wake one up in a surprising fashion.' We all became a degree more vigilant, for what it was worth, having never experienced the moodswing of a bear jolted rudely out of his slumber.

This time our trek became more like the proverbial wild bear chase. We skirted the river, getting somewhat strung out in the process. All over the muddy banks were spattered salmon, their insides torn apart, and the stench of fish was overwhelming. We had about three sightings – one of a mere shadow flitting between the trunks of trees, another of a huge male lumbering into the river, and a third of a female and her cub heading off for their siesta.

We returned to the camp for a lunch of fish soup, smoked salmon and caviar. In the afternoon, Victor two, a professor of volcanology, took a small group of us to see some hot springs, where he explained the fault lines, caused by clashing tectonic plates. On a short trek, we discovered some Martian-coloured grasses, boiling mud-pots and strange chemical residues.

Later he gave us a lecture, supposedly on 'The Life Cycle of the Salmon' but which spun off into what I could only imagine were typically Russian ruminations on the nature of existence, the fall of Soviet Communism and the beguiling beauty of Kamchatka. His volcanology was hard science but he invoked the fish as metaphors of the unrelenting power of destiny – and I felt his mind was pulled in two directions by the opposing forces of the seismic and the salmonid.

We ate heaps of the stuff: salmon roe for breakfast, salmon soup for lunch and cold, cured salmon for starters at dinner. If you think only a freakish aristocrat could ever utter the words 'Oh, I am so sick of caviar and smoked salmon', then try Kamchatka. But fortunately, there were also delicious bowls of borscht, tasty pork dishes and the occasional tipple of vodka.

GONE FISHING

Two more trips to the bear river, one that evening and another the next morning, found us in the capable hands of Victor the Third. He was the owner of Two Yurts Camp, a veterinary surgeon and experienced hunter, and had flown in on his own chopper. He was carrying what looked like a pellet rifle that would, at best, deliver a delightful tickling sensation to an attacking bear – and he

'WE FOUND A SULPHUR-STAINED YELLOW CRATER, AT THE CENTRE OF WHICH WERE FUMAROLES AND GEYSERS, AND BUBBLING POTS OF GREY MUD POPPING AND EXPLODING.'

pointed out a dozen more bears. As well as drawing us deep into their lairs – again, the exploded salmon bellies and penetrating stink of putrefying fish – he got us close-up sightings and found wonderful viewpoints. At one point I stood on a bank looking directly at a huge male rearing up to his full height of eight or nine feet. Thankfully, he was too busy fishing and biting mosquitoes to be bothered crossing the river to get me.

A helicopter flight took us out of the wilds and into the man-made sections of the Russian Far East. En route by bus to the capital, Petropavlosk, where we would explore the volcanoes, I took a dip in the hot springs at Malki and ate two pies in the roadside village of Sokoch. The latter may sound unexotic for an overland adventure in Kamchatka, but – maybe because of my Lancastrian upbringing – I found it a curious fact that here, thousands of miles from Moscow and the industrial heartland, Russia is vaguely like northern England: the people were friendly, the weather was wet, and the pies were delicious.

SCRAMBLE THAT

What came next was a serious assault on a peak. We were taken by a 6WD all-terrain transporter to a lodge at the foot of the Avacha volcano. From the camp, we could see the perfect cone above. That night, we stayed up too late, drinking vodka and chatting to our new guide, another volcanologist (surprisingly, not called Victor).

The next day, I cursed the nightcaps, but the truth is that there's no easy way up Avacha. It wasn't just the scree that slipped down as you tried to step forward. Nor was it the bitter cold of the dawn, the breathlessness, and the lack of perspective. Above all, it was that the cone, so perfect to look at, made for the very worst kind of climb. At a constant 25 to 30 degree angle (it felt like 50), progress was slow.

THE FORCE OF NATURE

A small group of us made it to the top, leaving the others at the collar. Here we found a sulphur-stained yellow crater, at the centre of which were fumaroles and geysers, and bubbling pots of grey mud popping and exploding between some black boulders that had presumably been blasted from miles beneath the earth's crust only to land back in the hole. It was awesome, stupendous, frightening… but I was so exhausted that I lay down and dozed off before making the epic, knee-busting descent.

Bears and volcanoes. You don't get more human-repellent than these two forces of nature. Indeed, I never got a sense that humans – even if there were 30 of them for every bear – had anything like dominion over Kamchatka. As I flew back to the airport on our last helicopter journey, I stared down, dazed, at a carpet of forest, broken only by the occasional craggy peak of a volcano. Somewhere down there was a bear sitting on a muddy riverbank, whose only concern was whether or not to dive in for another salmon. It's a comforting thought. ●

WHEN TO GO
Midsummer, between 10 July and 30 August, is the only good time to explore Kamchatka.

GETTING THERE
Petropavlovsk-Kamchatsky can be reached via Moscow on Aeroflot (www.aeroflot.co.uk); buses and a helicopter then take you into the park.

ORGANISING YOUR TRIP
Explore's 'Bears and Volcanoes' tour of the area, including helicopter flights. Book well in advance (www.explore.co.uk).

COST
The two-week trip costs £2,875 (before flights).

AM I UP TO IT?
The bear 'hunts' and glacier treks are straightforward enough and should be feasible for just about anyone. However, you'll need strong legs and a good general level of fitness to climb the volcano.

MORE LIKE THIS
Katmai National Park (www.nps.gov/katm) in south-western Alaska is superb territory for bear-watching – and you can climb no end of volcanoes in Chile or New Zealand (try Villarrica and Ngauruhoe respectively), or Mount Fuji in Japan – but Kamchatka is something else.

FOR REFERENCE
Steller's History of Kamchatka: Collected Information Concerning the History of Kamchatka, Its Peoples, Their Manners, Names, Lifestyles, and Various by Georg Wilhelm Steller is an 18th-century classic travelogue and natural history.

Castles in the sand

Ros Sales walks across the Libyan Sahara and sleeps under the stars.

WHAT	HOW LONG
Trekking in the Sahara	Seven days
WHERE	THRILL FACTOR
Southern Libya	● ● ● ● ○

We pitched our tents on sand, beside high, stepped rocks. Above us the stone slab had split in two, creating a thin, sand-filled gully we could climb and follow down to the other side. We were in the middle of the Acacus Mountains in the Libyan Sahara, one of the world's most dramatic desert landscapes – and as I looked out across the parched plain from the camp, my caravan of trekkers felt like nothing more than a microdot on the sand.

Little-visited Libya isn't an obvious holiday destination. The oil-rich country acquired international pariah status for its support of terrorism in the 1980s, but these are changing times. In the 21st century, the country has changed direction under the maverick leadership of Colonel Gadaffi: its nuclear and biological weapons programme was abandoned in 2003; there was an early denunciation of the 9/11 attacks; and the colonel even met with Condoleezza Rice. Today, Libya is keen to welcome visitors and although travel is generally only possible with a Libyan guide (and usually as part of an organised tour), its scenic riches make it well worth the effort. The Sahara desert, which covers most of the country, encompasses everything from vast, featureless plains and salt flats, to valleys lined with melodramatic rock formations, to immense sandy seas.

DESERT HIGHWAY

After an internal flight to Sebha, 500 miles south of the capital, Tripoli, we set off in 4X4s for the Jebel Acacus (Acacus Mountains), an isolated region in the south-west of the country – and another 300 miles away. The road from Sebha was long and straight; the gradients flat; and the land almost entirely barren and featureless, with black smoke from distant oilfields occasionally visible.

We off-roaded after the dusty desert outpost of Al-Alweinat and soon found ourselves in an exciting new world of dark escarpments and improbably hewn, gravity-defying rock forms, with rivers of ochre sands flowing in between. As the eyes adapt, the brain translates the shapes into familiar forms: the famous 'finger rock', a fox's head, a couple kissing, mushrooms…

As we prepared to trek 60 miles over the next five days, camping in a different place each night, we said goodbye to all but the two trucks that would carry food, water and tents – leaving just the trekkers, the crew and a wide open desert.

ROCKS IN A HARD PLACE

As if the scene hadn't already provided ample drama and suspense, during the first night under canvas, the wind got up and blew the fabric of our tents in and out like lungs; there was even a little light rain. After breakfast, we packed up, put on our boots and began to walk. We started with a swift climb up a rocky slope and a descent into a sand-filled dip, but that was unusual. Much of the terrain consisted of sandy plains, where the occasional solitary desert bush seemed like something of a miracle. Sometimes we walked between small egg-like dunelets topped with scrub, other times the landscape was all-black – an endless, pitiless plain of black basalt, devoid

'THE SENSE OF WONDER COULD EASILY MUTATE INTO SOMETHING VAGUELY FEARFUL; THE SILENCE, THE UNENDING EMPTINESS OF THE LAND AND THE PAUCITY OF LIFE LENT AN EDGE OF MENACE.'

of vegetation, that stretched ahead into infinity, broken only by the distant, glowering hills of rock.

The rock outcrops of the Acacus were a constant, silhouetted against a cobalt sky. From afar they were dark brooding shapes; close up, we saw that the rocks were textured and layered by desert winds. There were high ledges, overhangs at ground level creating mini caves, rock keyholes, bulbous rocky globes and table-tops.

Walking 13 miles a day in temperatures well into the 30s is no easy stroll; we were equipped with three litres of drinking water a day, and we needed every drop. But the wonder of the surroundings and group camaraderie eased the

way. As did the relief of lunch out of the midday sun, followed by a long siesta in the shade of rocks until the hottest part of the day was over.

BACK TO BLACK

On the tough third day, only three of the group resisted the offer of a lift in the trucks and endured a full day's walk across hot black basalt. We all noticed – especially when tired – that the sense of awe one felt at the desert could easily mutate into something vaguely fearful; the silence, the unending emptiness of the land and the paucity of life it could support lent an edge of menace.

Signs of life in today's Acacus are few and far between: a few birds, a shrub, a chameleon, a rare desert bloom. Every morning, however, we were reminded that we weren't entirely alone by the presence of animal tracks in the sand: the marks of a Saharan fennec fox or the winding line of a snake trail. That anyone or anything resides in this harsh landscape defies logic, yet apparently around 12 Touareg families live in the area. We saw no human life while we were there, but we did stop beside a poignant cemetery, where a few modest mounds of earth marked with stones reminded us of their presence.

'THE OLDEST CAVE PAINTINGS IN THIS REGION DATE FROM 10,000 BC, WHEN THE SAHARA WAS COVERED IN SAVANNAH.'

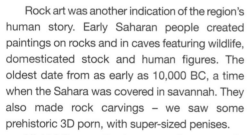

Rock art was another indication of the region's human story. Early Saharan people created paintings on rocks and in caves featuring wildlife, domesticated stock and human figures. The oldest date from as early as 10,000 BC, a time when the Sahara was covered in savannah. They also made rock carvings – we saw some prehistoric 3D porn, with super-sized penises.

Night fell promptly at seven, and we generally arrived at camp around five, so the first task was always to put up the tents. Washing was a lesson in water conservation – a couple of inches in a small plastic bowl. Then it was time for a hot pre-dinner drink: whoever thought Nescafé with powdered milk could taste this good? Dinner began with soup, followed by couscous, or macaroni with meaty sauces. We ate under the stars, a surreal and shadowy scene.

DUNE DRIVING

After five nights in the Acacus, we met a new crew of 4X4 drivers, and a different phase of our desert journey began: the drive north to the Ubari Sand Sea. The change of pace came as a shock. From

living and walking in the middle of the desert, we were now passengers speeding through classic car ad territory – long, wide avenues of sand, bordered by the ever-present rock forms. The sound of tyres on the sand resembled a plane on take-off. If the velocity was surprising, so was our re-entry into a world of people. In the last five days our world had shrunk to our group of 12 and the crew, so we observed the signs of human civilisation with distorted interest as we approached the desert town of Al-Alweinat: chickens, simple dwellings, and then people.

Our drivers took us up near-vertical dunes, plunged us down terrifying descents, and raced each other when the sand was flat. This was driving as showmanship. Once our cars drew level at the peak of a dune and then stopped: ahead lay the magnificent vista of Madara – a palm-strewn oasis that looked too kitsch to be real. We camped in the Ubari for two nights, amid dunes of warm, fine sand with knife-sharp peaks that you could climb up and then run down.

There was one more adventure before returning to Tripoli: swimming in the salt lake of Gebraoun. Except that we couldn't really swim. The water is so salty that backstroke is the only option. After dousing ourselves with freshwater from a well to remove the salt, we drove to a camp for a final lunch, and bid farewell to our crew. There were a few tears behind sunglasses as we thanked them for sharing their desert.

There had been moments when walking across a hot desert seemed a preposterous task, but mostly it felt like a privilege. Travelling on foot revealed its unimaginable vastness and barrenness, as well as all those small signs of life that proved that even in the most inhospitable places on earth, nature adapts to survive. ●

WHEN TO GO
In spring and autumn, daytime temperatures climb into the 30s, while nights are usually cool but not cold. In winter, the daytime high is a pleasant 20 degrees, but night temperatures can sink to freezing. Summer is too hot for desert trekking.

GETTING THERE
This trip is really only practicable on an organised tour, leaving from Tripoli. The Libyan government insists that foreign travellers are accompanied by a guide.

ORGANISING YOUR TRIP
The author travelled with Walks Worldwide (www.walksworldwide.com).

COST
From £995 for a 12-day holiday, including seven nights' camping, with five days' trekking in the Acacus Mountains and two days' driving in the Ubari Sand Sea. British Airways flies to Tripoli for around £350.

AM I UP TO IT?
Hot weather makes walking more arduous, but the distances are achievable for anyone who takes regular exercise.

MORE LIKE THIS
Jordan has similarly magnificent desert scenery, along with the archaeological site of Petra.

FOR REFERENCE
A History of Modern Libya by Dirk Vandewalle is the first history of modern Libya for two decades. *In the Country of Men* by Hisham Matar, which was shortlisted for the 2006 Man Booker Prize, describes the effects of the 1969 Libyan September revolution on a nine-year-old boy who is struggling to understand his family's plight.

Top of the world

Henry Wismayer breathes, occasionally uneasily, the rarefied air at the top of Mount Damavand, the highest peak in the Middle East.

WHAT	HOW LONG
Mount Damavand ascent	4-5 days
WHERE	**THRILL FACTOR**
Alborz Mountains, Iran	● ● ● ● ●

My body was too panicked for sleep. At altitudes like this – 4,380 metres above sea level – arteries contract and blood pressure amplifies. Hypertension follows, as the heart beats hard and faster to compensate for the lack of oxygen. Stricken by the inadequacies of biology, I lay with eyes wide open, almost hyperventilating, while my impoverished blood slowly starved.

Through the base camp shelter's semi-opaque window, a faint sliver of light heralded the arrival of my date with destiny. Outside was the highest mountain in the Middle East and in half an hour our team would begin its push for the summit, still another 1,300 metres above.

IRANIAN ICON

If you know your world topography and you're quick at sums, you'll have calculated that I was languishing on a fairly substantial kink in the earth's crust. But if this is the first time you've heard of Mount Damavand, don't worry – you're not the only one.

Damavand's height status depends on whose tape measure you trust. Either it is the highest point on the Eurasian landmass west of the Hindu Kush, standing at 5,671 metres – if you believe any one of numerous dubious internet sources. Or it's not: 5,610 metres If you're from the credible-sounding Statistical Centre of Iran, which would make it a three-storey building shorter than Georgia's Mount Elbrus.

Either way it's big, and in Iran it has been venerated for generations. Located in the heart of the Alborz Mountains, some 40 miles north-east of Tehran, this was the volcano that once cast a shadow over trading caravans on the Silk Road to Byzantium. Today, in the Islamic Republic, it looms over a band of asphalt, shuttling traffic from the capital to the Caspian coast – but the symbolism remains.

Three days earlier, hurtling down the same road, we gazed in awestruck silence as the mountain filled the Land Cruiser's windscreen. A vast, near-symmetrical pyramid, its flanks scarred by titanic ridges and sheer glaciers, Damavand appeared to hold absolute dominion

over the surrounding peaks, like an emperor encircled by throngs of genuflecting subjects.

I comforted myself with the knowledge that, despite appearances, we were about to embark on a relatively straightforward climb. In mountaineering terms, Damavand is a cinch, even for five hopelessly underprepared Englishmen: put one foot in front of the other; don't slip; don't go for a nap in the snow; turn back if you get a headache.

Drawn by the ascent's lack of technical challenges and keen to stand on top of this great icon of their homeland, Iranians have been climbing Damavand for decades. Meanwhile foreign climbers, put off by an endless cycle of social unrest and diplomatic hostilities, have elected to stretch their legs elsewhere.

The mountain's unpopularity among the mountaineering cognoscenti makes for solitary slopes, free of the crowds that can undermine your escapism on other peaks. This is a serious mountain climb for people who thirst for adventure and yearn for the remote, but recoil from the idea of dangling from a belay – people like me.

AT THE BOTTOM LOOKING UP

Our ascent began where the dirt road ended at Gardaneh-Sar: a cluster of low buildings with flat stone walls and wattle-and-daub roofs. There are numerous established trails to the summit, each emanating from one of the ramshackle villages – all breezeblock walls and muddy lanes – that pockmark the mountainside.

Ably shepherded by our guides, Mohammad and Nasir, we were to approach from the north-east route, harder than some but purported to be among the most rewarding. The total distance from here to the crater is slight – a smidgeon over 16 miles – but the hefty gains in altitude place great emphasis on the need for gradual acclimatisation. Non-technical it may be, but Damavand has claimed the lives of ten summiteers in the last decade, most of them victims of Acute Mountain Sickness, the

mountaineer's *bête noire*. In our efforts to avoid contributing to this statistic, we would be taking three days to reach the top. Harried by a fusillade of barks from the settlement's posse of belligerent dogs, our expedition took to the hill.

At 3,000 metres, summer on Damavand is a time of plenty. Poppies, lavender and thistles carpet the wind-ravaged plains in a fretwork of red and purple that hums with the industry of insects. Beekeepers wearing shalwar khameez and chitral caps harvest honey from hive boxes while grizzled goatherds mark the mountaineers' passing with disdainful stares.

Within an hour, we came across the great salient features of Damavand's north face: two enormous geothermal bulges, each 100 metres broad, that looked as if the great three-headed dragon of Zoroastrian legend, Azi Dahaka (rumoured to live chained within the mountain), had been slamming against the earth from below, in a bid to escape. 'We call those Damavand's balls,' chirruped Mohammad, pointing at his crotch with disconcerting enthusiasm.

Damavand's metaphorical genitals allude to the mountain's earthly purpose. This is the tallest volcano in Asia, a giant cauldron of molten rock built by nature to relieve the earth-shuddering friction at the conjunction of the Arabian and Eurasian plates. Since its last eruption, some 10,000 years ago, Damavand has brooded

'THIS IS A SERIOUS MOUNTAIN CLIMB FOR PEOPLE WHO THIRST FOR ADVENTURE AND YEARN FOR THE REMOTE, BUT RECOIL FROM THE IDEA OF DANGLING FROM A BELAY – PEOPLE LIKE ME.'

Scorning all the admonitory signs, our single file trudged on, the hypoxia really showing now: frowning expressions, weary steps and pauses for breath. Relief came in the early afternoon: a half-barrel-shaped silhouette emerging through the mist. This was base camp, one of four rudimentary mountain refuges that encircle the mountain at around 4,400 metres. We stepped over the threshold just as a deep rumbling above announced the arrival of a snow-storm.

WEATHERING THE STORM

While the maelstrom raged, the remaining daylight hours were spent playing cards, munching on pistachios and pestering Mohammad to translate the hut's Persian graffiti. Then darkness fell and with it came my futile attempt to sleep. Finally, at 4am, a rustling from below told that the guides, who had slept like contented babes, were preparing the packs for the day ahead. Half an hour later, galvanised by chocolate, flatbreads and a packet of cheese triangles, we gathered on a broad rocky buttress in five centimetres of snow.

From beneath our feet the ridge soared uphill to where the peak's year-round ice-falls, clearly visible against a cobalt-blue sky, were turning orange in the sunrise. In the other direction, the spine swept eastwards, a peninsula of rock jutting into an ocean of low-lying cloud, punctured here and there by a lesser peak.

dormant, its slumbering crater belching sulphurous smoke. But one day it could blow, taking most of this rustic idyll with it.

4,000 METRES HIGH AND CLIMBING

The next day, after a fitful night's rest, we broke camp at dawn before continuing uphill enveloped in the clouds. Above 4,000 metres, Damavand shows a face more becoming a mountain of its standing. The landscape is dominated by scree slopes of nuggety, light brown pumice and streaks of ice, the melting outstretched fingers of the glacial ice-falls that shoot down from the summit in every direction.

OUT OF THIS WORLD

The scene was suitably otherworldly, given Damavand's rich Persian mythology. According to the *Shahnameh* (the Epic of Kings), the Persian poet Ferdowsi's tenth-century epic, it was on these slopes that the hero Fereydun vanquished the evil king Zahhak, a tyrant said to have fed his pet serpents with the brains of his subjects. Fereydun imprisoned Zahhak in the mountain and usurped the crown, going on to rule for 500 years. In the centuries since, the great ridge on which we stood, which delineates much of the north-east route from here on up, came to be known as the Takht-e Fereydun – Fereydun's Throne.

For us there was somewhat less at stake – just ego-gratification – but it still suddenly felt like a big deal. To stay in one piece, every climber must douse their ambition with a realistic awareness that so many variables lie outside of human control. But then you get on the mountain and the sweet taste of challenge seems to overtake all else. Suddenly, the notion of not making it to the top seemed to us like the end of the world. With the sun rising at our backs, we set off up the slope.

Three laboured hours passed and the display on Nasir's GPS flickered past 5,000-metres – steady progress by Mohammad's reckoning, but even our guide's apparent serenity could do little to hide the deteriorating conditions. The morning's plucky breeze had become a blustering gale, coming from the furious-looking cloud swirling around the summit.

PEAK FITNESS

Barely visible against this slate-coloured penumbra, we could just discern the outline of 'the gate', a gap between two rocky outcrops, like a half-finished barricade, through which lay our destination, the summit plateau. It looked – and was – painfully far away.

Had we capitulated at this point, we wouldn't have been the first to fall foul of the mountain's chicanery. As is often the way with prominent peaks (and Damavand is the twelfth most prominent in the world), the weather is powerfully unpredictable. Back in 1971, the Tyrolean climber Reinhold Messner, who would later become the first man to scale all 14 of the world's 'eight-thousander' peaks, failed to overcome this relative trifle when a storm sabotaged his summit bid. Henceforth, Messner would describe Damavand as 'the little hill that defeated me'.

Continuing uphill felt akin to an act of faith – a mental fog of groin-deep snow and freezing temperatures, of numb fingers and even number toes. We plodded upwards, heads bowed in deference to the headwind – with no inclination to stop and marvel at the translucent curtain of the Yakhar Glacier; no happiness as the expected storm failed to converge. Just the act of placing one foot in front of the other – ten drunken steps then an exhausted pause – and half-hearted mutters of encouragement.

Enfeebled by the thin air and convinced that all the winds of Asia were conspiring to stall our progress, I tackled each precipitous snow-field with eyes fixed on the ankle of pace-setter Nasir's trailing leg. Accidental glances downhill brought fits of vertigo – who said this wasn't supposed to be steep?

UP ON THE ROOF

There was only one hundred vertical metres left to climb, but the atmospheric oxygen concentrations were down to 50 per cent of their value at sea level. I urged Nasir onwards and upwards with what was supposed to sound like bravery but came out as a whimper. 'Ten minutes from here,' he replied, exhibiting the classic motivational mendacity of the mountain guide.

Forty minutes later, the terrain beneath his boot-heel changed from snow to stones, made gnarled and jaundiced by the same fumaroles that had begun to contaminate the thin air with a noxious mixture of gases from the belly of the earth. At around midday, I lumbered through the gate, and up to the crater rim.

Now, we stood on top of an Iranian icon, the roof of the Middle East. The huge country spread out in every direction. We couldn't see any of it of course – the cloud had seen to that. But we knew that, far below us, people were slaking their thirst with bottles of 'Damarvand' brand mineral water, purchased with 10,000-rial banknotes decorated with a monochrome image of this mountain's snow-streaked profile. And, this time round, that was more than enough for me. ●

WHEN TO GO
Conditions are most hospitable in July and August, when summit temperatures rarely fall below minus 10ºC.

GETTING THERE
Fly into Tehran (carriers include Qatar Airways and Emirates). Depending on your route up the mountain, the road journey from the capital to the mountain villages takes between two and four hours by car.

ORGANISING YOUR TRIP
Tehran-based outfitters Iran Mountain Zone (www.mountainzone.ir) can arrange and guide your ascent. From 2009, Explore (www.explore.co.uk) will be running the package 'Classic Damavand Trek' in July and August.

COST
There is a US$50 entrance fee for the national park. The cost for guided climbs varies depending on the agency. Expect to pay at least US$500 for a fully inclusive summer

ascent. The Explore package costs from £895 for ten days, excluding flights.

AM I UP TO IT?
You don't need to know your crampons from your karabiners, but this is a serious climb. The summit day is arduous and not for the faint-hearted, and you'll be exposed to extremely high altitudes; if in doubt, consult your doctor.

MORE LIKE THIS
From the remaining six of the volcanic seven summits – the roll-call of the highest volcanoes on each continent – Georgia's Mount Elbrus (5,642 metres) and Tanzania's Kilimanjaro (5,895 metres; see page 218) are similar in terms of scale and challenge.

FOR REFERENCE
Iran Mountain Zone (www.mountainzone.ir) is a mine of information on the mountain's routes and history. Damavand features prominently in *the Shahnameh* by Abolqasem Ferdowsi, the great masterpiece of Persian literature.

'MAN CANNOT DISCOVER NEW OCEANS
UNLESS HE HAS THE COURAGE TO
LOSE SIGHT OF THE SHORE'

ANDRE GIDE

Going to extremes

Pleasure and Paine

Ismay Atkins finds paradise at the end of a long, dusty road.

WHAT	HOW LONG
Torres del Paine trek	4-10 days
WHERE	**THRILL FACTOR**
Southern Patagonia, Chile	● ● ● ● ●

Standing on the shores of the Last Hope Sound, the Patagonian wind beating against the seams of my anorak, I tried to imagine if anywhere could feel further from home than Puerto Natales. This remote waterside outpost, a weathered settlement of battered tin roofs and sleepy streets, is just a few score miles away from the southernmost tip of the continental mainland. It seemed the very picture of solitude.

Only dedicated travellers make it to this remote corner of Chile – usually via a long bumpy bus journey across the Patagonian backcountry. Nearly all of them come to trek Torres del Paine: one of the world's most electrifying walks, taking you past blue and green glacial lakes, formidable ice-pocked peaks and dense forests.

As I made my way from El Calafate, just across the border in Argentina, to Puerto Natales – our elderly bus crawling through mile upon mile upon empty mile of lifeless plains – I found it increasingly hard to credit the existence of such a colourful wilderness. Patagonia is a vast region shared (not particularly harmoniously) between Chile and Argentina. For all its famous natural highlights (the Perito Moreno Glacier, the Lake District, the sealife of the Valdés Peninsula), most of what you see on a visit here is barren, undulating deserts of *meseta* (treeless plains). A constant wind bends everything to its will, colours are muted – dull grassy tans, greys, browns – and dust covers everything with a gritty coat.

THE BOUNDLESS PLAINS

There was nothing to see for hours as I stared out the bus window, save for the odd sheep (which outnumber people by a factor of 5, 10 or 20 to one, depending on who you believe), a Patagonian hare or a startled *guanaco* (a pretty, local version of the llama). Nevertheless, I couldn't take my eyes off the shrubby desert;

'GREY GLACIER ENTERS INTO VIEW WITHOUT FANFARE, ITS VARIEGATED BLUE-GREY CUTS AND CREVASSES APPEARING TO EACH HIKER LIKE A THRILLING PRIVATE DISCOVERY.'

it was mind-bending in its relentlessness, interesting despite its apparent dearth of interest.

The arid plains of Patagonia have been exerting a peculiar fascination on visitors for centuries. Among the more illustrious, Charles Darwin ponders the *meseta* in *Voyage of the Beagle* (1839): 'These plains are pronounced by all most wretched and useless… Why, then, and the case is not peculiar to myself, have these arid wastes taken so firm possession of the memory?' He later postulates that 'it must be partly owing to the free scope given to the imagination. The plains of Patagonia are boundless, for they are scarcely practicable, and hence unknown.'

Intrigued though I was by the austerity of the terrain, this didn't by any stretch of the imagination mean that I wanted to trek through it for five days. Arriving in Puerto Natales, the jumping-off point for Torres del Paine, knowing I was marooned by hundreds of miles of Patagonian wasteland, I caught myself thinking: it had better get considerably better than this.

RISING FROM THE RUBBLE

Fortunately, the hyperbole I had read about Torres del Paine is amply justified. Rarely does nature offer such rich visual rewards for your footwork as in this most dramatic of South American national parks (decreed a UNESCO Biosphere Reserve in 1978). The scenic diversity is extraordinary: milky-green lakes, steep valleys,

granite mountains, pretty meadows, pre-Andean desert, lush forests and giant creaking glaciers (eerie relics of the last Ice Age) are all arranged as if by some omnipotent set designer around the Paine mountain range, an eastern spur of the Andes that rises formidably, and most improbably, out of the barren steppe. The namesake *torres*, or 'towers', are the set piece – three polished granite needles carved by glaciation with picture-perfect precision.

Aside from its string of natural jewels, the beauty of trekking the Torres del Paine national park is its accessibility – guides aren't necessary, and anyone with good all-round fitness, basic common sense and a serious coat can take on the challenge independently (those concerned about fitness or map-reading should stick to the shorter, less isolated 'W' trek). Even as the park draws increasing numbers of hikers, and facilities expand year on year, you still get to live out your very own Patagonian survival odyssey: pitching your tent in the howling wind; drinking clear, clean water straight from the icy rivers; and willing your tired legs on to the next camp before nightfall. There are no cars, no ATMs, no phone reception and no mains electricity.

PREPARATION AND PLANNING

The park's headline trek is the ten-day Paine Circuit, which circles the entire Paine range. This challenging walk, a shoo-in to any list of the world's top-ten treks, offers constantly changing views of the Paine massif. For those with a little less time or stamina, the 'W' circuit (four to five days), so named after the shape it traces on a map, allows you to skip the 'less exciting' sections through the forest and pampas, taking you straight to the big hits: Grey Glacier emptying into an iceberg-spotted lake; the vertiginous path up the Valle Francés; the striped Cuernos (Horns) del Paine, standing at 2,600 metres; and the needle-like Torres del Paine.

In the minibus and over breakfast, between bursts of 'my tent's lighter than your tent' one-upmanship, we heard trekkers ruminating on the best way to tackle the circuits. Part of the fun is in planning your own itinerary – it's advisable to pencil in your overnight stays before starting (wild camping is prohibited in the park), bearing in mind realistic daily distances and keeping a close eye on the time and remaining daylight hours. The official maps are available online at www.pntp.cl, though you'll also be given one on entry to the park.

CARRYING THE WEIGHT OF YOUR WORLD

It is now theoretically possible to do the entire Paine circuit without a tent, hopping from one *refugio* (mountain cabin) to the next. But the lodges are relatively costly and fill up fast. For the maximum sense of achievement – and greater flexibility – we opted to carry all our kit and supplies, brave the night temperatures (which rarely fall below zero in summer, but are equally never balmy) and cook our own dinners. Mercifully, all trekkers are spared the weight of litres of water, as you can fill up straight from chilled streams, which taste almost sweet after chlorinated tap water.

And so we stood, poised to tackle the trek, on the banks of Lake Pehoe, the weight of food for five days, tent, thermal sleeping bag, inflatable mattress and a skeleton kitchen already exerting unwelcome pressure on our shoulders. With a degree of trepidation, we watched as those finishing their trek lined up for the ferry: some limping, others having resorted to flip-flops to air their blisters, and all looking unnervingly feral, with wind-matted hair, battered cheeks and mud-splattered clothing.

ICE WITH THAT?

The first leg took us along the banks of Lake Grey and eventually to Grey Glacier: the largest glacier in the park, and part of the vast Southern Patagonian Ice Field. Just as I was wondering if the shrubby steppe would ever end, I rounded

'IT IS BIZARRE WHEN, IN THE SPACE OF A FEW HOURS, YOU HAVE TO SWITCH FROM SHADES, SHORTS AND SUNBLOCK IN A FLOWER-STREWN MEADOW TO RAIN GEAR AND THERMAL GLOVES AT THE BASE OF A MOODY-LOOKING MOUNTAIN.'

the bend and stalled – eyes bulging in the manner of an exaggerated cartoon character. Chunks of ice the colour of blue curaçao were floating on the lake, like an accidental paint spill over the subdued Patagonian palette; they had

been discarded by Grey Glacier, still tantalisingly out of view. We turned back and watched as other trekkers stopped in their dusty tracks, slowly absorbing the spectacle. This sight, and the knowledge that an unimaginably huge ice machine lay only a few miles ahead, administered a natural high that propelled us the rest of the way to Camp Grey, and the foot of the glacier.

Even those who have seen many glaciers will marvel at the scene – no hordes, no railings, no dedicated 'picture op' spot. Glacier Grey enters into view without fanfare, its variegated blue-grey cuts and crevasses appearing to each hiker like a thrilling private discovery.

FOUR SEASONS IN ONE DAY

As we picked our way up the sharp incline of the Valle Francés (French Valley), following the fast-flowing river towards its source in the

mountains, the mood changed. A sighing forest gave way to a desolate new world of screaming high winds laced with ice; long-dead tree trunks, gnarled into sinister shapes; and dirty-grey glaciers clinging to mountains, occasionally calving lumps of ice. At the top we arrived at a huge natural amphitheatre, a clearing circled – on a grand scale – by spiked mountains, granite walls and, far below, a series of chalky grey-green lakes.

So violent a climatic and scenic change is typical of Torres del Paine. Patagonian weather is notoriously volatile, and nowhere more so than here, where landscapes and ecosystems start and finish with surprising frequency. It doesn't matter how many times you're told to prepare for all eventualities – it is still exciting and bizarre when, in the space of a few hours, you have to switch from sunglasses, shorts and sunblock in a flower-strewn meadow to protective rain gear and thermal gloves at the base of a moody mountain. While packing for your trek, it's worth keeping in mind the old adage: 'There's no such thing as bad weather, only bad clothes'.

NATURE'S PLAYGROUND

We had planned the trek to end with a towering finale: the three granite spires known as the Torres del Paine. After a knee-grinding boulder ascent, the toughest section of the trek, you are repaid with one of the world's most dramatic spectacles. In a beautiful piece of natural plot suspense, trekkers are kept guessing until the last moment, with only the very tops of the spires in view for most of the climb (and providing little by way of encouragement). With little warning, the scene unfolds and, like so many in the park, it is fabulously far-fetched: a trio of granite spires soaring above a cirque, neatly carved by millennia of glaciation. Its bed is filled with a pistachio-coloured tarn, fed from high above by the drip-drip of glacial melt, whose rivulets paint mint humbug stripes down a colossal wall of granite.

After days of natural theatre, I should have expected nothing less of the Torres del Paine. But still the finale left me reeling as I dragged myself back down the valley to the exit, before wending my way back through the rubble of the Patagonian wasteland to more mundane sights. ●

WHEN TO GO
November to March (which is spring/summer in Chile), when the weather is most favourable; the park is at its most crowded in December, January and February. Winter treks are possible but challenging.

GETTING THERE
Minibuses leave from Puerto Natales in the early morning to make the 75-mile journey to the Torres del Paine national park. Most visitors fly into El Calafate across the border in Argentina, or into Punta Arenas in Chile; buses run on both routes (book in advance).

ORGANISING YOUR TRIP
There is no need to pre-book your trek but if you intend to stay/eat in the lodges rather than camp, reserve your place (www.fantastico sur.com or www.andescapetour.com). On arrival, register your details with the park ranger (*guardaparque*) and pay your entrance fee. In advance of your trip, you can plot your route and overnight stops using the official maps at www.pntp.cl.

For the ultimate post-trek pamper, check into Indigo (www.indigopatagonia.com) in Puerto Natales, where roof-top hot tubs look out across the sound towards Torres del Paine.

COST
Entry to the park costs 15,000 Chilean pesos, campsites and lodges extra. There are some free campsites but these offer limited facilities (in general, just a cold tap or two and a toilet).

AM I UP TO IT?
No specialist skills are required, but the trek is strenuous in parts (particularly on the longer circuit), more so if carrying kit and food.

MORE LIKE THIS
There are few national parks as diverse and pristine as Torres del Paine that can be tackled independently. Other great multi-day wilderness treks that can be embarked upon without a guide include the Overland Track in Tasmania (see page 182) and the Milford Track in New Zealand through Fjordland National Park.

FOR REFERENCE
The website for the national park (www.pntp.cl) is translated into English and contains essential information about activities, lodges and transport, as well as printable maps.

Patagonia: A Cultural History by Chris Moss gives you the long view of Patagonia and Tierra del Fuego, with accounts of explorations by the likes of Magellan, Drake and Darwin.

Snow motion

Ismay Atkins sleds across Lapland, powered by a team of huskies.

WHAT Dog-sledding in the Arctic Circle	**HOW LONG** 5 nights, 4 days
WHERE Karasjok, extreme north of Norway	**THRILL FACTOR** ● ● ● ● ●

Before departure, I had willingly absorbed all the cheery Lapland clichés about dashing through the snow, bobble hats and winter wonderlands. All of which facile notions did precious little to prepare me for the realities of life in the Arctic region: the severity, the solitude, and the fact that a bobble hat offers minimal protection at 25 below.

As the taxi crunched along the deserted, snowy roads from Alta airport (an atmospherically remote point of entry on the fjords) towards Karasjok, the driver pointed to the outside temperature showing on his dashboard: minus 27°C. I shuddered, feeling the beginnings of a compulsive fascination with life this far out on the edge: the dark, the cold, the sparseness of human life.

'Do you ever get used to the cold?' I ventured. The driver looked at me, with the faintest of knowing smiles: 'Only as much as you get used to putting your finger in a flame.' The analogy, I saw later, was entirely apt. Super sub-zero temperatures feel less like the 'icy grip' prevalent in poems, and more like a Chinese burn. In extreme cases of exposure, the skin blisters in much the same way as it does in intense heat. The flame image stayed with me, as we ploughed on for hours through an otherworldly landscape of frozen forests, lakes, canyons and mountains: scenes devoid of all signs of movement (even wind), frozen into a long winter pause, and illuminated with surprising intensity by the light of the full moon reflecting off the snow.

SUN DOWNER

We arrived in the dark at husky headquarters in Karasjok, a small Sami settlement in the Norwegian region of Finnmark. We had also left the airport in the dark. And we were, in fact, going to spend most of every day in the dark. This was the Arctic Circle in the middle of December, and the sun wouldn't be putting in a full appearance until February. Sitting in the comparative warmth of my wood cabin, I contemplated four days of darkness, while tuning in to the hush of the forest and an occasional chorus of wailing from the kennels of the nearby dog yard.

DRIVING SCHOOL

In the morning, kitted out with snow suit, snow boots, triple-layered mittens and reindeer-fur cap, I shuffled over like a puffed-up moon-walker to meet my team of huskies and receive some dog-sledding training. Banking on a cautious first day, I coolly took in the short lesson on how to drive a sled: the soft and hard brakes; how to shift your weight on corners; and, most importantly, tips on how to hold on to your sled if you fall off, to prevent the dogs from running to the hills without you. Sounded straightforward enough.

I stepped on to the sled, one foot on a 'runner', the other pressed on the 'hard' brake and took a firm grip of the curved wooden hand bar – I released the brake and the huskies flew. For some reason, I had pictured slow, quaint traverses of frozen flats. So it came as an adrenaline-pumping, knuckle-whitening surprise to find myself, within a few short minutes, slalom sledding at what felt like turbo speed, powered by six panting huskies of clear athletic pedigree. Crashing into the bends and eventually losing my balance, I took a dive into

'THE SUN BRUSHES CLOSE ENOUGH TO THE HORIZON TO SCATTER THE PRETTIEST OF PINKY-PURPLE RAYS.'

the snow, instinctively using my hands to break the fall instead of heeding the advice about detaining the dogs – a big no-no.

When we reached the frozen Karasjohka river at the bottom and the orderly train of five sleds (huskies follow a line trailing from the sled in front with incredible precision) took a pause, my pulse returned to normal, and I quickly upped my mental game.

Although there's something inherently peaceful about dog-sledding – the perfectly still surroundings, the silent athleticism of the huskies – it's a much faster, more active and more exciting sport than most people imagine. As a sledder,

your role is more participant than passenger: moving your weight subtly to maintain balance on bendy sections; 'pedalling' up steep inclines to rally the dogs (pushing using one foot on the ground while the other remains on the sled); crouching quickly to avoid a lashing from low-hanging branches; and applying your weight to the sled in the event of a fall to halt your team.

THE SILENT ENGINE

Dog-sleds may no longer be the only way to transport supplies through deep snow in polar regions – as they were before the advent of snowmobiles, roads and planes – but it doesn't take long to realise their potential for power and efficiency. Like a natural engine, the dogs respond briskly to the lead musher's quiet commands (not shouted, as stereotype might have you believe); slow quickly on feeling the tug of the brake; and, as a team, can reach speeds of up to 15 miles an hour (in racing conditions).

Fortunately for beginners, it is a sport that allows for quick and satisfying progress. By the second and third downhill runs, I had gained confidence (the dogs aren't keen on driver hesitancy), managed to unlock my knees and body from their position of rigid fear, and realised that the falls were actually very safe and soft – all but the most brittle of bones can handle sinking into a metre of snow.

ALL WHITE NOW

It was only at this stage, emerging from my first successful 'slalom' through the woods on to more manageable frosty tundra (the name given to huge treeless plains of the Arctic region), that I dared to take my eyes off the path and look around. A fresh deep-pile carpet of snow lay ahead as far as the eye could see, fringed at the sides by twinkling trees dressed up in an array of delicate interlocking white ornaments crafted by the hoar frost (or 'white

'SUPER SUB-ZERO TEMPERATURES FEEL LESS LIKE THE "ICY GRIP" PREVALENT IN POEMS, AND MORE LIKE A CHINESE BURN.'

frost'). Distinct from ground frost, hoar frost forms at sub-zero temperatures and drapes surfaces in a pretty white-ice coating.

A scene of great purity – of snowy blankets, icicles and crystallised snow-tinsel on branches – I might have imagined from home, but what I hadn't anticipated, given the latitude and the season, was a spectacle of exotic light and colour. In December, the sun never rises above the horizon, instead diffusing a disorienting light for a few hours that feels like a strange mixture of both dusk and dawn. But the sun brushes close enough to scatter the prettiest of pinky-purple rays – deep pink at its greatest concentration on the horizon, baby pink covering a distant hill, and pale Parma violet hues everywhere else.

DEEP FREEZE

When we stopped for lunch, our leader Christel, a no-nonsense Norwegian musher of mildly intimidating pragmatism (three knives strapped to her belt, self-made reindeer-skin trousers and a friendly but firm treatment of beginners), built a roaring fire in the forest with expert speed. As we huddled around it on reindeer pelts, pink hands lunged as close as was bearable to the flames, the dogs rested in the snow.

It was only when I opened my bag to find everything, including my sandwiches (and my contact lens solution, fruit, water), frozen solid that I realised: the fire, an instant flame-grill for our sarnies, was less about adding an adventurous flavour to proceedings than a practical imperative.

DISCOMFORT AND JOY

The cold had bitten with varying intensity during the day, but it was ever-present, causing an unnerving numbness in at least one peripheral area at any one time – usually the nose, toes or a thumbs. Back in the cabins, roasting red in front of the wood-burning stove, the rookies had lengthy clothing discussions in preparation for the next day's sledding, increasingly determined to conquer the cold. Three pairs of socks or four? Wool or fleece? Scarf arrangements were rehearsed to cover as much facial skin as possible, while still allowing for breathing and seeing. Mittens not gloves (the proximity of the fingers keeps them warm). Loose not tight (tight clothes aren't as effective).

By the last day, I was quietly confident with my line of attack: three merino base layers, one hollow-fibre roll neck, one chunky-knit lamb's

> ## 'IT DOESN'T TAKE LONG DRIVING A WELL-HONED TEAM OF HUSKIES TO REALISE THEIR POTENTIAL FOR POWER AND EFFICIENCY.'

wool jumper, a goose-down body warmer… and that was just the underclothes. This latest ensemble yielded some improvement – and I fancied there were even moments of vague thermal comfort – but at temperatures colder than the average household freezer, in reality this was a war I could not win.

Back at the lodge on the last night, the memory of a five-minute-long frostbite panic earlier in the day (the result of a careless mittenless photography session) still very much with me, I quizzed the owner Sven Engholm about life in the Arctic. Sven, the 11-time winner of the Finnmarksløpet 1000 – at 1,000 kilometres, the longest dog-sledding race in Europe – answered my basic survival questions and told me of his impatience during summer months for the onset of winter. Gently spoken, and possessing a quiet, rugged confidence, he seemed to command the sort of instant respect one earns from a lifetime voluntarily embracing some of the most inhospitable terrain in the world.

TESTING HUMAN BOUNDARIES

In the end, it was the alluring romance of survival – nature's practical challenges and man's practical solutions – as much as the chimerical landscape and invigorating expeditions that inspired and stretched the mind. Long after it became feasible to live somewhere more clement, the native Samis have stayed in Lapland, and others – passionate Arctic dwellers like Christel and Sven – have moved in. As I made my way back to Alta airport

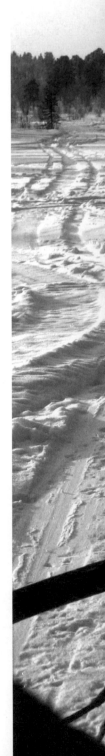

– the sun partially rising behind me at 10.30am and taking a pink highlighter to the branches of the trees – I realised that my initial curiosity had evolved into a deep respect.

A short trip to the edge of the world, and to the boundaries of my comfort zone, had been exhilarating enough to cause a profound comedown. Still, that didn't stop me flying in to Heathrow with a pleasing new take on English winter: land of bright skies, long hours of daylight and balmy temperatures. ●

WHEN TO GO
Dog-sledding expeditions in Lapland take place between the start of December and the end of April.

GETTING THERE
Fly to Alta then transfer (2-3 hours) to Karasjok.

ORGANISING YOUR TRIP
The author travelled with Activities Abroad (01670 789 991, www.activitiesabroad.com).

COST
£1,115 excluding flights for four nights and three days (at full-board).

AM I UP TO IT?
No previous experience or training is required for dog-sledding; you will, however, need to be able to stand for many hours in sub-zero conditions.

MORE LIKE THIS
Dog-sledding tours take place in a variety of snowy places, but for wilderness outings the Arctic region is best, in particular Alaska, Greenland and northern Canada.

FOR REFERENCE
Arctic Dreams by Barry Lopez.

Diving into the abyss

Joe Mackie swims between tectonic plates in the crystal-clear waters of an Icelandic lake.

WHAT	HOW LONG
Scuba-diving the Silfra Crack	One day

WHERE	THRILL FACTOR
Thingvellir Lake, Iceland	● ● ● ● ●

Two metres of water and eight millimetres of neoprene. That's all there was between me and the most powerful, apocalyptic force on the planet. Lurking beneath the surface of a glacial lake, somewhere between Europe and America, is the Silfra Crack, a huge rip in the earth's crust that scythes through Iceland, the towering walls of rock on either side the final frontiers of the North American and Eurasian continental plates.

Sealed in a dry suit, I took another breath through my regulator and watched the bubbles spiralling towards the sunlight. Looking right and left again, I tried to engage my mind with the surreality of being suspended between two continents – and the fantasy of a journey to the centre of the earth. At Thingvellir Lake, the fissure in the earth cuts through some of the world's clearest water. With visibility at over a hundred metres, Silfra is the perfect portal into the underworld. It's as though there were no barrier at all between you and the very forces that shape our planet, as you mingle with Arctic char, brown trout and three-spine sticklebacks.

GOING UNDER

Divers need to get their PADI qualifications before venturing to the glacial north, but Silfra is a shallow dive and there are no exacting technical demands – apart from mastering the buoyancy balancing act of the dry suit; experienced guides and equipment are provided by the lakeside dive centre. Fortunately for non-divers, the water is shallow and clear, and you can get almost as complete an experience by snorkelling on the surface. You won't be journeying any closer to the centre of the earth, of course, but you still get a window on this unique underwater spectacle.

We arrived at Keflavik Airport the evening before our dive, and it was a short drive to the capital through the soupy half-light of a high Arctic evening. After a strong dose of Reykjavik nightlife, my head was heavy as we headed out of the mini-opolis the next morning. Not the ideal way to prepare for a slice of the life sub-aquatic perhaps, but as the sun rose higher and my personal fog lifted, Iceland poured irrepressibly through the windows of the 4X4. The landscape is alive with the forces that are forging it: without the passage of time to soften their contours, waterfalls crash over sheer cliffs and only the first beachheads of vegetation blanket the rock in a primordial green. Apart from the odd, empty road there's barely any sign of human presence, and everywhere you sense the sculpting fingers of glaciers at work.

DONNING THE DRY SUIT

Thingvellir Lake is an hour's appetite-whetting drive from Reykjavik and, after a short briefing, it's time to pull on the dry suit. The mercury never gets too excited in Iceland, even in summer, and the lake itself is fed by a chilling underground flow of meltwater from the Langjökull glacier, 32 miles away. This ensures the water is incredibly clear,

'VOLCANIC ISLANDS PUT ON A SHOW OF PLANET-SHAPING FORCES, WITH A CAST OF GEYSERS, GLACIERS AND WATERFALLS.'

and so pure you can drink it, but it also makes it several degrees the wrong side of balmy.

A dry suit keeps the water out, sealing you in a bubble of body-warmed air. It also means a hood that presses like a circus strongman on your temples, and a weight vest (to counter the suit's buoyancy) that makes for an energetic shuffle to the lakeside dive platform. Once in the water, though, it's effortless. The gentle current of the subterranean stream carries you over the initially shallow crack, then the lake floor drops away – about 20 metres at first, then gradually sloping deeper into the distance. Sinking below the surface, you're powered by the gentle drift and the occasional flick of a fin.

MIDDLE EARTH

As the crack widens and the rock walls lengthen on either side, you find yourself drifting, with just enough elbow room, between continents – and you can't fail to feel the thrill. Known as 'the Cathedral', this section of the crack is on a grand scale, reaching a maximum depth of 65 metres.

The underwater scene is of jagged rocks – mountains in miniature on the lake bed and sheer cliffs framing it on either side. Submerged vegetation clings to nooks and crannies on the bed and the walls, hiding the odd darting fish. Though the sight was spectacular in itself, my thoughts kept drifting back to the plates. As still as they seem, you know the walls can move with incomprehensible power. They're diverging at the overall rate of roughly two centimetres a year, though thankfully their movement isn't

constant. The plates stay motionless for hundreds of years until enough tension builds, then they rip apart in a mighty wrench – something the forecasters keep a close eye on, in case you were wondering.

For 20 minutes or more, I floated on through 'the Cathedral'. With no sound but the amplified cadences of my own breathing, it was easy to lose myself down there. Occasionally, like a signal from the world above the water, the sun emerged from behind a cloud, kaleidoscoping through the ripples above to bathe everything below in a new light. The crack widened and narrowed, grew deeper and shallower, with new life clinging irrepressibly to its ragged contours in shades of green. Then, after around 500 metres, the cavern widened and joined the main lake. A few minutes later, I hauled my weighted body out of the water feeling as though I'd returned from somewhere much further away than a few metres below the surface.

'I TRIED TO ENGAGE MY MIND WITH THE REALITY OF BEING SUSPENDED BETWEEN CONTINENTS – THE FANTASY OF A JOURNEY TO THE CENTRE OF THE EARTH.'

FEELING THE FORCE

After the sweet release from the grip of the dry suit and a warming cup of tea, I was eager for more geological drama – and Iceland has a greater concentration of that than any country in the world. A number of portals to the underworld lie within a short drive from Thingvellir.

The geothermal show of the Haukadalur Valley, one of only 50 or so geyser fields on earth,

is essential viewing. The pools steam in a constant reminder of the forces that are lurking below, and then every five minutes the star turn – the Strokkur – lets rip. Haukadalur's most active geyser spurts water 30 metres into the air, and standing a few metres away, I could feel the heat and the spray.

Besides the shifting tectonic plates and the geothermal show, the so-called 'Golden Circle' – a loop out of Reykjavik – also does an impressive line in water power: it's fast-moving at Iceland's poster-boy waterfall, Gullfoss, and sedate at Langjökull glacier, the country's second largest, feeding both Thingvellir Lake and the Haukadalur geothermal geysers. As I'd come to expect, Langjökull hides its own geological secret: deep beneath the ice sheet lies the Langjökull volcano, a huge, brooding, active monster which is just waiting to blow its top; and it's not a question of 'if', but 'when' it will erupt, melting the glacier and unleashing a biblical flood that will reshape the land.

Fortunately, the volcano-monitoring stations had concluded it wouldn't be on the afternoon after my dive. So, on with the second ridiculous suit of the day, followed by a bumpy 4x4 drive over the scree, fording a couple of rivers of glacial run-off. Past the wind-sculpted edges of the glacier, there was a transfer to snowmobiles waiting to take us out across the pocks and ridges of Langjökull's surface for another close encounter with a natural force. The engines are a drop in the ocean compared to the power below, but they provide enough speed to turn your knuckles a shade whiter.

After our adventure on ice, we started the drive back to Reykjavik. Just before the sun set we passed another waterfall crashing over a huge, sheer cliff, with a rainbow just visible in its spray. It seemed a fitting end to the day. By the time we got back to the capital, it felt like I had returned from another world. The only forces left to reckon with were those of a Saturday night in Reykjavik – and the chilly embrace of a Viking beer. ●

WHEN TO GO
You can dive year-round, but scant daylight and plummeting temperatures in winter make May to September the best time to go.

GETTING THERE
Reykjavik is the best base for exploring Silfra and the 'Golden Circle'.

ORGANISING YOUR TRIP
Black Tomato (www.blacktomato.co.uk) organises three-day packages for the dive. You can arrange your dive independently with www.dive.is.

COST
The dive, including pick-up from Reykjavik, equipment and guide, costs €249. Black Tomato offers three-day packages from £1,300, including flights, transfers, accommodation, the dive and all activities.

AM I UP TO IT?
To dive Silfra, you'll need to complete the PADI Open Water Diver course (www.padi.com). It is, however, possible to snorkel it.

MORE LIKE THIS
Silfra's position between the plates is unique. However, the Blue Hole, 60 miles off the coast of Belize, is an almost perfectly circular 'hole' in the world's second-largest reef (www.travel belize.org) and a lot warmer.

FOR REFERENCE
Read up on Thingvellir National Park at www.nat.is/travelguideeng/thingvellir.htm. For information on Iceland, see www.icetourist.is.

Icy wastes

Juliet Rieden picks her way up the Fox Glacier.

WHAT	HOW LONG
Trek on Fox Glacier	6-7 hours
WHERE	THRILL FACTOR
South Island, New Zealand	

Our guide carved a new path through the ice with his pick and – feeling like explorers scaling the ice for the first time – we walked in a line behind him, literally in his footsteps for fear of slipping down a crevasse.

There's a sense of nature taking charge all over New Zealand, but nowhere more so than in Glacier Country, on the wild west coast of the South Island. Here, nature wears her history on her surly snowcaps, where the moving remnants of the Ice Age creak and scrape as they advance, eventually trickling down to feed into thick rainforests below. The incongruity of seeing ice faces and rainforests in the same frame feels otherworldly, like a day out in Middle-earth – but as I fitted boots with crampons, I began to feel decidedly more Ranulph Fiennes than Frodo.

EIGHT MILES OF ICE

Fox Glacier is the longest on the west coast, falling some 2,600 metres on its eight-mile journey from the Southern Alps. It has been advancing at a staggering rate – roughly 90 centimetres a day since 1985, approximately ten times the speed of most valley glaciers around the world. As a result, no two visits to Fox can ever be the same. New ice features form hourly, while others – if you're lucky – break off dramatically.

We climbed slowly up the ice face from the salt-and-pepper slush at the bottom, spiking with our crampons and pulling our weight up with the help of alpenstocks. We walked through ice tunnels, up to the sheer faces of electric blue-white ice mountains and into gaping ice caves. All around, pinnacles of ice were dusted with snow, juxtaposed with rounded Dalí-esque valleys of ice and plateaux cut with miniature jagged peaks.

We ate our lunch on a relatively flat part of the glacier and took in the sounds of silence – even the tour group sat in silence, listening only to the prehistoric creaking of the glacier on the move and the odd bird coasting on the breeze.

The descent was, if anything, tougher than the climb. Every muscle was concentrated on not slipping down the ice, which, melted by a day of dull sun, was now slightly wet. Even with aching muscles and the magical colours turning into a mundane grey slush and scree at the bottom, I was already planning a return trip. ●

WHEN TO GO
The glacier is open for treks year round, but November to April has the best weather.

GETTING THERE
The nearest airport is Queenstown. From there it's a five-hour drive north to Fox Glacier.

ORGANISING YOUR TRIP
Fox Glacier Guiding (www.foxguides.co.nz) runs tours; see www.newzealand.com for others.

COST
The all-day glacier walk costs NZ$135, including a guide, transport and all equipment.

AM I UP TO IT?
No specific training is required but you should have good all-round fitness and agility, and be able to breath comfortably at high altitudes.

MORE LIKE THIS
Short treks can be arranged on Perito Moreno Glacier in Argentinian Patagonia – one of the world's largest advancing glaciers, with pieces breaking off dramatically into a vast turquoise lake.

FOR REFERENCE
Parts of Peter Jackson's *The Lord of the Rings* trilogy were filmed in the Fox Glacier area.

A long way down

Ruth Jarvis hikes a vertical mile down into the Grand Canyon and – rather more painfully – back up again.

WHAT	**HOW LONG**
Climb to the floor of the Grand Canyon	3 days, 2 nights
WHERE	**THRILL FACTOR**
Arizona, USA	● ● ● ● ○

Beneath me was a chasm of dimensions that defied the imagination, above me the bluest, clearest sky, and to either side rock walls of startling beauty – and all I dared to look at were my own two feet plopping down on the path one by one, in a rhythmic, bouncy lope. Whichever way you go down the Grand Canyon, you can bet on two things: a steep gradient, and the possibility of falling to your death. Which rather focuses your attention – and your eyes – on staying upright.

The Grand Canyon isn't the world's deepest canyon, nor its largest, but it could well be its most dramatic. As well as almost unquantifiably vast vital statistics – the canyon is a mile deep, anywhere between 600 feet and 19 miles wide and 277 miles long – it has a unique profile, dropping abruptly off from the flat Colorado Plateau like a biblical crack in the earth. Weather systems trip at its verge, generating violent thunderstorms that look like mere celestial doodles from the opposite rim. Giant rock monoliths stretch out from its edges, eroded into shapes recalling religious architecture. The overall impression is one of beauty, but a disorienting beauty that is hard for human eyes to process – even the most die-hard atheist cannot but feel wonder at its creation.

WE'RE GOING IN!

Backpacks packed, checklists checked, nerves a-jangling, we presented ourselves at the park office to sign up for backcountry passes. The ranger grilled us about our plans, and issued some stern advice on taking it slowly and drinking water regularly and copiously – at least four litres each for each of the three days of our trip.

Ignore such advice at your peril. Conditions here are extreme, unique, counter-intuitive and fast-changing. It can be winter at the top and summer at the bottom, thanks to the elevation change. Shade is hard to come by, water often impossible, and the heat often furnace-fierce. And as for wildlife, I'd already spied a tarantula just half a mile down Hermit Trail. Even on the busy, patrolled main paths there are scores of casualties every year, most of them avoidable.

THERE AND BACK AGAIN

First-timers are advised to take one of these 'corridor' routes, and we duly set off on the wide, well-maintained Bright Angel Trail, early on a May morning. At first we felt conspicuously overspecced with our technical gear – we saw more high heels and flip-flops than we did water bottles. But as the trail descended we gradually shed the daytrippers: the last turned back after reaching the viewpoint at Three Mile Resthouse. Bright Angel is built around a wide geological fault, which creates a natural break in the cliff and makes for constant vistas: this is one of them.

Going over the edge plunges you into a new and marginal world of stone and trees. The path is graded into long steps and follows regular zig-zags; you swiftly settle into a rhythm, leaning slightly back uphill (and remembering to give way to mules). You measure your progress not in miles but in rock layers, descending from Kaibab Limestone (245 million years old) to Vishnu Schist (1.7-1.8 billion).

We reached our overnight stop at Indian Garden campground by mid-afternoon and pitched our tents. Then, glad to escape the weight of our backpacks, we set off again across

'WHICHEVER WAY YOU GO DOWN THE GRAND CANYON, YOU CAN BET ON TWO THINGS: A STEEP GRADIENT, AND THE POSSIBILITY OF FALLING TO YOUR DEATH.'

the blissfully flat Tonto Platform, to watch sunset from Plateau Point. It was a joy to lift our gaze to the desert landscape and the opposite canyon wall, closer now we were halfway down. And, beneath us, newly visible, the muddy yellow river.

After a porridge breakfast, both to sustain and warm, we dived back into the canyon. The path closed in as it followed creek banks and side canyons, and required nimble footwork. At times, the vegetation was dark and primeval, and the solitude unnerving. It was a relief to emerge to sunlight and the Colorado River view, though

journey's end was still quite a yomp away along a rocky riverside path: civilisation, in the form of the café at Phantom Ranch, was very welcome, along with a chance to nurse our blisters.

Getting down, of course, had been the easy bit. The gruelling ascent remained, pretty much a continuous nine-mile staircase with a 20 per cent gradient. Taking it slow, resting every hour, drinking regularly, not thinking too far ahead, talking as we went – these strategies all helped. There was less contemplation of scenery on the way back up: we were tired, for a start, and our backpacks punched their weight once refilled with the camping gear (a second night at Indian Gardens camp had allowed us to travel light on the previous day). And, instead of leaving the crowds behind us, we rose up to meet them, their bright chatter clashing with our quiet new thoughts on the immense.

Leaving the canyon would have been anti-climactic, had not a pair of the desert's rarest and most cherished animals, the bighorn sheep, mounted a rocky stupa just to our left to provide an honour guard as we climbed out. ●

WHEN TO GO
The best months to attempt the hike are May or October, when the temperatures are generally more bearable.

GETTING THERE
The nearest international airports are in Las Vegas and Phoenix. Arriving at either of these, you'll then need to rent a car. If you fancy turning up at the canyon in style, take the historic train: www.thetrain.com.

ORGANISING YOUR TRIP
All the information you'll need can be found at www.nps.gov/grca. There's no advantage to going with a group unless you are alone or taking a non-corridor route, in which case it is advisable.

COST
The park entry fee is $25 per car. Back-country permits cost $10 and camping is $5 per person per night.

AM I UP TO IT?
Yes, if you have a good level of cardiovascular fitness (ie play sport or use a gym regularly) or if you prepare with some steep hikes.

MORE LIKE THIS
The Grand Canyon is a one-off. Of the world's other legendary canyons, Mexico's Copper Canyon is the next most easily explored.

FOR REFERENCE
Hiking Grand Canyon National Park by Ron Adkison is the best trail guide.

The seventh continent

Matt Chesterton visits the world's harshest wilderness – the easy way.

WHAT	**HOW LONG**
Cruise to Antarctica	11 days
WHERE	**THRILL FACTOR**
Ushuaia to the Antarctic Peninsula	● ● ● ● ●

'd been told to expect the sublime in Antarctica, but this was ridiculous. In just one afternoon I had filled my logbook (what a notebook becomes the instant it crosses a gangplank) with the following:

Excursion to Mikklesen Harbour… Beach strewn with whale ribcages and half-buried planks from old skiffs (hard to tell one from other)… Trio of Weddell seals snoozing on the ice… Gentoo penguins are civil engineers: they build 'highways' in the snow and toddle along these compacted trenches in groups… Back on boat, crew hand out hot chocolate – tastes better than Krug in the context… Pod of humpback whales spotted: captain slows boat, no one speaks but 78 cameras whirr as two whales flash their flukes… Lecture: early British Antarctic expeditions didn't use dogs because public thought it cruel… Supper: gourmet empanadas, proof of chef's genius… Happy hour: whisky served with glacier ice – 30 per cent off!… Tomorrow we swim in a volcano…

It's hardly Scott or Shackleton; but then neither of them were tourists. The pioneers set out to conquer Antarctica; the modern traveller sets out to be conquered *by* Antarctica. And through the rapid accumulation of unique experiences and vivid impressions like those written above – encompassing the sensual, the intellectual and the downright hedonistic – this is usually what happens.

SHIP SHAPE

My logbook effusions were written six days into the expedition, but in fact I'd been won over from the moment I saw my cruise ship, the *Antarctic Dream* – for the simple reason that it didn't look like a cruise ship. It looked sturdy and utilitarian, the kind of boat that would rather be running into the teeth of a gale than hosting Strictly Come Grab-a-Granny nights.

My first impressions were spot-on. The *Antarctic Dream* is an 83-metre Chilean ex-Navy ship with capacity for 78 passengers and 43 crew, one of a number of vessels that carry tourists between Ushuaia, Argentina's southernmost port, and the Antarctic Peninsula. Choose your craft carefully: some of the ships are Cunard-esque floating condos where passengers get dressed up for dinner; smaller boats, like the *AD*, have a more informal, participatory atmosphere.

'DRAKE SHAKE'

Coracle or cabin cruiser, all ships bound for Antarctica must cross the Drake Passage, the body of water separating South America from the South Shetland Islands, which even some cruise company brochures dub 'notorious'. Swells can reach six metres or higher, causing even the largest vessels to pitch and yaw at alarming angles. For those who don't get sick, it's a thrilling ride; for those who do, the Passage becomes synonymous with dry crackers and disposable paper bags. Seasickness medication should be as high up your pre-trip shopping list as that nifty Gore-Tex jacket.

The two-day 'Drake shake' is, however, an opportunity for Dramamine-drowsy passengers to attend lectures given by the naturalists who lead the expedition, and to get acquainted with some of their fellow travellers. I instantly warmed to my cabin mate, David, a fiftysomething American who, being diligent, agreed to take notes at the lectures that I missed; and who, being teetotal, agreed to slip me his wine allowance at mealtimes.

Even without the double rum ration, I think I would have still spent most of my time staring out of the huge windows of the *AD*'s wood-panelled dining room, mesmerised by the noble aspect and parabolic flight patterns of the seabirds that were our constant companions. Wandering albatrosses, cape petrels, giant petrels and southern fulmars swooped and soared around us with ridiculous ease, using the very elements – the fierce winds, the mountainous waves – that were hampering our passage to facilitate their own.

'A PENGUIN MATERNITY WARD WHERE COUPLES ALTERNATE BETWEEN INCUBATING THEIR CHICKS AND COLLECTING STONES FOR THE NEST.'

On the third evening, after another of the gourmet four-course meals the chefs somehow managed to contrive in a bouncing kitchen, we went to bed feeling like kids on Christmas Eve. We would wake up in Antarctica.

PICK UP A PENGUIN

To be precise, we woke up in the South Shetlands. This chain of Antarctic islands, 75 miles north of the Peninsula, provides the first landing opportunity for expeditions en route to the ice continent proper. It also provides the first opportunity for passengers to debut their obscenely expensive 'outdoor performance' clothes – all four recommended layers of them. Life vests are a great sartorial leveller, however,

and by the time these were donned, everyone was looking equally foolish.

We piled into the Zodiac inflatable boats, introducing ourselves to those passengers who had emerged, queasy but not defeated, from their cabins for the first time in three days. First stop, Yankee Harbour. As the Melvillian name suggests, this spit of land was first used by American sealers in the 19th century, and several rusty blubber pots from that period still litter the shoreline. As if to fill out the narrative, a small herd of young elephant seals were lazing on the beach. A few of them checked us out with their rheumy eyes, but most ignored us, opting to get on with the serious business of scratching, yawning, snoozing and defecating.

The elephant seals would have had to spin beach balls on their noses while clapping out 'Jailhouse Rock' to get much attention from us, for penguins are the natural world's great scene-stealers. Further up the beach was a rookery of gentoos – in effect, a penguin maternity ward where couples alternate between incubating their recently hatched chicks and collecting stones for the nest. Arguments flare up over disputed stones but otherwise the colony is one harmonious huddle. Like the seals, the gentoos seemed oblivious to our presence. They did, however, keep close tabs on the skuas circling overhead. These dark, drooling birds – portrayed as mobsters in the film *Happy Feet* – will snack on the chicks if given the chance.

Penguins are usually described in anthropomorphic terms: they walk like drunks, they dress like nuns, and so on. But it's really their sheer, indefinable penguinness that makes them loveable. We sat quietly and watched them for about an hour, and returned to the boat.

THE ICEBERGS COMETH

We'd seen penguins; now we wanted icebergs. And as we pushed south across the Gerlache Strait towards the Antarctic Peninsula – suddenly visible in all its craggy, snowy glory, with glaciers running like smooth ice ramps from the peaks to the shoreline – we got them in increasing numbers. The Ancient Mariner, blown this way against his will, had a knack for iceberg sketches – 'And ice, mast-high, came floating by/As green as emerald' – but there were no Coleridges on board, so our games of Ice-Spy contained more pop culture gibberish than poetry. 'This one looks like a prostrate Barney from the Simpsons.' 'A used Ford Flex.' 'A pack of Marlboro Milds.' 'A giant's helping of cranberry sorbet.' It's a fair bet that Shackleton's crew were in better mental shape after two years stuck on an ice-floe, than we were after four days' easy sailing.

'WE ARRIVED AT THE ANTARCTIC: THOSE WHO HAD COME TO FULFIL THEIR AMBITION OF "DOING" ALL SEVEN CONTINENTS WOULD BE ABLE TO TICK THAT LAST BOX.'

STEPPING ON ANTARCTICA

The fifth day (which didn't dawn as such – at these latitudes the sun barely dips below the horizon) was the hinge moment of the expedition. We were to land at Charlotte Bay, on the Antarctic continental mainland: those who had come to fulfil their ambition of 'doing' all seven continents would be able to tick that last box.

Ignacio, our expedition leader, had advised us to spend some time exploring the landing area before glueing our eyes to our cameras and DV recorders. What we saw was a curved bay layered in deep virgin snow; and a shoreline ribboned with shingle and glistening ice shards, and covered in natural flotsam – in particular, colourful splodges of eerily inorganic-looking seaweed and lichen. Hills rose steeply from the bay – and, from the top of the hills, using their deep compacted 'highways', gentoo and chinstrap penguins were waddling their way beachwards, looking like ramblers returning from a day trip. Back towards the ship we saw tiny icebergs in the bay, each bathing in a pool of Bondi blue (the reflection from the mass of the 'berg beneath the surface).

It was snowing gently, and the wind had obligingly dropped to a murmur. The sun vanished behind a dirty blanket of clouds, and we had the illusion that the gleaming earth was lighting the dreary sky rather than vice versa. The snow was solid, not powdery: a snowball fight was quickly wound up when it became clear someone could lose an eye. The air may have been fresh, but it was also loaded with the acrid scent of penguin guano.

Trying to get down in words what it feels like to land on the ice continent is a descriptive challenge far greater than any of the other minor ones we faced (sinking waist deep into snow was as tough as it got). The evidence for this was in the furrowed brows and hovering biros of those writing postcards in the ship's lounge each evening. Few of the clichés seemed to help. 'Unearthly' is an adjective that crops up a lot in Antarctic travelogues. But the landscapes aren't

'IT IS HARD TO IMAGINE ANYWHERE MORE EARTHLY: ANTARCTICA IS MOTHER NATURE IN HER BIRTHDAY SUIT.'

'unearthly'. On the contrary, due to the almost total absence of human intervention, it is hard to imagine anywhere more earthly. Antarctica is Mother Nature in her birthday suit.

coloured but streaked with ice and orange lava rock, is entered through a narrow passage known as Neptune's Bellows. Inside is a landlocked caldera, above which drifts a sulphurous mist. It's part natural wonder, part Marilyn Manson video.

We landed on the black sands and explored the remains of research stations destroyed during several big eruptions in the 1960s. Our feet sank into dark ash and cinders, and we found 'cooked' krill on the beach. Even the handful of chinstrap penguins on the beach looked like strangers in a strange land. There are few places in the world that can be properly described as both

HELL FROZEN OVER

After another day nosing around the Peninsula, the captain pointed the *Antarctic Dream* back towards civilisation, and we began the long return. Threading our way through the South Shetlands by a different route allowed us to land on Antarctica's closest approximation to a tourist trap, the astonishing and much-visited Deception Island. This volcanic netherworld, obsidian-

picturesque and hellish, and this is one of them. A number of my brave shipmates took a dip in the (relatively) warm waters of the caldera. Shamefully, your correspondent wimped out, blaming a fictional head cold.

The Drake Passage was calmer on the way back. Most of us had got our sea legs and the breakfast queue was three times as long on day nine as it had been on day two. There was time

to exchange email addresses, play poker games, attend more lectures, toast the captain and his wonderful crew at a special reception, catch up with journals, and make wild promises about setting up Facebook groups.

I talked with Jan, a Prague pensioner in his seventies and the oldest member of our party. He was, as he proudly told everyone, 'Czech person number 21 to visit the Antarctica!' He had recently been diagnosed with a mobility disorder, and his doctor had advised him to get a DVD player and a bunch of movies, and to take things easy. Jan thanked the doc for his kind advice, went home,

and booked himself a berth on the *Antarctic Dream*. Crassly searching for a neat way to round off this piece, I asked Jan if this would be his 'last big adventure'. He gave me a look that was one part kindness, one part pity, and began to walk me through the itinerary of his next big trip.

But I knew that I was at least half right. There would be other expeditions, other thrills, other adventures: but Antarctica had been 'done', crossed off the 'things to do before you die' list, 'conquered' even. A void had been filled; a new one would be required. We needed an eighth continent. ●

WHEN TO GO

Between November and March. Go early in the season for penguin chicks and round-the-clock light. Late-season trips mean less ice and more whales. Caveat: conditions are always unpredictable.

GETTING THERE

Cruises leave from Ushuaia in the Argentine part of Tierra del Fuego; most visitors arrive by internal flight from Buenos Aires (Aerolineas Argentinas flies daily; www.aerolineas.com.ar).

ORGANISING YOUR TRIP

The author travelled with Cox & Kings (020 7873 5000, www.coxandkings.co.uk).

COST

For a berth on the *Antarctic Dream*, prices range from around £4,000 per person for a bed in a twin cabin (add on 50% for single occupancy supplement if you don't want to share) to around £8,000 per person for the top Cape Horn suite.

Cox & Kings offers a 13-night Antarctic Cruise itinerary leaving from the UK that combines a ten-night cruise on the *Antarctic*

Dream with two nights in Buenos Aires and a night in Ushuaia, from £5,350 per person. The cost without international flights is from £4,395 per person.

AM I UP TO IT?

If you can ascend and descend a flight of stairs without assistance, you're up to it. If you suffer from motion sickness, and don't respond well to medication, think twice before taking this trip.

MORE LIKE THIS

Other more affordable Southern Atlantic cruising destinations include the Falkland Islands and South Georgia. Or look north…

FOR REFERENCE

South, by Ernest Shackleton, is the great explorer's own account of his famous 1914 expedition – essential Antarctic reading. Apsley Cherry-Garrard's *The Worst Journey in the World* gives a harrowing, frank, but highly readable memoir of the 1910-13 Scott expedition; adapted for television in 2007. Good websites for reference include the *Antarctic Dream* website (www.antarctic.cl) and Cool Antarctica (www.coolantarctica.com).

'WE ARE HERE TO SHOW THOSE GUYS
INCHING THEIR WAY DOWN THE
FREEWAYS IN THEIR METAL COFFINS
THAT THE HUMAN SPIRIT IS STILL ALIVE'

BODHI, IN 'POINT BREAK'

Action stations

Powder play

Cyrus Shahrad hikes up Mount Tokachidake, then snowboards down.

WHAT	HOW LONG
Snowboard down a volcano	One day

WHERE	THRILL FACTOR
Hokkaido, Japan	● ● ● ● ●

There are few dress rehearsals more disturbing than learning how to dig your friend out of an avalanche. Our guide, Watanabe, showed us how to switch our tracking devices to search mode – reading the guidance beacons of other devices in the area as a distance in metres – before hiding one in the snow and having us converge on it from opposite sides of the car park, a process that took a distressing amount of time. He then schooled us in assembling probes and shovels – equipment I didn't dare ask if he'd ever had to use – while groups of skiers filed past and began ascents of their own on the slopes above.

No one gave us a second glance: this was essential training for anyone hoping to play in the powder fields of the smoking Tokachidake volcano, a mountain that regularly claims lives and has been known to throw skiers so far off course that they've had to dig snow shelters to sleep in.

WHITE GOLD RUSH

The island of Hokkaido – Japan's second largest and least developed land mass – is blessed with the sort of snow that most European skiers long

ago stopped believing possible, with the prevailing Siberian air mass annually delivering metre after metre of the lightest, driest powder imaginable. It was this that had brought me to the base of the region's most infamous mountain. I would be hiking up 800 vertical metres in order to snowboard back down – a run that a handful of articles in snowboard magazines over the last decade have described in language normally reserved for depicting the lives of saints.

Not that everyone embarking on ski or snowboard tours of Japan need engage in such daredevil pursuits. Those seeking more conventional runs will find lift systems, groomed pistes and well-equipped resorts. Contrary to appearances, Japan got a relatively late start in the world of winter sports. It wasn't until 1911 – when Austria's Major Von Lerch came to inspect the Japanese Army and, awed by the mountains in which he found himself stationed, began teaching local soldiers and postal workers to ski – that a national obsession started to take root.

Over the next 100 years, Japan went on to host countless World Cup events and two Winter Olympics, while the island of Hokkaido acquired ski resorts of all shapes and sizes. These now range from local municipality slopes like Santa Present Park, and privately run ski areas like Kamui, to major developments like the sprawling Furano resort. Accommodation runs from traditional Japanese houses – complete with robes, straw mat floors and futons (like the Tokiya Ryokan in Asahikawa; www.tokiya.net) – to the glamorous, wood-panelled La Vista Hotel in Daisetsuzan National Park (www.japan-ryokan.net/lavistadaisetsuzan).

Hokkaido's mountains are crowd-free (Australians constitute the only significant contingent of non-Japanese tourists) and offer a wealth of cultural experiences – replacing glutinous cheese fondues with steaming bowls of miso ramen, and après-ski gluhwein sessions with soothing soaks in geothermal hot springs.

CONTEMPLATING THE CONE

The previous afternoon, from our vantage point at the top of Asahidake – another active volcano dotted with vents spewing sulphuric steam, albeit one scarred with ski pistes and accessible by gondola – the peak of Tokachidake had looked no more threatening than a collapsed ice-cream cone, its silently smoking crater as cheerful as the chimney on a country pile. Yet Tokachidake is a mountain bereft of gondolas, groomed slopes or the potential intervention of ski patrols: those who brave it do so under their own steam, and entirely at their own risk.

Not that we were given long to contemplate the dangers: our guide Watanabe estimated that the currently sun-spangled peak would be hidden by heavy weather come lunchtime, so we saddled our bags, set our avalanche beacons to 'send' mode and began the four-hour trudge to the summit – which was now seeming as welcoming as Mount Doom did to young Frodo Baggins.

The ascent, difficult under any means, is decidedly easier with skis, which can be adapted with mohair 'skins' that allow skiers to shuffle uphill without sliding back down. Snowboarders

'WE SADDLED OUR BAGS, SET OUR AVALANCHE BEACONS TO "SEND" MODE AND BEGAN THE FOUR-HOUR TRUDGE TO THE SUMMIT.'

like us have no choice but to strap boards to their rucksacks and their feet into aluminium snowshoes, the increased surface area of which reduces the chances of sinking in waist-deep.

SNOWSHOE ASCENT

The early stages of the climb were unproblematic – the gradient was gentle and the snow still relatively secure beneath our feet – and the conversation was broken by fascinated silences as we took in the snow falling in glittering trails from trees and the green-leaved bamboo shoots poking from the snowline. An hour into the climb, the silence turned into one of exhaustion, with the mountain starting to throw us awkward angles and the snow three metres deep under our feet. We were sinking a good 30cm into the snow despite our snowshoes – and occasional powdery collapses revealed that we were actually standing on top of small trees, whose covering was far from settled. Hats, gloves and jackets were discarded despite the minus 10°C temperatures, then hurriedly replaced during our power-bar break, when the cold began to freeze our sweat and clutter our hair with micro icicles.

There was to be no stripping on the second half of the climb, though – above the treeline, we encountered a relentless 40-degree terrain, unprotected from the 45-mile-an-hour winds that forced the temperature down further. Clouds closed in and falling snow pixelated our field of vision – from above, I couldn't help

imagining that we looked like a line of arctic explorers, marching to our icy doom.

Not that there would be any such fate in store with a guide as scrupulous as Watanabe leading the pack. After the breathless hugs and handshakes that followed at the summit, he spent the best part of half an hour digging a pit to test blocks of snow for stability, only giving the thumbs up for the descent when he was sure the ground wouldn't give way at the first tumble or overly aggressive turn.

ON BOARD

Tentatively, we clipped into our boards, the run below – over a mile long – beckoning and taunting us with its immaculate powder and ridiculous steepness. Even then there was no rushing our route down: Watanabe skied ahead to test every hundred-or-so metres before giving us the all-clear to follow on the walkie talkie, a stop-start process

that gave us time to admire both our silent surroundings and the majesty of the snow beneath us. It was so deep and light that it felt as though we were not so much gliding on top of it as inside it, every turn kicking up arcs of spray that broke like waves overhead, every jump ending in a landing so soft that I felt as though I were still in the air. If snowboarding in deep powder is akin to flying, then this was the closest thing to travelling business class I'd ever experienced.

After the first few hundred metres of treeless faces we were back in the forest, weaving between snow-burdened cypresses and keeping our eyes peeled for the great bears that roam the area (and make for warming if reputedly tough winter stews), until we returned to the car park, breathless and beaming, our clothes saturated, gloves frozen, hats and goggles caked in snow.

Less than half an hour later we were soaking our exhausted muscles in the mineral-rich hot

springs at the foot of the mountain (the laid-back nakedness of Japanese communal bathing can come as a shock to Westerners convinced of the nation's social shyness), and contemplating the dreamlike nature of the day. Before setting off that morning, Watanabe had promised us that we were going to *omoide tsukuri* – 'make good memories'. He wasn't bluffing. Half an hour of snowboarding might seem a minimal payoff for a four-hour uphill slog through deep snow, but liberating oneself from the metal drudgery of the ski lift lends an appropriately Zen-like quality to what was, by some way, the most memorable run of my life. ●

WHEN TO GO
Hokkaido's snow season runs from November until June, but it's best to travel in February, when the snow is likely to be at its deepest and the harsh winter cold should have abated.

GETTING THERE
Flights with ANA (www.anaskyweb.com) to Asahikawa in Hokkaido operate from Tokyo's Haneda airport and take around 90 minutes. From there, it's best to hire a car to get to the region's various mountain resorts. Or navigate the region by rail (www2.jrhokkaido.co.jp), with services stopping at most major resorts.

ORGANISING YOUR TRIP
Hokkaido Powder Guides (www.hokkaido powderguides.com) operates out of Furano, and organises backcountry tours of Mount Tokachidake, as well as Asahidake and other mountains in the region. Furano Tourist Association (www.furanotourism.com) is the tourist office for Hokkaido's largest linked ski area, and a good source of information.

COST
14,000 yen (£100) per day backcountry riding with Hokkaido Powder Guides; 3,000 yen (£22) full equipment rental.

AM I UP TO IT?
Beginners should look elsewhere: even experienced skiers and snowboarders struggle the first time they encounter deep powder, which demands a different technique to piste riding – albeit one that half-decent riders can pick up as they go. Hiking hundreds of metres up steep snow faces is exhausting – a few weeks of exercise is good preparation.

MORE LIKE THIS
Most resorts offer backcountry skiing and snowboarding in some form, if not with quite the quantities of powder found in Hokkaido. In Europe, Chamonix is considered the champion: McNab Snowsports (www.mcnab snowsports.co.uk) organises tours in the valley. Canada's powder paradise is Whistler: engage the services of the Whistler Alpine Guides Bureau (www.whistlerguides.com) to explore the area's full potential. Finally, for a ski trip with a similarly unusual cultural bent, try the Iranian resort of Dizin, an hour's drive north of the capital Tehran (www.skifed.ir).

FOR REFERENCE
Ski Furano (www.skifurano.com) is a useful resource for Hokkaido's ski areas – from backcountry mountains like Tokachidake to purpose-built resorts like Tomamu (www. snowtomamu.jp). Snow Japan (www.snow japan.com) has a wealth of information on Japanese ski resorts. See www.snow-forecast.com/resorts/furano for an up-to-the-minute snow report for the region. The Japanese National Tourist Organisation website (www.seejapan.co.uk) contains essential information on transport and accommodation.

Sound waves

Daniel Neilson kayaks around the Scottish Highlands for an exhilarating communion with nature.

WHAT	HOW LONG
Sea-kayaking in the Sound of Arisaig	Six days

WHERE	THRILL FACTOR
West coast of the Scottish Highlands	● ● ● ● ○

Frantically, I dragged my paddle through the cold water. 'Harder! Faster!' my guide Myles yelled at me. As his instructions disappeared, whipped away on the wind, the next swell rose up behind me. With one final pull against the white-capped wave, the kayak was thrown forward and I struggled, using my paddle as a rudder, to wrestle it to the shore. Anyone who has surfed will know that harnessing the power of the sea is a rousing experience. But it's a fickle beast – earlier that day it had ravaged my kayak, its spray whipping my face and drenching my body; I cursed it.

I had travelled to the west of Scotland for a six-day kayak excursion through the cold sea that laps, or more often pounds, the coastline. On the train from London, I watched the countryside change: the glacier-scraped flatness of the Midlands gave way to the gentle, undulating landscapes, green fells and jagged heights of the Lake District, jutting into low forbidding skies. Nothing, however, that could prepare me for the drama of the Scottish Highlands.

BEACHES AND MOUNTAINS

With 6,000 miles of diverse, untouched coastline, the Highlands are a world-class destination for sea-kayaking. White sandy beaches can look decidedly Mediterranean when the sun comes out; ragged, sea-beaten cliffs and ice-veiled mountains drop into the sea; and basking sharks, orcas, dolphins, porpoises and otters mingle with sea-kayakers – often the only humans in sight.

En route to the launch, we headed east of Fort William and Ben Nevis, where one narrow road weaves its way through craggy glens, heading past Glenfinnan, where Bonnie Prince Charlie raised his standard in 1745 to unite the clans for the Jacobite rebellion, and then continuing on to Mallaig, where the road stops abruptly. Beyond is an epic and untamed landscape where wildcats and stags roam the storm-ravaged terrain. Much of it is inhospitable and inaccessible – except, that is, by sea.

My expedition was to circumnavigate the Sound of Arisaig. With the exception of a stop for a sneaky pint halfway, we were alone throughout, at the mercy of the land, sea and the

> 'FORMIDABLE MOUNTAINS FLANK THE LOCH. IN SUMMER, THEY ARE A BRIGHT GREEN BUT BY AUTUMN THE COARSE GRASS AND BRACKEN IS PAINTED RUST RED WITH AN AUTUMN BRUSH.'

notoriously changeable weather. The sea-kayaking season runs from early May until late September but, this being Scotland, the weather can range from mirror-flat sea and blue skies to raging gales at any time. Still, with the bewildering array of clothes I had to wear – quick-drying wicking shirts, waterproof trousers, fleece tops, kayaking jacket, spray skirt and, finally, a life vest – it felt as though nothing could hamper my progress.

HOLD YOUR HANDS UP

The journey started early in the morning in the relative calm of Loch Moidart. We loaded the kayaks with tents, dry clothes and food; everything we needed to survive for nearly a week in the wilderness. In the shelter of the loch, safety procedures and basic techniques – 'pedal your legs', 'use your back', 'hold your hands up' – were taught before moving seawards and into the choppier currents of the Atlantic Ocean.

Formidable mountains flank the loch. In the summer, they are a bright green but by autumn the coarse grass and bracken had been painted rust red with an autumn brush, picked out occasionally in magnificent amber sunlight. At the mouth of the loch loomed Castle Tioram (pronounced 'cheerum'), a defiant shell of a fortress and a Jacobite stronghold that has stood solid against the combined might of the ocean and the Scottish Crown since the 13th century.

MUCK, EIGG AND RHUM

During the day, our flotilla headed north, clinging closely to the coastline, bouncing and bobbing on the sea, navigating peninsulas and stopping for lunches of cold cuts and cheeses on sandy beaches. On land, red deer and wild goats chewed heather on the open moorland before returning to their shelter in some of the last remaining Atlantic oak woodland in the country. On the horizon we could just make out the ragged, sketchy outlines of the smaller isles of Muck, Eigg and Rhum – and, nearer to us, the dramatically intimidating peaks of the Cullin Hills of Skye.

We covered just seven to nine miles a day, but with stops at islands, lunch and landmarks, it amounted to a full day on the water – and, during the last few hours of paddling, daydreams of rest, food and water dominated my thoughts. We set up camp on peninsulas and islands with unpronounceable names like Eilean nan Gobhar, Peanmeanach and Smirisar. None of the campsites could be reached except by a small boat and, with the squally North Atlantic on one side and mountains on the other, a feeling of insignificance is tempered by the sight of the large teepee. We gathered in it each night to eat a solid supper – we even chowed on edible seaweed (kelp is delicious fried with olive oil and garlic) and gut weed, which (despite its name) is surprisingly appetising when flash-fried until crispy.

After dinner, you can forage for seaweed and mushrooms or go on a night kayak on the black-ink waters. In late summer, if you are lucky, the paddle strokes light up phosphorescent algae and you might see seals dart below the boats, creating luminous, glimmering trails behind them.

Thanks to a strict 'Leave No Trace' strategy, by the time we left each camp it looked precisely as it did when we arrived. We were asked not to ram kayaks up the beach lest we upset some earth or scrape off some harmful plastic. Tents were placed on durable surfaces, meals measured out to perfection and 'toileting' carefully considered.

OF MUNROS AND MOUNTAINS

On day three, we visited the narrow Loch Ailort, where 900-metre-high Munros, the highest mountains in Scotland (and their smaller cousins known as Corbetts) rose steeply out of the water, an icy waterfall crashing down hundreds of metres into the loch. When you're bobbing around a couple of inches above sea-level, they are an intimidating sight.

It was at this point, just as I was feeling more than ever like a vulnerable dot on the landscape, that the weather began to turn. Instead of gently rolling swells, white caps started to appear on the crests of the waves, and the winds began to lash stinging spray on to my face. Battling against the westerly gusts, my muscles burned as I urged the kayak forward. Around the exposed peninsula into Loch nan Ceall, boats were being tossed around like toy ships – and occasionally the tempestuous waves were high enough for us to briefly lose sight of each other. But putting our new skills and confidence into

'WITH THE WIND AT OUR BACKS, WE QUICKLY RODE THE SWELL AND SURFED THE WAVES INTO THE BAY.'

practice was thrilling – and we set up camp exhausted, but giddy on a natural high.

LIFE AT SEA

On the penultimate day, we explored the Skerries, a rocky outcrop near the final destination of the village of Arisaig. The whole Sound of Arisaig is a designated Special Area of Conservation, thanks to its unique sealife. Oystercatchers and red-throated divers compete with seagulls above for crabs and small fish, but the area is best known as a seal nursery. Hundreds dot the rugged land, and we bob around the Skerries within a few feet of the smelly beasts; their expressive faces returned mildly baffled glances.

On the morning of the final day, the weather can only accurately be described as 'Scottish'. The wind had picked up over night, and the waves were up. We loaded our kayaks one last time and began the paddle home. But with the wind at our backs, we quickly rode the swell and surfed the waves into the bay, with dreams of a hot meal, a warming whisky and a cosy bed drawing nearer with every tired stroke.

'On a river trip you can only go down the river, but in a sea-kayak you are free. You feel like a true explorer,' Myles mused later, over a dinner of local venison. As the whisky gradually warmed my body, and loosened my limbs, I agreed with renewed conviction. ●

WHEN TO GO

There are regular trips between May and September. June to August are usually the warmest months, but the weather is changeable all year.

GETTING THERE

From Glasgow, a Scotrail (www.firstgroup.com) connection can then be made to Fort William. Transfers from Inverness or Fort William.

ORGANISING YOUR TRIP

Wilderness Scotland (www.wilderness scotland.com). Travel insurance is a condition of making your booking.

COST

The five-night, six-day Sound of Arisaig trip costs £575; it includes food, tent accommodation and all equipment.

AM I UP TO IT?

The Sound of Arisaig trip requires some previous sea-kayaking experience, and the four-day introduction course is recommended. Sea-kayaking can be strenuous on the arms, shoulders, legs and back, so a good level of general fitness is required.

MORE LIKE THIS

Sea-kayaking is very popular on the Canadian Pacific coast around Vancouver Island, particularly as you'll often find yourself paddling alongside orcas. Northern Lights Expeditions (www.seakayaking.com) provides trips. Wilderness Journeys (www.wilderness journeys.com), the international arm of Wilderness Scotland, also organises sea-kayaking trips to the Galápagos, Norway, Italy and Greenland.

FOR REFERENCE

The '45 by Christopher Duffy is a colourful and comprehensive history of the 1745 Jacobite rebellion, a key event in the history of the area. The Essential Sea Kayaker by David Seidman is one of the best sea-kayaking manuals for all levels, and talks you through every step, from buying a kayak to learning the Eskimo roll, and navigation. And if you really want to live well in the wild, pick up The New Seaweed Cookbook by Crystal June Maderia.

High rolling

Helen Gilchrist tackles the Anti-Atlas on two wheels.

WHAT	HOW LONG
Mountain biking	8 days
WHERE	**THRILL FACTOR**
Anti-Atlas Mountains, Morocco	● ● ● ● ○

Stretching out ahead, the empty road curved under the lee of a dark, lonely peak – and the sky turned a moody grey. My bike quickly accelerated with the pull of gravity, I clicked into top gear, pedalled hard, leaned forward, easing into the first bend and then giving in to the speed of the ten-mile descent.

Whizzing past almond orchards and stone terraces, I rounded the final hair-pin bend and let momentum pull me towards Tafraoute, an ochre-coloured settlement nestled in a valley of the Anti-Atlas Mountains. It was market day and there was some traffic on the usually deserted roads as locals headed home to the satellite villages. Vans and pick-up trucks crammed with passengers chugged up the hill towards me, their roof racks loaded to the hilt with sacks of vegetables, chicken cages and the odd carpet – four people in the front, six in the back, three hanging off the tailgate. Swerving out of their way, I narrowly avoided skidding in the loose gravel at the roadside, steering through a fug of diesel fumes as they passed.

ROCKY RIDE

The rugged Anti-Atlas is the oldest mountain range in Morocco, formed some 300 million years ago when the tectonic plates that would eventually become Africa and America collided. Once higher than the Himalayas, the Anti-Atlas have eroded over the millennia to the point that they are now lower than the more recently formed High Atlas range that runs almost parallel, just to the north.

The elements, coupled with some serious volcanic activity, have shaped them into a landscape perfect for cyclists – in the visual as well as the muscle-enhancing sense: there is a huge network of endless, empty roads and unpaved dirt tracks or 'pistes'. You pass through deep gorges scarred with fissures and striations; towering, wind-smoothed boulders; enormous escarpments, high arid mountain plateaux and low rounded hills appearing out of vast desert plains.

The cycling is not always easy but it's never boring: flat roads meander along the floors of dramatic gorges; a gently undulating route might follow the spine of a high ridge; and long

sweeping descents with the wind in your hair turn quickly into equally long winding climbs, with switchback after switchback.

To get the most out of this corner of Morocco, all but the most advanced of navigators will need a local guide – the Anti-Atlas is no place to get lost.

FULL SUSPENSION

Our base for the first four days, the former French garrison town of Tafraoute, is set amid dusty-pink mountains, bizarrely shaped rocky outcrops and lush palm groves. It's now a laid-back, convivial outpost, the sort of place in which I could imagine kicking back for an afternoon, strolling the streets and nosing around the small markets and craft shops.

It was not to be. 'Switch on your suspension, and make sure your water bottles are full. We're going off-road for the next six miles and the Land Rovers won't be following us.' Mohammed, our guide, was signalling ahead across a barren plain that shimmered with heat haze. Until now, we'd enjoyed the reassurance that Abdul, Habdul and Big Mohammed – driving the Land Rovers with extra water, lunch, spare clothes and bike tools – were never far away.

Leaving the shade of the big argan tree where we'd stopped for lunch, we got back in the saddle and braced ourselves for the desert. Large, loose stones kicked my wheels unpredictably in different directions; I felt like I'd lost all co-ordination, drunk with the heat of the

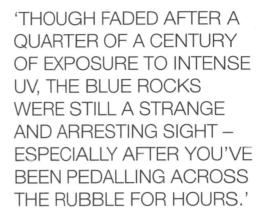

'THOUGH FADED AFTER A QUARTER OF A CENTURY OF EXPOSURE TO INTENSE UV, THE BLUE ROCKS WERE STILL A STRANGE AND ARRESTING SIGHT – ESPECIALLY AFTER YOU'VE BEEN PEDALLING ACROSS THE RUBBLE FOR HOURS.'

relentless afternoon sun. The going was slow. Eventually, the rocks became too big for our wheels, so we dismounted and pushed. Stopping for a swig of water, I gazed at the unforgiving terrain ahead, which extended to the foot of the distant mountains. On a large rock, the solitary figure of a Berber goatherd sat and gawped at us: tourists in shiny lycra clothes and helmets, pushing our bikes instead of riding them.

A little further on, a handful of tourist cars appeared out of nowhere, there to see the Painted Rocks: in 1984, Belgian artist Jean Vérame took six months, 18 tonnes of paint and a team of Moroccan firemen and their hoses to cover these giant granite boulders in blue, turquoise, red and purple paint. Though faded after a quarter of a century of exposure to intense UV, they were still a strange and arresting sight – especially after you've been pedalling across the rubble for hours.

VILLAS AND VILLAGES

On another outing out of Tafraoute, we climbed slowly through the Ameln Valley towards the mighty peak of the Djebel el Kest. The valley's many traditional Berber villages and almond terraces shored up against sheer stone walls are now interspersed with painted villas fortified with imposing gates, turreted walls and security

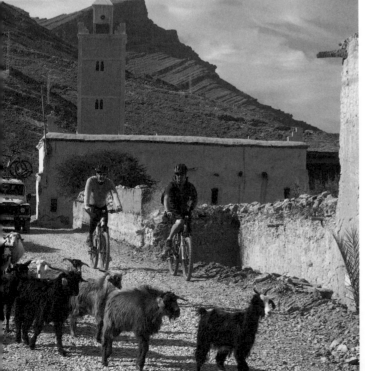

'A CYCLIST'S DREAM: FLAT ROADS THAT MEANDER ALONG THE FLOORS OF GORGES TO UNDULATING ROUTES THAT FOLLOW HIGH RIDGES; FROM LONG SWEEPING DESCENTS WITH THE WIND IN YOUR HAIR, TO LONG WINDING CLIMBS.'

systems, the holiday homes of businessmen who've made their money in the cities.

Then came a gorgeous long descent. As we sped along the empty road from the village of Tleta Tazrite to Aït Mansour, the road twisted and plunged, clinging to the gorge's steep rose-coloured sides before unfurling along its palm-filled floor. In the space of about half an hour, we had been transported from barren mountain roads to dense groves of palms, and streams. After splashing through a shallow ford, we sat beside the river, eating satsumas beneath rustling leaves.

Descending further, the dense palmeries of the wider Afella Ighir Valley, watched over by ancient kasbahs and crumbling agadirs, gave way to another parched orange canyon and a stony piste by a dried-out riverbed, the mountains' vertical strata a vivid reminder of the seismic forces that shaped the land.

PARADISE FOUND

Finally, a break from the bike. We transferred by Land Rover to Immouzer (waterfall) des Ida Outanane in the High Atlas, and we spent a night in the Hotel des Cascades, where lush gardens tumble down to the 'waterfall' – now run dry due to years of drought. After a fish tagine and a cosy

evening round a log fire, we were on the road again – for the final 18-mile descent to the Atlantic coast.

Then, paradise: Paradise Valley, that is. This area of sublime natural beauty was a popular hangout on the Moroccan hippie trail of the 1960s and '70s. We flew past pine trees, a whitewashed mosque atop a precipice, jagged escarpments and countless cafés with panoramic terraces down to the bottom of a tight gorge, where a clear blue river ran over time-smoothed yellow stone.

The hard part over, it was time for a ritualistic scrub-down at a hammam in Agadir, on the coast, to banish every last trace of dust and chain grease. Lying on the warm tiled floor in a steamy room full of naked women, I winced while a large, pink bra-ed Moroccan lady rubbed every inch of my body with a coarse black kissa glove. After a week of seeing veiled women watching us curiously from a distance, we were finally mixing.

An invigorating massage – pleasure bordering on pain – was the right way to end this particular adventure. The climbs were tough, the long descents revitalising, but the scenes flashing past were always stirring. Travelling on two wheels through the Anti-Atlas, you feel you are viewing the earth's ancient bare bones up close. That you are experiencing it all in the open air, powered by your own energy, adds deeply to the pleasure, and makes up for all the aches, pains and strains. ●

WHEN TO GO
Cycling here is best in early spring or late autumn, when the days are warm with clear skies and refreshing breezes. Summer is unbearably hot and winter subject to snowfall at any time.

GETTING THERE
Agadir is the closest international airport to Tafraoute, which is around three hours' drive away. There is one bus a day from Agadir to Tafraoute, via Aït Baha.

ORGANISING YOUR TRIP
The author travelled on Explore Worldwide's (www.explore.co.uk) new Anti-Atlas Adventure tour (from £645, excluding airfares), which included seven nights' B&B accommodation, the provision and maintenance of mountain bikes, two local guides and three local support drivers.

COST
If you're not taking your own bike or joining a tour, bikes can be hired in Tafraoute for around 70dh per day (check the brakes).

AM I UP TO IT?
A good level of fitness is needed for this trip, especially for some of the climbs. If you can manage a few long hill climbs before you go, it'll help. Our group was mixed and included some with very little cycling experience, who loved it. Padded cycling shorts are highly recommended, as well as warm clothes for evenings.

MORE LIKE THIS
With a mountain bike, any legal terrain is your oyster. Notable areas to target are the Southwestern USA with its iconic desert slickrock (particularly Moab), and the Alps, where many resorts continue to run lifts in the summer. You can ferry your bikes up to the top and tackle downhills from the near-suicidal to the ambling. Morzine is one noted resort.

FOR REFERENCE
www.ctc.org.uk – although it's UK-based, the Cyclists' Touring Club website is a good resource for planning your trip. Michelin Map 959 (1:1,000,000) – good for route planning rather than micro-navigation.

Surf safari

In the quest for the perfect wave, **Alf Anderson** charters
a boat to surf pristine reef breaks off the Maldives.

WHAT Charter a surf yacht	**HOW LONG** One to two weeks
WHERE The Maldives	**THRILL FACTOR** ● ● ● ● ○

Non-surfers tend to look upon the dreamy atolls of the Maldives as a honeymoon destination of impossible picture perfection – a place to laze, loiter and luxuriate. And they're right, of course. It may be the smallest Asian country, but with over 1,000 miniature islands trimmed with soft white sands and coconut trees, circled by turquoise seas, it has no shortage of sandy stretches on which to live out your very own Bounty advert.

But surfers look to the seaward side of the tranquil atolls to see fantastically consistent Indian Ocean swells thumping into the offshore reefs, creating some of the loveliest waves in the world – warm, clear and clean. Few of the Maldives' breaks can be reached from the shore and, while some surfers base themselves at holiday resorts on one of the 26 different atolls that make up this oceanic nation, there is no better way to surf the Maldives than chartering a live-on yacht, anchoring off the reef and jumping over the side when you get to a sweet spot. A boat charter isn't a cheap ticket, but most surfers will get more good waves in a two-week 'surfari' in the Maldives than in a year at their home break (unless, of course, they live in Hawaii).

JUST SWELL

The swell had been coming through before we arrived and was still coming through when we left – in fact, our surf guide said it never gets flat in the Maldives, even in the supposedly 'flat' season (generally coinciding with the northern hemisphere winter). During two weeks of sailing from atoll to atoll (an atoll is a coral island encircling a lagoon) aboard the 75-foot motor vessel *Rani*, our group of seven long-time surf buddies never had a day when the surf was lower than head-high, and on several sessions it was double overhead – which was plenty big enough for most of us. The Maldives is surfed by everyone from intermediates to world pros but experience of big reef breaks is essential.

Charter boats invariably head north from the capital Malé to a string of unpronounceable atolls from which perfect lefts and rights roll into deep-water channels. Having a boat at your beck and

'FANTASTICALLY CONSISTENT INDIAN OCEAN SWELLS THUMP INTO THE OFFSHORE REEFS, CREATING SOME OF THE LOVELIEST WAVES IN THE WORLD.'

call means that if one break isn't working or is too crowded you can head to another. With one exception, all of the breaks we surfed were within an hour or two's sailing time of each other so we didn't lose much time roving the high seas instead of surfing them.

The captain of the *Rani* had a lifetime's experience of surfing the region's waters and he was accompanied by a local surf guide who knew exactly when and where the best waves would break. That said, you may not get the waves all to yourself – or not often, at least. Some get pretty busy, with maybe 20 surfers on a peak, but since the peaks will shift a little depending on the size of each set, you can still catch plenty of waves whether you wait out the back or pick off the smaller inside waves. And the crowds tend to fluctuate dramatically too – we found that if we sat it out on deck while a particular break was busy, the numbers would invariably thin out as people paddled in for a meal break. On other occasions, it just seemed that a herd mentality ruled: people were surfing a particular break simply because other surfers were on it, while an equally good wave on the other side of the atoll was going unridden.

BARRELS OF FUN

As for the typical Maldivian surf experience: picture a perfect aquamarine barrel peeling shorewards; the water temperature is 27°C year-round; the waves aren't too heavy; and the reefs aren't too shallow. For your average recreational surfer, this is as good as it gets. There's a fairly even distribution of lefts and rights too, so whether you're natural (left-foot forward) or goofy (right-foot forward), you'll find your wave.

'WE WATCHED DOLPHINS SURFING THE WAVES, MANTA RAYS FLAPPING BEYOND THE BREAK, AND FISH AND TURTLES UNDER THE BOAT.'

As a natural footer, my favourite breaks were Sultans, Ninja's and Cola's. Sultans is a world-class break that is consistent and long, with a super-fast, hollow inside section (and there's the bizarre left-hander of Honky's on the other side of the peak, which actually gets bigger as you ride it); Ninja's, according to most surf guides, is a short, 'mellow' wave popular with Japanese surfers (although if this is 'mellow', I'd like to see a few more mellow waves back home in Wales); and Cola's is a heavy, exciting wave that picks up plenty of swell.

SURF SURVIVAL

The Maldives has a hot, tropical climate, so prepare accordingly. Take plenty of sunblock, a rash vest and maybe even a hat to protect yourself against the sun when you're out in the surf. Reef boots are also a good idea to guard against cuts and grazes. And, above all, drink plenty of water. We all suffered dehydration at some point during the trip, which not only makes you feel awful but means you miss out on the surf action. You should drink at least three litres a day.

During breaks, we snorkelled the underwater world, spotting turquoise parrot fish, turtles, dolphins and octopuses, with their ever-changing shades, in the gin-clear waters. From the deck we watched dolphins surfing the waves, manta rays flapping around beyond the break and all manner of fish and turtles beetling about beneath the boat. There was no question of us getting bored on board: the boat had comfortable ensuite twin cabins, a sound and viewing system for downtime and an on-board chef serving up the kind of enormous meals (usually local fish) needed after a day's surfing.

ON SHORE

Nowhere in the Maldives is more than three metres high, making it the world's flattest nation on average, and the only settlement of any size is the capital Malé, a surprisingly affluent little city that makes for a diverting jaunt when your boat goes to port for supplies.

It's worth remembering that the Maldives is a Muslim country (although its cultural roots are Buddhist), so don't expect to be boozing in your shore time (although beer can be – and is – drunk aboard the surf yachts). You'll also see that various cultures have left their mark – from architecture to religion – with the Portuguese, Dutch and British having had a presence here until independence in 1965.

An island visit will also help you appreciate the advantages of living on a boat. The Maldives is only three degrees south of the equator, and the heat and humidity on land, even if it is surrounded on all sides by the Indian Ocean, can get intense. On board the surf vessel there was always a cooling breeze to take the edge off the sun's intensity. It was also our launchpad for finding the best waves of our lives – not just on one day, but every day of the trip. ●

WHEN TO GO
The main surf season is March to November, with the biggest waves in July and August. Outside this period, the surf tends to be smaller, the winds onshore and the weather less reliable.

GETTING THERE
Malé international airport is the point of entry, with direct flights from the UK but not the US.

ORGANISING YOUR TRIP
For more information on surfing the Maldives, and chartering a surf boat, go to www.maldivesurf.com; for general information on the region, see www.themaldives.com.

COST
Surf boat charters cost from €120 per person per day (www.maldivesurf.com), including transfers and meals. Watch out for the possible surcharge for surfboards on your flights.

AM I UP TO IT?
You need to feel comfortable surfing reef breaks while riding waves that are well over your head. This is the ideal place to develop your skills but it's definitely not the place to *learn* how to surf reef breaks. And note that there are no beach breaks if you find you can't handle the reefs.

MORE LIKE THIS
Similar tropical surf boat charters are available in Indonesia (www.baliwavehunter.com), New Caledonia (www.wavehunters.com) and Tahiti (www.theperfectwave.com.au). Beginners wanting to have a go at easier reef breaks from the shore with an exotic backdrop should try Sri Lanka or Costa Rica.

FOR REFERENCE
For up-to-date comments on surf spots in the Maldives, check out the surf atlas at www.wannasurf.com.

Paddle your own canoe

Following in the wake of the earliest Canadian voyagers, **Daniel Neilson** navigates the great northern lakes.

WHAT	HOW LONG
Canoe expedition	One week
WHERE	**THRILL FACTOR**
Algonquin Park, Ontario, Canada	● ● ● ● ○ ○

Morning on Burnt Island Lake and only a laughing loon broke the silence. Mist rested on the mirror-flat water and, as we placed our canoe in the lake, the reflection of pines and reddening maples broke into a satisfying ripple. We pushed off the rocks, and in rhythm, plunged our paddles into the lake, gently drawing them back – at first, it felt effortless. In the distance, a moose, having a good scratch, looked up, and an otter popped above the surface before disappearing back to the inky depths.

It was the first full day of a canoe trip into the forested wilderness of Algonquin Park in northern Ontario – and the conditions were perfect. For seven days, we paddled through dozens of lakes, portaged (carried canoes) across wooded islands and cooked over open fires. Save for moose, a few critters and two very tired Torontonians (portaging really takes it out of you), we hardly saw a soul.

CANADA'S EARLY EXPLORERS

Albeit with the aid of tinned food and head-torches, we liked to think we were following in the slipstream of native Canadians, who have been paddling and exploring these wild, fertile lands in search of cherries, fish (trout and bass) and white-tailed deer for over 5,000 years.

The First Nations people pioneered the plank canoe, realising how these simple birch-bark boats could silently approach hunting targets and be used to transport heavy cargos with little effort. 'What the camel is to desert tribes, what the horse is to the Arab, what the ship is to the colonising Briton, what all modern means of locomotion are to the civilised world today – that, and more than that, the canoe was to the Indian who lived beside the innumerable waterways of Canada,' wrote the Canadian historian William Wood in 1915. Later, French and English explorers also used the canoe to penetrate this

'RACOONS SNIFFED AROUND OUR TENT AT NIGHT, WHICH, TO A PARANOID MIND, SOUNDED EXACTLY LIKE A BEAR.'

vast country of lakes: it was sturdy enough to carry food and tools, and light enough to be easily carried over land.

Even today, the canoe occupies a unique place in the Canadian psyche – something the late former prime minister Pierre Trudeau appreciated with rare poetry for a politician. 'What sets a canoeing expedition apart is that it purifies you more rapidly and inescapably than any other. Travel a thousand miles by train and you are a brute,' he said. 'Pedal 500 on a bicycle and you remain basically a bourgeois; paddle a hundred in a canoe and you are already a child of nature.'

Every summer, thousands of Canadians take to the water to fulfil their seemingly innate need to be in 'the Great Outdoors'. Say 'canoe trip' to a Canadian and they look wistful as they recall learning the paddling techniques: the 'J-stroke', used to keep the canoe on course by making a J-shaped motion in the water, and the 'C-stroke' to turn the canoe quickly. But it's the serenity of a canoe trip – the quiet splash of the paddle and the gentle glide – that keep Canadians coming back. And there is no better place to experience it than

Algonquin Provincial Park, a northern idyll of lakes, islands and woodland. Although thousands descend on the park every year, solitude is easy to find in its 2,300 square miles.

You can set out from one of several ranger stations, but the most popular is Canoe Lake, a five-hour drive north of Toronto. Canoes, paddles, lifejackets and equipment can be hired from outfitters around the visitors' centre. Once you have registered a route with the park ranger, you'll have just a map and a compass to guide you.

GOING SLOW

At the launch point, we passed other campers: families laden with food supplies; men escaping their wives, equipped with fishing rods and beer; and hardened outdoorsy types complete with bushy beards and 'survivor' smugness.

We loaded our 15-footer with two backpacks filled with camping gear and food, and then carefully stepped into the tipsy boat. I was assigned to the bow, while my Canadian wife took up the stern. The canoe is guided from the back, and a basic knowledge of the 'J' and 'C' strokes is required to keep the boat heading straight.

We started to cut slowly (canoes don't do quickly) across Canoe Lake, the spot where influential Canadian artist Tom Thomson drowned under mysterious circumstances in 1917. His Algonquin paintings inspired the country's most significant art movement, the Group of Seven, famous for its bold northern landscapes.

'LOOK OUT FOR FUNGI AND ORCHIDS – THAT'S IF YOU CAN SEE THEM FROM UNDERNEATH YOUR CANOE AND THROUGH THE SWEAT POURING DOWN YOUR FACE.'

CARRY THAT WEIGHT

Portaging involved emptying a 23-kilogram canoe and lugging it across muddy, root-covered trails. The lengths varied between a third of a mile and two or three miles, and the person not carrying the canoe carried the backpacks. 'Light, light, light' is the mantra when packing food and equipment, and hiring a canoe; we chose one made from Kevlar, a synthetic material – not very traditional, perhaps, but lighter than wood and aluminium. Doing a portage isn't always fun – it's the most demanding part – but you are at least rewarded with an up-close encounter with wild and woodsy Canada.

Algonquin Park is a greatest hits of Canadian woodland: it mixes the iconic coniferous woods of the north – pine, spruce and balsam fir – with the colourful deciduous trees of the south (sugar maple, yellow birch and beech). In the woods, we encountered another Canadian icon: the

majestic moose, which stands up to two metres high. Even though the conditions – having our heads under a canoe and sweating profusely – weren't ideal for flora-spotting, we also managed to spy fungi and orchids in the dense vegetation.

INTO THE UNKNOWN

On the first day, keen to get beyond the day-tripper range, we pushed ourselves and completed four long, hard portages. By nightfall, our shoulders and lower backs throbbed. We picked a campsite on a deserted peninsula and lit a fire. Night after night, we settled into a routine: we leapt naked into the still lake – surprisingly bearable even in September – while the sun silhouetted the pines; collected dry wood, found kindling (it is good etiquette to leave some dry kindling for the next campers) and sparked a fire; then we cooked sausages, pasta, mashed potatoes and baked beans (it was always baked beans).

After dinner, the backpack with the food was hoisted high into the trees to deter bears (you are unlikely to see any, but rangers give bear advice before you depart). Racoons sniffed around our tent at night, which, to a slightly paranoid mind, sounded exactly like a bear. Chipmunks jumped on to our makeshift tables and would, if allowed, have taken food straight off our plates.

We planned our route on the recommended nine to twelve miles a day. Navigation required concentration: landmarks on maps are often unrecognisable from your canoe; signs mark portages and designated campsites, but they were not always obvious. We quickly learned to use a compass, but occasionally a lake would turn into a stream and we'd reach a dead end.

By day, the scenery changed constantly: marshy lakes teeming with fish were followed, after a portage, by deep black lakes and rocky islets. On land, moose nibbled lakeside shrubs and great blue herons soared overhead. There is an infinite array of possible courses but avoiding long portages is key: our longest was two and a half miles and it nearly finished us off.

As we paddled the home straight, we were already planning our next trip. A canoe expedition feels like an exploration of endless possibilities. As philosopher Henry David Thoreau once said: 'Wherever there is a channel for water, there is a road for the canoe'. And nothing beats the satisfaction of paddling your canoe along its own watery path. ●

WHEN TO GO

The ice usually melts around the end of April, returning late October. From mid May to the third week of June, black flies are out in abundance. From late June until the first week in August, the mosquitoes take over, but they are more tolerable. Late August, September and early October are usually free of bugs.

GETTING THERE

The nearest air hub is Toronto. Buses leave Toronto for the park every day.

ORGANISING YOUR TRIP

Friends of Algonquin (www.algonquinpark. on.ca) and National Parks (www.ontarioparks. com) have weather forecasts and information. Portage Store (www.portagestore.com) and Algonquin Outfitters (www.algonquinoutfitters. com) organise guided tours, or provide the equipment you need for an independent trip.

COST

A five-metre Kevlar canoe, including paddles and compulsory lifejackets, costs CAD$32 per

night (five nights or more). A park permit is required (CAD$9.90 per adult, per night) and includes parking at entrance points. An overnight guided tour costs CAD$155 per person per day, including equipment and food.

AM I UP TO IT?

Anyone can paddle a canoe, but long trips put a strain on arms, shoulders and backs. You also have to be capable of carrying a 23-kilogram canoe, though shorter journeys without portaging are possible.

MORE LIKE THIS

Canoe and kayak trips can be taken all over Canada. The lakes around the Laurentian Mountains in Quebec are similar to those around Algonquin Park; there are outfitters in Mont Tremblant. River trips can also be taken along the Yukon with Sea to Sky (www.seato skyexpeditions.com), among other outfitters.

FOR REFERENCE

A Paddler's Guide to Algonquin Park suggests hundreds of routes.

'I SAW THAT MY LIFE WAS A VAST
GLOWING EMPTY PAGE AND I COULD
DO ANYTHING I WANTED.'

JACK KEROUAC

Journeys of the imagination

Discover the city from your back pocket

Essential for your weekend break, 25 top cities available.

POCKET SIZED
from £6.99

Football crazy

Daniel Neilson joins the chorus at the world's wildest football match: Boca meets River at La Bombonera.

WHAT	HOW LONG
Argentinian derby match	One day
WHERE	**THRILL FACTOR**
La Boca, Buenos Aires, Argentina	● ● ● ● ●

The sky turns momentarily white with ticker tape as Boca Juniors emerge on to the pitch. Blue and gold then resume their place as the dominant colours as smoke machines blast out dye. The roar of 50,000 of Argentina's most fanatical fans fills the Bombonera stadium, or the 'sweet box', so named because of its vertiginously steep tiers. Shoulders, elbows and bare chests flail and barge. Shirts are swung, songs screamed. On the east stand, drums thump and horns blare, while on the tier above them, the enemy, dressed in the red and white jerseys of River Plate, try to drown out the Boca crowd as if their lives depended on it. And, when that doesn't work, all manner of chairs, coins and bodily fluids land on the Boca crowd below.

In the unlikely event that residents four miles away had managed to remain oblivious to the weeks of build-up, round-the-clock media coverage, the cancellation of buses, taxis and the closure of public offices, they would still know that Boca Juniors were about to kick off against River Plate. How? The ground shakes.

WHEN TWO TEAMS GO TO WAR

The Argentinian *superclásico* (superderby) at La Bombonera stadium is, quite simply, the most visceral football experience in the world. It is often said that in Argentina football is a religion. In fact, it is much more than that. In a country of near-constant political strife and frightening financial unpredictability, the hopes, fears and passions of the people are concentrated in football – and belonging to one of the rival churches of Boca and River (which 70 per cent of the nation do) means nurturing a unique fervour. The influence even extends into the afterlife; there is a Boca cemetery, and even a funeral director who makes Boca coffins (and refuses to make River ones).

Preparations for the game begin months in advance. Police demand that extra officers in the area are on call, cafés and bars take on extra staff, and travel agents around the world hawk tickets to the game and flights to the Argentinian capital. The most extensive preparations, however, take place among the dedicated hardcore of fans, known in Latin America as the *barras bravas*. These organised groups plan fireworks displays

and paint banners big enough to cover the side of a stadium. The flags are emblazoned with the faces of past legends and the former leaders of the *barras bravas*. These are coveted positions that command big bucks through touting tickets, flogging parking spaces and drug sales. And when the rival factions meet, something the police try desperately to avoid, violence is often the outcome (recent leaders of the Boca and River fanclubs are currently in jail).

THE CLASS DIVIDE

The teams' mutual loathing can be traced back more than 100 years. Italian sailors founded Boca Juniors in 1905, in the port district of the Argentine capital known as La Boca; River Plate was founded four years earlier in the same neighbourhood, and a local derby was born. River moved first to Palermo and, in 1923, the club shifted to the wealthy neighbourhood of

'THE ARGENTINIAN SUPERCLÁSICO IS, QUITE SIMPLY, THE MOST VISCERAL FOOTBALL EXPERIENCE IN THE WORLD.'

Núñez, subsequently garnering the nickname *Los Millonarios* (the Millionaires). As the two teams rose to become the most successful in Argentina (to date, River Plate have won 33 domestic titles, 11 more than Boca, but Boca have won 13 more international titles), their rivalry only intensified. Yet it is the supposed class divide that has come to represent the fans, and the differences are keenly played up – many River fans arrive in the Boca neighbourhood with clothes pegs on their

noses (admittedly, the nearby Riachuelo river is rather pungent), while Boca fans cart along live chickens in a nod towards River's derogatory epithet *gallinas* (chickens).

The build-up on match day is electric. Fans congregate early in cafés and bars in the area, manned by dicky bowed-waiters in grubby tuxedos. Here they drink cheap lager, or the Argentinian favourite Fernet and coke (made with a bitter Italian herbal liqueur). Once suitably lubricated, it's time to progress, with due rowdiness, south towards La Bombonera.

Up and down the metre-high pavements, so built because of the area's tendency to flood, thousands of fans walk in convoy, singing, dancing, waving flags and thinking up increasingly offensive remarks with which to insult the enemy's mothers. Out the windows of the colourfully painted corrugated iron-tenement shanties in La Boca, residents cheer along the congregation. Beer is lowered down. There is time to stop for the classic game-day snack *choripán*, a sausage in a bun doused in spicy *chimichurri* sauce.

THE BEAUTIFUL GAME

Spectators are directed by the police down one of two routes, depending on which team they have chosen to support. (If ever the two sides meet, you don't want to be there.) After being frisked several times at the entrance, you're in.

No matter how many football games you have seen, nothing can prepare you for the feeling you get as you walk up the stairs out into La Bombonera. Some get a lump in their throat, some get butterflies, some get giddy, some are simply scared. Forget Wembley (even the old one), Barcelona's Nou Camp and Madrid's Vicente Calderón. This is football Argentinian style and it really is like no other. Boca's most famous fan (and ex-player), Diego Maradona, can often be spotted hanging out of his box, security guards clinging on to him, as he leaps and chants. The atmosphere is almost unbearably intense. And then Boca score… ●

WHEN TO GO
Boca Juniors and River Plate clash twice a year in a league fixture, usually in April and October.

GETTING THERE
If you aren't going to La Bombonera stadium with an organised group, take a radio cab directly. It's not in the best part of town, so it's better not to walk.

ORGANISING YOUR TRIP
Check the official Boca website (www.bocajuniors.com.ar), with English translation, for a fixture list for the year. Otherwise it is best to go along with a local.

COST
Tickets for the derby are only available to members and tour groups; otherwise, expect to pay a tout up to US$150. Tour agencies in BA usually charge around US$50 for travel, ticket and a guide. *Popular*, the cheapest section, is also the most dangerous so we don't recommend it.

AM I UP TO IT?
Bear in mind you will be jumping and singing for 90 minutes – dress comfortably and keep your wits about you.

MORE LIKE THIS
Boca and River occasionally meet in the off-season between December and February, and in other championships throughout the year. If you miss the big game, remember that any football match is still likely to be an adventure.

FOR REFERENCE
Mad For It: From Blackpool to Barcelona: Football's Greatest Rivalries by Andy Mitten includes an in-depth history of the long rivalry between Boca and River Plate.

Among beasts

Claire Boobbyer climbs on an elephant in search of rhino.

WHAT	HOW LONG
Rhino safari on elephant back	3-4 days
WHERE	**THRILL FACTOR**
Chitwan National Park, Nepal	● ● ● ● ●

Chhannou, our guide, looked solemn. 'People have died, you know,' he said. 'Impaled on the horn?', I enquired, affecting nonchalance. 'No, that's what most people think. In fact, they die from injuries caused by the razor-sharp tusks inside the mouth.'

When man confronts beast, it's always better to be the larger of the two. Emboldened by the height of the Asian elephant I was about to ride, I settled into the howdah with three others. Our convoy set off at a waddle, fording a streamlet, then entering the thicket of the sal forest. In the heart of the Chitwan National Park in southern Nepal, we were on a mission: to catch a glimpse of the rare one-horned rhinoceros that inhabits the lowlands of Asia.

The Chitwan National Park, a World Heritage Site, lies in the flood plains in the jungle-covered Terai, the southern lowlands of Nepal. Bounded by four rivers, the 360-square-mile area was a royal hunting reserve between 1846 and 1951. After the demise of the ruling Rana regime and the eradication of malaria in the area, Chitwan opened to visitors in 1973.

The endangered Indian rhinoceros, also called the greater one-horned rhinoceros, numbered less than 100 during the 1960s. But the Nepal government and WWF moved to halt the decline – and largely succeeded. Chitwan now supports the world's second-largest rhino population. Numbers had increased to about 600 prior to the recent Maoist insurgency, but then figures declined to 372 in 2005 owing partly to an increase in poaching. The reason? The trade in rhino horn. In many Asian countries, it is considered an aphrodisiac and a cure for everything from food poisoning to fever. The current figures – a 2008 survey detected 408 rhinos – suggest a quiet comeback.

ON THE SCENT

At first, the view from the back of the elephant was a blur of narrow, chalky-white trees. The elephant ripped up the jungle, tearing at thick, leafy branches as he shuffled through. Twigs cracked and branches thwacked as he curled his trunk, stuffed food into his mouth, chewed, munched and then ejected football-sized turds on to the narrow path.

Suddenly, and in spite of what proved to be disturbingly ineffectual protests from the mahout, the elephant decided to veer to the left and crashed headlong through what had seemed to me to be impenetrable jungle. A tangle of vine, grass and branches was mown down with surprising ease as a passage, of sorts, was forged. We eventually emerged, covered in debris, into an area carpeted by bun mara (forest killer), a vine that destroys everything in its path. In the calm, the mahout carefully brushed away the foliage from the elephant's head and we continued with our plodding wander.

'THE SKIN ON THE RHINO'S THIGHS DROOPED AND FOLDED, AS IF SHE WERE WEARING GREY BLOOMERS.'

To maximise our chances of spotting wildlife, the safari was conducted in silence – with occasional whispering. The sounds of dung thudding to the ground and streaming ponds of piss were broken only by the aerial manoeuvres

of a langur (long-tailed Asian monkey), whose landing released a shower of leaf confetti. This prompted a shift in our vision and, as a result, we spied spotted deer skulking in some greenery not far away. We ambled on, eyes peeled.

Without saying a word, our mahout pointed his finger and there, just four metres away to the right and sunk knee-deep in a stew of green, was the *Rhinoceros unicornis*. She raised her horned head, and locked her eyes on the invading party. Although almost two metres high, and weighing in at around 2,000 kilos, she looked reassuringly small from the top of an elephant. Her rotund

milky-grey body was saddled with large, taut skin plates. Her eyes were small and set well below the big, cylindrical-shaped ears. Rhinoceroses have terrible eyesight, but their myopia is more than compensated for by one of the most sensitive nasal detection mechanisms in the animal world: the two nostrils flaring at the side of the mono-horn can detect a scent as far as 300 metres away.

ARMOURED AND DANGEROUS

Disturbed by the nosy pachyderms and their riders, the rhino trundled off into the thicket, showing off her huge behind. The skin on her bulky thighs drooped and folded, as if she were wearing enormous, grey bloomers. As the elephant turned, I let out a muffled shriek as we spotted a baby rhino. Half the size of its mother, it was almost hidden by the dense bush.

The lumps and bumps on the rhino's armoured skin give it a curiously prehistoric look (indeed, early explorers thought these strange–looking creatures were unicorns). According to Rudyard Kipling's wonderful story about *How the Rhinoceros Got His Skin*, the one-toed ungulate takes its skin off to bathe, only to come back and find that a vengeful Parsee (the rhino had eaten the Parsee's cake on a previous occasion) had filled the skin with stale cake crumbs. In an uncontrollable fit of itching, he rubs his skin vigorously against a tree trunk – hence the rhino's crumpled skin (and its grumpy nature).

BATHING BEAUTIES

After our first brief encounter with a rhino, this small parade of elephants steered towards the lake edge. Abundant vegetation gave way to a sandy bank.

There, submerged in the water, were two more rhinos, basking happily. The one-horned rhino is a keen bather: we heard gurgles and nostril clearances as the beasts swam about in the reedy water. Another rhino was spotted closer to us, at the lake's edge. As we approached, its ears twitched furiously. Snorting, it nose-dived into the water and paddled to the opposite bank.

The mahouts commandeered the elephants out of the jungle into the elephant-grasslands. The flatlands were populated by mammoth clumps of pale golden grass (*Saccharum spontaneum*) that squeaked with dew as the elephants stamped through. Up to two metres high, the feathery grass provided a good hiding place for wildlife – and brilliant scarlet dragonflies hovered like mini 'copters overhead.

A little way on, the elephants stopped without warning, and began to shiver and shake. Their trunks rose and they let out a piercing trumpet call as they backed away from a clump of grass. The mahout's foot dug into the flapping ears as he tried to control them. Above the commotion,

'IF A RHINO CHARGES, RUN IN A ZIGZAG, AS IT CANNOT SEE WELL. IF YOU SEE A TIGER… JUST PRAY.'

the mahout whispered that two Asiatic black bears, the most fearsome animals in the park, were hidden in the undergrowth.

EASY, TIGER

The next morning, at 5.30am, fat dewdrops splashed down from the trees giving the impression of rain. An ethereal mist had enveloped the lodge and thick opaque cobwebs spun across low ground. Chhannou gave us a pep talk before we set off early, this time on foot.

'The rhino, tiger and bear are the most dangerous animals in the park. If we see a rhino, climb or stand behind a tree. If it charges, run in a zigzag, as it cannot see well. The bear is black and aggressive and is the most dangerous animal. If we see it, don't run; stay in a group and bang the ground with the staff. If you run away, they will follow us.' He continued: 'We may see a tiger. They are very territorial, so don't run away and don't turn around, as they attack from behind. The only thing we can do is… pray to God.'

There are only about 60 tigers (Panthera tigris) in Chitwan, but sightings are not as uncommon as you'd think. We began with a marching pace through the sal, stepping over rhino dung and swerving around termite mounds. I carefully eyed up vines and trees that might offer a leg-up should the need arise. A blood vine – a big choking creeper that spiralled helter-skelter around a tree – drew our attention to a bear hole at the base of the tree. With no sounds heard from within the cavern, we pushed on to an open area with a semi-dry riverbed.

There were dozens of tiger paw marks imprinted in the sand; I felt my lip tremble with

fear. The jungle noises were suddenly amplified as my eyes frantically scanned the dense forest. Chhannou pointed out fresh tiger scratches on tree trunks, there to mark territory. From this point on, with the unsettling knowledge that a tiger had probably seen us even if we hadn't seen it, I was keen to get back to the lodge. We pushed on, returning around breakfast time, knowing that with the morning broken in and the heat rising, our chances of spotting wildlife were slimmer.

NIGHT MOVES

That evening, at sunset, we gathered on the deck at Temple Tiger lodge and looked out over the flood plain. The Himalayas that had been visible during the day were disappearing in the fading light – and the pale silhouette of the Mahabharat mountains now backed the jungle. Night herons and other birds skimmed the water. Out of the silence, the water gurgled; there was a purr, a snort and a nose-blowing stutter. With the water birds starting to screech, the grey water rippled as a rhino swam in our direction through the riverine grass. Its single horn glided stealthily like a submarine on a mission. Our mission accomplished, we sat under the stars and listened to the water splash, as the morse-code flickering of fireflies lit up the night sky. ●

WHEN TO GO

The best months to go are outside the monsoon months: between September and April. Wildlife-spotting opportunities increase in March/April, when the trees lose their leaves.

GETTING THERE

From Kathmandu, it is a five-hour road trip to Chitwan National Park (included in Temple Tiger rates). Alternatively, you can transfer to Baratpur, the nearest airport, and travel from there to Chitwan (half an hour); taxis are available.

ORGANISING YOUR TRIP

We recommend Himalayan Frontiers (www.himalayanfrontiers.co.uk), which organises tours out of Temple Tiger, a lodge occupying a superb location deep in the park; transfers can be arranged from Kathmandu or Pokhara. Cheaper tours can be arranged from Sauraha, a touristy outpost on the edge of the park.

COST

The cost of a three-day, two-night stay at Temple Tiger lodge costs £260 per person, for two people sharing, and includes road and boat transport to and from Kathmandu, accommodation, three meals a day, guides, park entrance fee of US$14 per person per day, and all elephant rides, walks, canoe trips and jeep trips.

AM I UP TO IT?

Basic fitness is necessary (for walking in the heat of the jungle and clambering in and out of howdahs).

MORE LIKE THIS

Chitwan is one of the best places in the world to observe the greater one-horned rhino at close quarters. Other spots around the world for observing rhinos include the Palmwag rhino camp in Damaraland, Namibia, where you can see desert-adapted black rhino and elephants; the Selous Game Reserve in Tanzania, home to the black rhino; and Kaziranga National Park, Assam, India, where you can arrange elephant tours to spot the Indian one-horned rhino, as well as wild buffalo and tiger.

FOR REFERENCE

Rhinoceros by Kelly Enright is full of fascinating facts. The International Rhino Foundation (www.rhinos-irf.org) and www.savetherhino.org.

City on the edge

Michael Hodges ventures back to battle-scarred Beirut.

WHAT	HOW LONG
Weekend break in Beirut, Lebanon	Two-four days
WHERE	THRILL FACTOR
Lebanon, Middle East	● ● ● ● ●

My head smashed against the concrete, the glass shot from my hand and the world was inverted. I saw stars – not *Tom and Jerry* stars, but the sparkling Middle Eastern sky, dotted with constellations and astral bodies. Then the stars were joined by concerned Arab faces, and hands came and pulled me up. 'I told you, that hashish is very strong,' said one of the men, before they carried me to my hotel and left me in an armchair in reception.

There was a time when Lebanon was mainly known in the UK for its hashish. During the 1970s, much of London was lost in a fug of Red Leb fumes while the country of its origin was suffering a calamitous civil war that tore apart Lebanon's fragile ethnic and religious mosaic of Sunni and Shia Muslims, Maronite Christians, Druze and Palestinian refugees. Rather than the pleasantly soporific – though dangerous if you are perched on a stool – effects of its drug crop, Lebanon became famous for death and destruction.

We haven't the space for more than a brief résumé of Lebanon's tortured recent history, but there's been plenty of it: a civil war from 1975 until 1990; the 1978 and 1982 invasions by Israel; the occupation of much of the country by the Syrian Army (ended by the Cedar Revolution in 2005); bombings in 2006; a campaign of car bombing; and, in May this year, another, small civil war. Each of these conflicts has left its imprint – many buildings still show the mark of bullets and shells.

But at time of writing Beirut was safe. No one was bombing or shooting anyone in Lebanon – except in Tripoli in the north and isolated incidents in the south – and kidnappings of Westerners were a thing of the past. You won't get mugged, you won't have your pocket picked and outside of the high-end hotels, no one will charge you £4 for glass of cold beer. Beirut is safer than Tottenham, cheaper than Soho and substantially more fun than either – a city that appears to be involved in a perpetual and particularly loud party.

MARTYRS AND MOSQUES
The city sprawls along a natural cove punched into the side of Mount Lebanon, not one mountain but a range that reaches 3,000 metres and marches along the Mediterranean coastline to define Beirut's limits.

'MUCH OF LONDON WAS LOST IN A FUG OF RED LEB FUMES WHILE THE COUNTRY OF ITS ORIGIN WAS SUFFERING A CALAMITOUS CIVIL WAR.'

After parking up and wandering around, I returned to find an irate soldier by the car. 'Is this yours?' 'Yes.' 'Don't leave it alone.' Car bombings have left everyone nervous of lone cars parked in unlikely places. The most famous victim of a car bomb was Sunni prime minister Rafik Hariri.

Below downtown lies Martyrs' Square, scene of the protesters' camp during the Cedar Revolution and site also of a giant Sunni mosque built by Hariri with Saudi cash. At the side of the square nearest the sea you can still see the evidence of the car bomb that killed Hariri. The blown-out building makes for an unnerving monument. Beirutis, however, drive blithely past. They have seen too much death to stop, and they're probably thinking about their next meal.

FEEDING FRENZY

Food is the national obsession. Lebanese cuisine mixes traditional Arabic cooking with Turkish – a leftover from the Ottoman Empire – and French, who were colonial masters here from the end of World War I until the end of World War II. From restaurants to street stalls, it's all good.

But this is, above all, a Mediterranean city, and seafood restaurants abound. Along the Corniche Beirut, the stretch of seafront that was the walkway of the demi-monde when the city

was the 'Paris of the Levant', young men dive from the sea wall into the waves and old men fish.

Behind the Corniche, the standards of the Shia Hezbollah movement are pinned to lamp posts alongside portraits of Hezbollah's leader, Hassan Nasrallah. The east and south of the city are Shia strongholds and, if you *do* go into a Hezbollah area, on no account take photographs, as you may well be taken for a spy.

Everywhere else, it's fine to snap away (but don't point your camera at soldiers). Lebanon's two prime photo opportunities – the Roman ruins at Byblos and the cedar trees – are at least an hour and a half's taxi ride from the city. But if you travel to the towns and hamlets dotted along the ridges that overlook the city, you'll discover lesser-known sites that are just as revealing.

In the morning, a mist comes surging off the Mediterranean and up the mountain. Time it right, and you can watch the blanket of fog flood into town, effectively turning Broumanna into an island, almost a lost world. You'll need to get up early to catch it, which is easy if you've spent the night in an armchair in reception. ●

WHEN TO GO
Late spring (April) is the best time to visit.

GETTING THERE
Beirut International Airport is three miles from the city centre; British Airways flies daily.

ORGANISING YOUR TRIP
Few companies offer city breaks, but a number of websites can help you; try www.downtown beirut.com, www.lebanontourism.com and www.travel-to-lebanon.com.

AM I UP TO IT?
Visas are available at Beirut airport. Take care to avoid restricted areas (see the Foreign Office website, www.fco.gov.uk, for details).

MORE LIKE THIS
Other great cities opening up to visitors include once-avoided Bogotá, now cleaned up and bristling with energy; small, historic Sarajevo, which has risen impressively from the ashes of its turbulent past; and the Estonian capital Tallinn, whose gorgeous medieval old town has survived the series of attacks the city has endured in the 20th century.

FOR REFERENCE
Read *De Niro's Game: A Novel*, by Rawi Hage, the story of two men caught in a Beirut crossfire, or watch *West Beyrouth*, a slice of life from the West Beirut of 1975. Listen to RGB's *Ya Wled Loubnan*; Lebanese rap is starting to find its natural rhythm with this outfit.

Mas hysteria

In Port of Spain, **Yolanda Zappaterra** dresses up,
and gets down, at the world's wildest party.

WHAT	HOW LONG
Playing mas at carnival	Two days to two months.
WHERE	**THRILL FACTOR**
Port of Spain, Trinidad	● ● ● ● ●

Wa' you wanna be? You wanna be jab jab? A midnight robber? A moko jumbie? A pierrot grenade? Or you wanna play bikini mas and experience the sheer exuberance of carnival in your sheer tights and sequins as you roll your bum-bu-lums and practise your chippin' and winin' on the road march? You can be whatever you want in 'mas', Trinidad and Tobago's carnival (mas is short for masquerade) – but whatever you do, don't miss the build-up.

Many visitors fly into Port of Spain just in time for the two-day event, before making a sleepy recovery on the island's white sands. But, as with so many things in life, when it comes to mas, anticipation is everything – and the partying and the preparations, the soca and sequins, start months in advance in Trinidad. As one masquerader put it: 'This is a two-day event that starts immediately after Christmas and ends on Ash Wednesday.' Determined to experience the real spirit of mas, I arrived two weeks before carnival, and got busy.

It was during the frenzied preparations for my first mas that I started to realise how the country's history and cultural diversity had shaped the celebration in unique ways. Everyone, from the scary-looking bootleg vendor downtown to ancient men splitting coconuts with machetes on Queen's Park Savannah, the huge park in the middle of the city, would ask, 'You playin' mas?' The affirmative response would trigger enthusiastic mini-lessons in history, anthropology, music, dressmaking and even dancing – and a picture began to appear of the event's dark underbelly, rooted in the slave trade, pagan rituals and religion, as well as centuries of conflict and servitude to different masters, on both a personal and national level. These elements, played out in a stirring spectacle of music, costume and dance, combine to make Trinidad and Tobago's carnival different from – and better than – any other in the world.

IMPS, BATS AND THIEVES

Trinidad's carnival, like any other, has had multiple roots and versions. The key narrative is this: in the 18th century, when French sugar cane

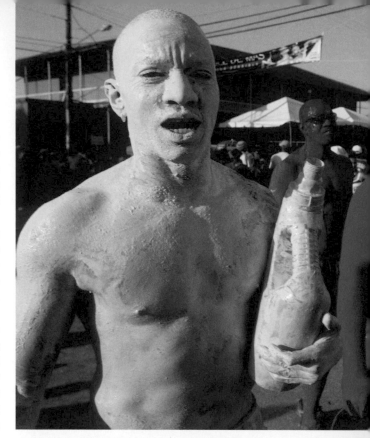

planters held elaborate masked pre-Lenten balls, their slaves soon started parodying these with their own versions, introducing African and Creole elements and gaily subverting the upper classes with characters like the Dame Lorraine, men dressed as women in flouncy frocks, big wigs and even bigger boobs and behinds (made of pillows).

Dark elements played their part too; an undercurrent of violence informed the characterisation of the masqueraders and, when devils, imps, bats and midnight robbers took to the streets in the years of wild post-emancipation celebrations, people took cover.

By the 19th century, contemporary carnival had started to emerge – spontaneous street parties and house balls merged into an organised parade of 'bands', devised and dressed by talented, dedicated band leaders like Harold Saldenah, George Bailey, Irwin McWilliams – and later 'masman' Peter Minshall, who in the 1970s brought his artist-trained eye back home from the Central School of Art and Design in London to add a touch of drama to proceedings. The bands grew, and grew, and one band can now number thousands. It's easy enough to join in: you sign up, pay up and turn up, and spend the carnival in a whirl of dancing and drinking on the streets of Port of Spain.

SOCA, SO GOOD

A descendant of soul and calypso, its more traditional forerunner, relentlessly uptempo soca is now the carnival soundtrack of choice. My mas preparation started with a handful of 'fetes', huge outdoor parties where Trinis from all backgrounds and visitors dance to the year's best soca beats until daybreak – the frenetic, insistently joyful soca (Machel Montano, say, exhorting us to 'push our flags up, big it up, jump up, spread our wings and fly away come carnival morning') armed me with a headful of songs I simply couldn't stop singing.

A quick confab with locals revealed that Under the Trees at the Normandie Hotel, a series of concerts, is an essential part of the build-up.

'ISLANDERS AND VISITORS DANCE TO THE YEAR'S BEST SOCA BEATS AND BANDS UNTIL DAYBREAK, FUELLED BY AS MUCH FOOD AND DRINK AS NECESSARY.'

For a whole week before carnival, the tropical grounds of the hotel host every big soca and calypso star on the island – the likes of Bunji Garlin, Machel Montano, Destra, Denise Plummer, Sparrow, Shadow, Black Stalin and David Rudder. Tickets cost around £30, but they include local dishes like roti, curried goat and doubles (channa, or curried chickpea, sandwiched between flat bread and topped with hot sauce); all the beer and spirits you can drink (rum is the carnival fuel of choice); and some of the hottest sets you'll see on the island. Best of all, they finish just when the panyards start swinging into action at about 11pm.

PAN-TASTIC
By day, some panyards look like scrubby concrete lots that you wouldn't dare venture into after dark, but once the sun sets, they are the best place to feel the energy of carnival. I wasn't convinced I liked the steel drum sound until I heard it in the panyards, but then it got me, and I got it: the different sections of the band; the intricacy of the arrangements; the subtle nuances of the bass and tenor pans; and also the fact that the instrument itself is so entwined with the cultural and political heritage of the islands.

The origins of pan music can be traced back to the early 20th century, when workers, previously

deprived of drums by fearful colonialists who thought they were using them to communicate, began to tap out rhythms with bamboo stems of varying sizes (known as tamboo bamboo). This music, banned by the British in 1935, foreran the playing of discarded oil drums used by the US Army based here in the 1940s.

But most stirring of all was the stamina and commitment of the orchestra members. A full-scale pan band comprises around 100 musicians, all working every night in the run-up to Panorama final, a huge competition held on carnival Saturday at the huge stages of the Savannah (visitors welcome).

FANTASTICAL FINALE

By rights I should have been completely exhausted from all the party nights, but daytimes spent lazing in the shade of the coconut trees at Maracas Beach provided ample recuperation, which was just as well since the big one, J'Ouvert (pronounced 'jouvay' and meaning daybreak), was just around the corner.

For many locals, this street party to end all street parties is the carnival finale, the cue to head off to Maracas Bay or Tobago for a few days of well-earned limin' and chillin' on the island's glorious beaches. But technically speaking, J'Ouvert is just the beginning: daybreak on carnival Monday morning, a point marked traditionally with a primal gathering of revellers immersing themselves in 'otherness'. A pretty woman might make herself look ugly, a macho man will dress as a woman, and a professional could wear nothing but a nappy. It is a strange, surreal experience, particularly as celebrations begin in the dark at 4am, with people taking to the streets covered in cocoa powder, motor oil, axle grease, mud, blue or black paint (or, more recently, chocolate) in a party that must be the closest there is to the devilish days of early mas.

Forewarned, we did J'Ouvert in old T-shirts and shorts, and loved every nervy minute of it. The darkness gives J'Ouvert a distinct edge –

and if you're planning on just wandering the streets aimlessly you will feel it – but most people these days join a band and parade with them. Do the same and let go – to subvert an old saying, 'You can't 'fraid mud and play J'Ouvert'. Suitably dishevelled and feeling that we'd welcomed the day sufficiently, we headed back to clean up and sleep before the final act of excess: mas.

CHIPPIN' AND SIPPIN'

We had wanted to play the nearest thing there is to traditional mas, 'pretty' mas with Brian McFarlane's band (twice winner of Band of the Year), but signed up too late, so instead we made do with sampling the more lurid, pumping 'bikini mas' or 'fete mas' (essentially a party on the move). The parade is made up of huge bands like Tribe, Elements and Harts, and their equally huge

trucks, band-members-only articulated lorries with everything from soundsystems and DJs to showers and chill-out rooms, plus smaller trailers acting as mobile bars and cafés. All around, the masses dance, sip and 'chip' behind the trucks. Chippin' to the beat is an essential mas move – a half-walking, half-dancing shuffle.

With more than 100 bands and 100,000 masqueraders playing modern mas, many of them interchangeable in terms of scale and energy, it was tempting to just stand on the sidelines and enjoy the peripheral activities of the dwindling moko jumbies, fancy sailors, robbers and imps. But not to play mas, at least once, is to miss out on the true spirit of the Trinidad carnival. So I donned my outfit, customised to my heart's content, and got stuck into the best bacchanal on earth. ●

WHEN TO GO
Carnival is held on the two days before Ash Wednesday. Preparations start two months in advance, but fetes, concerts and panyard rehearsals peak in the fortnight before carnival.

GETTING THERE
There are direct flights from the UK, US and Canada to Piarco Airport, Port of Spain.

ORGANISING YOUR TRIP
One of the most informative insider carnival sites, with links to all the mas bands' sites, is www.trinidadcarnivaldiary.com. For fetes and to book tickets, see http://trinidadfetetickets. blogspot.com. For the fete lowdown, see www.tntisland.com, which also has a full list of the panyards.

COST
From £1,000 for a week (mas costume and all-inclusive participation £300; accommodation £700; concerts £30; fetes £30).

AM I UP TO IT?
Anyone can take part – but remember to wear comfortable shoes and to drink plenty of liquid.

MORE LIKE THIS
Other world-famous carnivals include: Venice, where the weather in late winter may not lend itself to bikinis, but the location is extraordinary; Rio de Janeiro, the world's biggest carnival, with samba on the sound systems; and New Orleans, where you can watch the carnival krewes on Fat Tuesday, the day that gave Mardi Gras its name and the final day of revelry before Ash Wednesday.

FOR REFERENCE
Read *Miguel Street* by Trinidadian VS Naipaul, a collection of short stories set in Port of Spain; *The Dragon Can't Dance*, a penetrating portrait of carnival by Trinidadian author Earl Lovelace; and lavish photographical tome *Moko Jumbies: The Dancing Spirits of Trinidad*, by Stefan Falke.

In deepest Siberia

Chris Moss boards at Moscow bound for Siberia's great lake.

WHAT Epic rail journey	**HOW LONG** 10-12 days (train trip 8 nights)
WHERE Moscow to Beijing, via Lake Baikal	**THRILL FACTOR** ● ● ● ● ●

boarded the No.10 at Moscow's Yaroslavsky station in late April, just as the ice was beginning to thaw. Considered the most luxurious of the Trans-Siberian services – because it has a cold shower in some coaches – it only goes as far as Irkutsk, by Lake Baikal, but that was enough for me. For the moment.

Immensity and extremity are what Siberia does best. Skies and steppe swept away to the distant horizon and, as I chugged relentlessly through five time zones for five days, I had no shortage of time to contemplate it. For the first couple of days, I enjoyed the usual emotional cycles of rail travel: leaving Moscow, arriving in major, but mysterious, cities (Perm, Omsk, Novosibirsk), buying fresh bread at the platform *produkty* shops. But this is a long, stretched-out journey and most of my days, and nights, revolved around my compartment – I was sharing with an army officer who slept 18 hours a day – and getting hot tea from the samovar.

I read books, listened to music, occasionally shared a vodka and smoked fish with fellow passengers, and learned to look out of the window for hours: at steppe, at forests of silver birch, at dun-coloured skies and at grim factories built in Soviet times. Winter lingers long in central

'I LEARNED TO LOOK OUT OF THE WINDOW: AT STEPPE, AT FORESTS OF SILVER BIRCH, AT DUN-COLOURED SKIES AND GRIM FACTORIES.'

Siberia and there was a dusting of snow for most of the journey, and vast swathes of deep snow for miles before and after freezing Krasnoyarsk.

LAKE BAIKAL
The planet's oldest, deepest lake, Baikal is right at home in vast, underpopulated Siberia. It's not quite the world's biggest, but it's still the size of Belgium. More importantly, Baikal's steep bowl holds a fifth of the world's fresh water. If the world's taps were switched off tomorrow, Baikal's 5,663 cubic miles could keep all six billion of us sated for about 40 years.

I had my first taste of Baikal on the train. Filtered and purified by epishura, voracious sponges that live in its depths, the water in the whole lake is drinkable, making Baikal the source of some 20 per cent of the world's unfrozen fresh water. After a particularly prolonged vodka session with a soldier and his wife, the water was more than welcome. And after four nights in a second-class compartment, so was the lake.

SPRING IN SIBERIA

It was spring and snow was melting, birds singing. En route, I had seen the great rivers – the Volga, the Ob, the Yenisey – flowing freely without bergs. But the smaller tributaries were rock solid – and Russia was still unquestionably cold.

Lake Baikal is the most popular stop for Trans-Siberian travellers – it's an opportunity to exercise limbs, breathe clean air and eat wholesome food. I was staying at Listvyanka, the small resort town on the lake's south-western shore. From here, Baikal extends north like a crooked finger for some 400 miles, covering a surface area of 12,200 square miles – equal to about 2,140 Windermeres. As well as being the oldest and deepest, it's also the world's most transparent lake. In the fantastic little museum in Listvyanka, I learnt many more world record facts and figures, and saw all the weird gastropods

and algae (1,085 species) that inhabit the lake, as well as the pressure-resistant, see-through golomyanka fish that live in the depths.

But I couldn't really feel the statistics. What I saw as we drove past the landmark of Shaman Rock was surely one of the planet's most awesome visions. The entire lake was frozen. Pure white and shimmering, it looked too pristine to be true. Sunglasses donned, I could make out walkers, sleds pulled by huskies, a kite-skier, some kids playing football with a black ball and two fishermen sat around a small hole casting lines.

COMFORT FOOD

Before such a huge natural wonder, with its blinding light and impenetrable face, we all naturally seek out comfort zones. There are private and communal *banyas* (saunas) all over Listvyanka, and there is a special pleasure to be had in looking out of the window at the cold blue from a cosy wooden cabin set at a permanently tropical temperature. Afterwards, there's always black tea – after everything there's black tea – and a chat.

'THE ENTIRE LAKE WAS FROZEN. PURE WHITE AND SHIMMERING, IT LOOKED TOO PRISTINE TO BE TRUE.'

Listvyanka, which is basically a church, a port and some log cabins, is sweet enough and, at weekends, a market set up at the edge of the lake provides a social hub. There are souvenirs – wooden wall-hangings, animals stretched into furry scarves, necklaces made from the local violet charoite stone – and dozens of stallholders selling fish – pike, sig fish, and the local favourite, salmon-like omul – smoked in birch wood.

A bracing wind was blowing off the lake on the day I strolled round the market but for Russians – all of them in serious winter gear and big hats – this fresh spring day was no obstacle. Family groups stood around tearing off slices of oily fish along with bread, dumplings and bottles of Baltika beer.

The food was even better at my accommodation. I had been wary when I was told I was having a 'Siberian homestay'. It sounded like the kind of euphemistic invitation they may have offered to Solzhenitsyn before shipping him to a gulag. But it's the done thing in Listvyanka, where the hotels are pricey and still controlled by the supremely inefficient Intourist organisation dating back to Soviet times.

TIPTOEING ON ICE

On my second day, we walked across the ice to Port Baikal. Although the lake is at roughly the same latitude as London, it had snowed heavily during the night. Siberia is wide open, with lots of steppe and few high mountains to temper the winds, which bring in extreme weather. In summer there's no relief: massive electric storms are created when cold air settles above the warm lake, and the lake gets as choppy as an ocean.

It was hard to imagine waves that morning. I was not overly keen on walking on the ice: it was ice-rink slippy, the new snow covering hid any potential cracks, and I wondered how safe it was so late in the season. 'No problem,' Valery assured me. 'It's about 1.3 metres thick. Look, there are cars crossing right now.' A minute later his foot went through right up to the knee. Changing a sock, he muttered something about this being 'unusual' and 'must be a hole for fishing'. We continued on tiptoe. Both of us occasionally slipped on the wind-polished ice – and I slipped discreetly into single file behind Valery.

Ringing the lake is dense, dark taiga – the classic Russian forest of silver birch, silver fir, spruce, evergreen pines and amber-orange larch, skeletal in spring. There are still industrial pressures on the lakeside – pulp and paper plants are the main culprits, although they may soon close – but, since 1996, Baikal has been UNESCO-listed as 'the most outstanding example of a freshwater lake', and a string of national parks protects its forests and the elk, bears, ermine and snow rams that live there.

Hard as it was to imagine on my visit, from mid May onwards the ice breaks up and there are four months of fluid water for sailing and windsurfing and, in the shallower, warmer coves, swimming – and boats ply up and down the lake visiting islands and remote bays.

Before leaving the region, I visited the town where the train terminates – Irkutsk. It is the other reason why everyone breaks their journey at Baikal, for this is the so-called 'Paris of Siberia', a nexus of history, culture, architecture and religion. Like many other Siberian settlements, it was once a dumping ground for dissidents, criminals and assorted non-Russians. It has also long been a trading post for Buryats, Mongolians and other nomadic peoples. Tamara, my host, was a 69-year-old linguist. She filled me in on the local mafia, on life in Vietnam and Siberian weather – and made me a slap-up meal of chicken and mash, knowing I'd be on hydrogenated food once I got back on the train.

MOVING ON TO BEIJING

It was time to move on. I was taking the Trans-Manchurian, a decidedly unluxurious railway service that connects Moscow with Irkutsk and then carries on to Beijing, taking a long sweep round Mongolia to pass through Harbin – China's ice capital. There were no soldiers on this service. Just packed six- and four-berth compartments, full of families and young Chinese expats in pyjamas, who spent all day chatting and eating pot noodles – while sitting on my pillow. After Russia, there was almost a party atmosphere on board – as you cross the border you feel you are entering a busy, noisy, more optimistic country. It was comforting, but somehow less enthralling than the grey middle zone of Siberia.

Baikal and the Trans-Siberian go together. They are both big, strange and utterly unique. Much of Russia is an ecological desert, and the plains look parched, acidic and doomed, especially when you see them turn dirty yellow as the winter finally loosens its skeletal grip on the land. But Baikal is a gasp of hope for Eurasia and a blast of healthy living to break up a long sit-down train odyssey. It takes considerable effort to get there, but, on balance – taking into account the smoked fish, the steam baths, the views and the cool beauty of the taiga, as well as the dry food, the tedium and too much vodka – it's worth it. ●

WHEN TO GO
Trans-Siberian services run year-round.

GETTING THERE
Fly into Moscow; board at Yaroslavsky station.

ORGANISING YOUR TRIP
On The Go (www.onthegotours.com) has a 13-day Moscow to Beijing itinerary with an (extendable) stop at Lake Baikal.

COST
On the Go's 13-day trip from Moscow to Beijing, with a stop at Baikal, costs from £950, excluding flights.

AM I UP TO IT?
The only things likely to disqualify travellers are an intolerance of long periods of window gazing and an inability to sit still.

MORE LIKE THIS
There are three key Trans-Siberian routes to choose from: from Moscow to Beijing via Ulaan Bator, Moscow to Beijing via Harbin, or from Moscow to Vladivostok.

FOR REFERENCE
The Great Railway Bazaar: By Train Through Asia, by Paul Theroux, has colourful passages on the Trans-Siberian.

Eating the east

Time Out food and drink editor **Guy Dimond** samples the good, the very good and the ugly in Hanoi, street food capital of the world.

WHAT Adventure eating	**HOW LONG** 2-7 days
WHERE Hanoi, Vietnam	**THRILL FACTOR** ● ● ● ● ○

Many Western visitors to Hanoi avoid the street food, thinking that they'll get food poisoning at first bite. But if you're adventurous, you'll quickly discover that the street food is far preferable to the bland tastes proffered by many tourist restaurants. In fact, the Vietnamese capital excels at street food, topping even the night markets of Thailand, southern China or Malaysia for vibrancy and variety. In a week of scores of snacks and meals, I didn't once get an upset stomach.

A week is barely enough to discover the hundreds of Hanoi street food dishes, so you'd best start as soon as possible, at a *bia hoi*. Some of these 'pubs' have no signage, and are little more than a chilled barrel of beer with a hose to siphon the watery lager into glasses, a few low stools and some plastic tables set in the shade. Other *bia hois* have remarkably large menus (in Vietnamese), and can cook up a dozen or more types of snack to order; some have no written menus (see what other diners are eating and gesture that you'd like the same). Find your seat, order a *bia* (beer), then pick some snacks; when you're done, throw the debris on the floor (everyone else does).

DIY FOOD

Some dishes are self-assembly. Pigs' ears, for example, are served in strips, dusted in flour and served with rectangles of rice paper. You roll the meat inside the rice paper, as you might roll a cigarette, together with a leaf or two of the large, bay-like leaves provided; then dunk the roll in the dip. The result is an exciting contrast of textures and flavours, as with many Vietnamese dishes.

Street food is invariably cheap – most dishes cost pence, and an entire meal for two with beer is unlikely to cost more than a couple of quid – which allows for daredevil ordering. Dishes that don't sound appealing can be surprisingly tasty, such as *cháo lòng*. *Cháo* is the Vietnamese name for *congee* (rice porridge), a popular breakfast dish in southern China, some parts of South-east Asia and Japan. *Lòng* roughly translates as offal – specifically the stomach, liver, tongue and a type of blood pudding, which are all mixed in. The

'HANOI EXCELS AT STREET FOOD, FOR VIBRANCY AND VARIETY TOPPING EVEN THE NIGHT MARKETS OF THAILAND.'

tongue is particularly tasty, though the gristly-looking blood vessels in the liver can be a little off-putting. *Trung vit lon* is considered a big delicacy, but for me, eating duck embryo cooked in its shell – boiled egg of sorts with bits of beak and bone – was an experience I am in no rush to repeat.

Apart from the *bia hois*, there are many small, open-fronted caffs that specialise in just one or two dishes. Some of these dishes are famous, and caffs specialising in a particular dish tend to cluster in one street. Dishes such as *bun cha* (pork patties served with cold rice noodles and deep-fried Hanoi spring rolls), *pho* (a soup of meat stock with rice noodles), *bahn cuon* (a rice pasta wrapped like a pancake roll around a mushroom filling) and *cha ca la vong* (fried fish served with fresh dill, fresh turmeric and rice noodles) are all must-try dishes. You can get creditable versions of all these dishes throughout Vietnam – and quite possibly at a Vietnamese restaurant near you.

What you're unlikely to find in Surbiton, Salt Lake City or Sydney is a café specialising in water buffalo penis. Hanoi has several, where the member is steamed slowly to tenderise it. Many Vietnamese believe eating it is good for male stamina and sexual vigour (their own, that is, not the water buffalo's).

DOG IS THE DINNER

If you're visiting Hanoi, you will almost inevitably also be visiting the beauty spot Ha Long Bay, around 100 miles away. A stream of tourist buses runs to Ha Long Bay down a busy road peppered with humble roadside restaurants advertising *thit chó* or sometimes *thit cây*. *Thit* means meat; *chó*

is dog; *cây* is puppy. Northern Vietnam, like Korea, parts of China and South-east Asia, is dog-eating territory and, although it's hardly a staple of the diet – most Vietnamese people eat dog meat very infrequently, if at all – there is sufficient demand to keep many small restaurants busy. Dog is considered to be a 'heating' food, and so it's most popular in winter, accompanied by *nêp duc*, 'sticky rice wine', a potent drink with a sweet, fermented flavour.

In Hanoi itself, the *thit chó* restaurants cluster along the Red River (Nhat Tan) dyke. Most of them are fairly basic places and can feel like a scene out of *The Deer Hunter*, but they are popular with small groups of men and the occasional post-wedding party. Dog meat is prepared in several different ways. It might be minced and formed on to skewers like satay, minced into blood sausages and deep-fried, or roasted, cut into slices and served like cold roast ham.

Dog is one rare meat that doesn't taste like chicken; in case you've ever wondered, it tastes like fatty lamb (a meat normally absent from the Vietnamese diet, which may explain the popularity of dog). Dog meat is accompanied by fresh herb leaves (just like many Vietnamese dishes), also by a stinking, bubbling fermented shrimp paste called *mám tóm*, which is far more challenging to eat than the dog meat. Or you can simply eat the roast meat with salt, lime juice and a little chilli.

This begs the question: where do the dogs come from? A variety of dog breeds are kept as much-loved pets in Hanoi, the same as they are in any city. But these dogs, for obvious reasons, tend to be kept on leashes. In the Hanoi food market called December 19, you can see entire dog carcasses on sale, both raw or whole and roasted. These edible dogs are not pets – they have been raised in special dog farms to the south of Hanoi in a town called Nhât Tân. Dog farming really took off in the 1990s; trade between China and Vietnam eased, resulting in a flow of electrical goods from China to Vietnam, and dogs from Vietnam to China. So far, exports to the West have not taken off. ●

WHEN TO GO
Hanoi is cold in winter, hot in summer. Autumn (September to December) and spring (March and April) are the best times to go.

GETTING THERE
There are frequent flights to Hanoi from Bangkok, Hong Kong and Ho Chi Minh City.

ORGANISING YOUR TRIP
You need to be adventurous to explore the street food of Hanoi – and travel independently. Go as part of a package trip, and your guides will invariably steer you away from anywhere serving challenging dishes, or with less than five-star hygiene; a whole industry has arisen serving bland food in overpriced settings to tourists. You can, of course, just walk into any café and point and order, but chances are you won't be able to work out what you're eating or what the dish is called, unless you speak Vietnamese. To get the most out of Hanoi, use the services of a local guide. They are highly trained, inexpensive (around £30 per day) and – if you're lucky – will make your trip much more rewarding. Our excellent guide, Hai (Nguyen

Thanh Hai, tourguidehai@yahoo.com) met us at Hanoi airport. He was booked through Exotissimo Travel (www.exotissimo.com), but many reputable companies can also arrange experienced local guides.

COST
Street food is very cheap – a couple of pounds per meal is usually more than sufficient. The cost of hotels racks up the cost; from £50 to £100 per night for Western-standard accommodation. From the UK, return flights to Hanoi cost around £500 to £600.

AM I UP TO IT?
If you have any specific food allergies – peanuts or sesame, for example (both used widely in Vietnamese cooking) – make sure you travel with a guide who understands the problem.

MORE LIKE THIS
Ho Chi Minh City also has many good street food stalls and cafés; to a lesser extent so does Hué. Neighbouring Thailand, southern China, Malaysia and Indonesia are also street food hotspots.

Mountain meditations

Amar Grover takes thousands of steps to heaven.

WHAT	HOW LONG
Part of the Char Dham Hindu pilgrim trail	4-10 days
WHERE	**THRILL FACTOR**
Garwhal, Himalayan India	● ● ● ● ○

If pilgrims were the world's first tourists, then the Indian Himalayas are the world's oldest tourist attraction. Hindus have been going on pilgrimage in India for some 4,000 years, following an elaborate network of sacred trails and spiritual nodes that can take a lifetime to complete. Having ten days, I opted for spectacle over endurance and went to the lofty valleys of the upper Garhwal region in Uttarakhand state to attempt part of the Himalayan Char Dham or 'Four Abodes' route.

Many ancient Hindu texts laud the act of pilgrimage, and lines like 'Flower-like are the heels of the wanderer/Thus his body grows and is fruitful/All of his sins disappear/Slain by the toil of his journeying' do much to set the tone. Barely 175 miles north-east of Delhi, my journey was already beginning to feel two yards short of oblivion. Wedged into a tatty bus that careered through umpteen tight bends high above a wooded valley, I thought about karma and wished I had somehow oiled mine more thoroughly down in Haridwar, the 'Gate of God', the city where the River Ganges emerges from the hills on to the hot and dusty plains.

The Himalayan Char Dham comprises Yamunotri and Gangotri – the respective traditional sources of the Yamuna and Ganges rivers, and settings for various myths – and the temple sites of Kedarnath and Badrinath. Most pilgrims visit them in this sequence, though Badrinath, being the northern point of the great all-India route, is the most visited and important. I opted for Yamunotri and Gangotri, as they are slightly less commercial and the source of rivers have an aesthetic appeal.

PILGRIM'S JOURNEY

Having dipped my toes and paid my dues at Haridwar, the usual pilgrims' launch pad for all four sites, I set off by bus through Rishikesh and the tortuous road deep into the hills. For

'FOR CENTURIES, THESE HIMALAYAN ROUTES WERE USED SOLELY BY RAGGED MENDICANTS AND HARDY TRAVELLERS PREPARED TO BRAVE THE SOMETIMES DANGEROUS TERRAIN.'

centuries, these Himalayan routes were used solely by ragged mendicants and hardy travellers prepared to brave the demanding and sometimes dangerous terrain.

Much has changed: army-built roads blasted through the valleys now link settlements that were previously days' walk apart. Today's modern pilgrims mainly come by bus and jeep, and you are as likely to see middle-class families from Delhi, Varanasi and Mumbai as country folk from the foothills. Arduous ten-day coach tours often attempt the four sites, puffing up one valley, then down and across to another. While the distances are not so great, few vehicles manage more than 15 miles an hour.

Leaving behind golden terraces of lowland wheat and then worming through the dark chasm of Hanuman Chatti hamlet – set in a defile in the mountain – the Yamunotri road makes one final thrust up to Janki Chatti. The terminus for jeeps and vans, it's a functional place enclosed by steep picturesque hills. The main trail winds through a modernising village of balconied houses and simple inns before climbing steadily through forest above the Yamuna River.

It's a lovely, undemanding one-day walk. There are few mountain views until the end, but you can view the relatively wealthy, who seem to abhor walking: for around 800 rupees, or £10, four bearers will whisk individuals all the way to the small, plain temple set at the foot of Banderpoonch peak. A hamlet of sorts has been built up around it: grubby-looking hostels and restaurants; stalls hawking pious paraphernalia from gaudy pictures of deities to vivid powders; and even coconuts to cut as offerings.

Pilgrims often bring portions of food to tie in cloth and immerse in a steaming hot spring beside the temple. So 'cooked', they're offered to the deity and, thus sanctified, taken home for a friend or relative who had not the will or stamina to come here. As for the Yamuna River, its true source lies half a mile higher at a rarely visited glacial lake.

GETTING TO GANGOTRI: SOURCE OF THE GANGES

Two days later, on another public bus, I was rattling up the longer and more theatrical road to Gangotri amid forests of pine and cedar. Dotted with lively hamlets and villages, it follows the Ganges (or, strictly, its principal tributary, known on this youthful stretch as the Bhagirathi) all the way, crossing it several times on narrow bridges and climbing two-dozen hairpin bends to Sukhi Top (which is 2,744 metres high), only to plunge into the valley once more.

I found myself marvelling at the couple sitting in front, their two young children crammed between, seemingly oblivious to the discomfort, cold and high altitude. Gangotri village stands at 3,048 metres, so it's quite possible you will awake with a headache in the morning if you haven't arrived with one in the evening.

MORNING IN THE MOUNTAINS

Morning dawned crisp and clear with a dazzling cluster of muscular snowy peaks filling the valley's head. It's a busy little place with Western hikers rubbing shoulders with shopkeepers and sadhus, wandering ascetics with shaggy beards and brilliant saffron robes. Pilgrims milled about, thronging the bazaar and filling the main temple, some later casting adrift little flower-laden, candle-lit leaf rafts on the surging Bhagirathi.

Few head up to the river's main source, 12 miles away at the snout of a vast glacier. At nearly

'PILGRIMS OFTEN BRING PORTIONS OF FOOD TO TIE IN CLOTH AND "COOK" IN A STEAMING HOT SPRING BESIDE THE TEMPLE.'

4,000 metres, Gaumukh, or 'Cow's Mouth', is the journey's true climax. As I hiked up-valley, coniferous forest faded into strands of straggly birch, and I paused intermittently to fuel up with tea and instant noodles at the rudimentary tent cafés lining the route. A handful of frozen-looking pilgrims were riding ponies but even they could trot no further than Bhojbasa, just a few miles short of Gaumukh.

There's a small government hotel here but I opted for a simple ashram at which all are welcome. At dinner about 20 of us sat cross-legged on the floor. Obligatory prayers were recited – several Hindi words at a time, like at school, so everyone could follow – and then chapatis and lentils were slopped into steel bowls. I ate like a horse and slept like a shepherd in a cell-like room with a couple from Spain.

GAUMUKH

Amid a glorious amphitheatre of 6,000-metre peaks, including the much-admired Shivling, the path climbs steadily to the retreating Gangotri Glacier. Pilgrims traditionally bathe in the frigid waters emerging from a blue-tinged ice cave and a few even venture madly into its mouth, blissfully ignoring the considerable risk of falling ice.

An elderly yet lithe Japanese man arrived with a small entourage, disrobed and proceeded to meditate on a rock like a sage from a scroll.

'He can levitate,' claimed an Indian companion matter-of-factly, so I waited expectantly but in vain. For a while, I perched on a nearby boulder before moving to the riverbank to thaw in the sun alongside men nonchalantly drying themselves with tea towels.

Minutes later, that warmth treacherously loosened some huge rocks and ice that crashed down just yards from where I had sat. I would surely have leaped in panic and – who knows – broken a leg or cracked my skull. Was I lucky to escape or unlucky with time and place? In the Himalayas, perhaps your fate really is in the hands of the gods. ●

WHEN TO GO

The best months to go are May, June, September and October, with travel in July and August hampered by the monsoon. The Yamunotri and Gangotri temples (and therefore much of the tourist infrastructure) close from Diwali (late October/early November) to late April/early May.

GETTING THERE

New Delhi is the most convenient international airport. Several express trains run daily from New Delhi station to Haridwar. Regular buses connect Haridwar and nearby Rishikesh with up-valley destinations via Tehri. For Janki Chatti (Yamunotri), reckon on about 9-10 hours; for Gangotri allow 12-13 hours with a likely bus change at Uttarkashi.

ORGANISING YOUR TRIP

You can simply turn up and do the pilgrimage independently. However, several UK tour operators visit the area: Mountain (formerly Himalayan) Kingdoms (www.himalayan kingdoms.com) offers a two-part ten-day trek that visits Gaumukh; KE Adventure Travel (www.keadventure.com) provides a strenuous

14-day trek that climbs beyond Gaumukh to cross into the Kumaon region; Explore (www.explore.co.uk) has a 16-day Garhwal and Kumaon tour that includes Badrinath.

COST

A Rs150 (about £2) fee is charged on the edge of Gangotri to enter the Gangotri National Park when walking towards Gaumukh.

AM I UP TO IT?

You should be reasonably fit to walk, though some bearers carry pilgrims all the way to Yamunotri. The longer Gangotri–Gaumukh walk is more demanding because of altitude; the Janki Chatti–Yamunotri is more leisurely.

MORE LIKE THIS

Other mountain pilgrimages include: Mount Emei (Emei Shan) in China's Sichuan Province, a monastery-scattered mountain sacred to Buddhists; Mount Athos, the Orthodox 'monks' republic' in Halkidhiki, northern Greece; and Mount Kailash in western Tibet, among the world's holiest mountains and sacred to Buddhists, Hindus and Tibet's old Bon religion.

'LIFE'S BATTLES DON'T ALWAYS GO TO
THE STRONGER OR FASTER MAN. BUT
SOONER OR LATER THE MAN WHO WINS,
IS THE MAN WHO THINKS HE CAN.'

VINCE LOMBARDI

Personal best

Tall ships

Seasoned sailor **Libby Purves** takes to the high seas in a square-rigger.

WHAT		**HOW LONG**	
Crewing a Tall Ship		A week to two months	
WHERE		**THRILL FACTOR**	
All over the world		● ● ● ● ●	

Barrelling down-Channel with a sunny autumn gale behind her, the square-rigged *Tenacious* rose and fell, smashing her long golden bows into the rising seas. I was off-watch, stretched out on a cushion between the varnished wooden frames of the mess deck after three hours of hauling and lurching on deck as we brailed the upper topsails and braced the yardarms.

That might sound like sailor talk, but it merely consists of ruching up the higher sails to prevent too much wind pressure, and pulling across the heavy beams on which the sails hang, so that the ship can alter course and not bang into the isle of Jersey. In a wind like this, bracing takes ten of you on the uphill side, and a couple easing the lines gently off the pin rails on the other side-deck. There was some giggling, a bit of swearing and rope-burn for those hardy enough to do without gloves. When it was over, the ropes coiled and hung up and the big ship snug again, the watch on deck returned to steering and lookout, the galley team sloped off to peel potatoes, and we on the off-watch retired to bunks or mess deck with our books. And we were all happy.

SHIP'S COMPANY

This particular trip was not a race, merely an end-of-season delivery, but it brought back a host of memories: the North Sea race, for example, from Newcastle to Norway, when a third of the international Tall Ships fleet retired in dreadful weather – but we plugged on, and anchored at last in a remote fjord close to one of our rivals, the *Shabab Oman*. We had thought we were tired after a week of watch-keeping day and night, but the Omani crew came aboard *Tenacious* with their Arabic musicians and taught us some wild dances. After a few hours all the girls on board were wearing the guests' turbans and bopping around.

Then there was the race on *Lord Nelson* in the Baltic: Gdansk to the Aland islands in shimmering summer heat, ghosting along with every sail we could hang, teenagers singing to a guitar on the bow at dusk. And a dozen other voyages on other ships – Norwegian, Dutch, British. Huddling from a bunk in the small hours for my 2am watch, staring out over tumbling foam on a wild night, lying in oily calm watching for ruffles of wind... all of it has been magical, a step out of time in an older, simpler world.

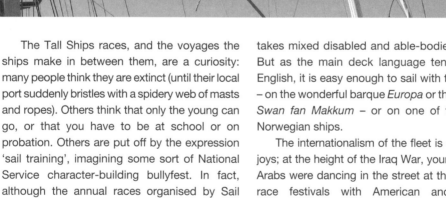

The Tall Ships races, and the voyages the ships make in between them, are a curiosity: many people think they are extinct (until their local port suddenly bristles with a spidery web of masts and ropes). Others think that only the young can go, or that you have to be at school or on probation. Others are put off by the expression 'sail training', imagining some sort of National Service character-building bullyfest. In fact, although the annual races organised by Sail Training International (STI) stipulate that half the ship's company must be between 16 and 25, there are places for others even on race legs.

AIN'T NUTHIN' BUT A NUMBER

I was 45 when I first signed up on the Norwegian ship *Staatsraad Lehmkuhl*, climbed my first rigging and slept in my first hammock (few ships have them, but they are surprisingly comfortable). *Tenacious* – like *Lord Nelson* – belongs to the British Jubilee Sailing Trust, and takes mixed disabled and able-bodied crews. But as the main deck language tends to be English, it is easy enough to sail with the Dutch – on the wonderful barque *Europa* or the elegant *Swan fan Makkum* – or on one of the three Norwegian ships.

The internationalism of the fleet is one of its joys; at the height of the Iraq War, young Omani Arabs were dancing in the street at the end-of-race festivals with American and British teenagers. At the height of the Cold War, the noble Russian ship *Kruzhenstern* was already a favourite of the fleet; after the Falklands, the first Argentinian ship in a British port was their *Libertad*. The Mexican *Cuauhtémoc* is happy to join a European fleet racing towards Finland. And so it goes on.

ALL HANDS ON DECK

There is something about joining the Tall Ships fleet that defies cynicism. Sailing these great vessels is not just sport, and not just

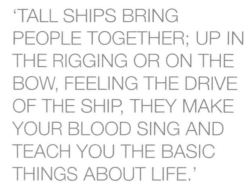

'TALL SHIPS BRING PEOPLE TOGETHER; UP IN THE RIGGING OR ON THE BOW, FEELING THE DRIVE OF THE SHIP, THEY MAKE YOUR BLOOD SING AND TEACH YOU THE BASIC THINGS ABOUT LIFE.'

sentimentality. It fuses the old sea skills of laborious teamwork and communal courage with a new pattern of adventure and internationalism. Even the most timid and unfit desk workers find themselves rising to the task, inspired by the natural beauty of the sea and the human beauty of the great ships, and the people who sail them.

On one gruelling upwind race, from Antwerp to Aalesund in north Norway, nearly everyone on *Europa* had some kind of sprain or bruise, and Captain Klaas Gaastra came down from the bridge to one crew meeting and looked around in the drizzle at the bandaged, exhausted figures (we had been having 'all-hands-on-deck' every two hours for three days), saying cheerfully, 'I feel like Jesus, coming to the halt and the lame...' Ania, a broke but resolute arrival from the old East Europe, paid her last few euros to join at Antwerp and eccentrically went barefoot in all weathers. 'It keeps my feet in touch with Neptune,' she said. 'And saves me the sickness.'

VIRTUE REALITY

Tall Ships – of all rigs – bring people together; up in the rigging or on the bow, feeling the drive of the ship, they make your blood sing. They teach you the most basic things about human life and history. They introduce you to the reality of many disciplines: engineering, physics, geography, history, psychology, poetry. The engineering wisdom of the ages formed their blocks and gear and the cobweb certainty of the high rigging, yet it is instantly apparent that these things can do nothing at all without human muscle and weight.

It is the opposite of a computer game, and it demands trust and teamwork. A shanty is not a museum piece, but a vital way to make you lean and pull together. A curt order from the bosun is not oppression, it is essential: he can see what is happening high up at the far end of the line you are hauling. As a watch, you work together; at the end of it, you fall into your bunk and trust the next watch to keep you safe. It's a lesson in being part of the human race. Adrian Seligman, who sailed with the last grain ships in the 1950s, put it best: 'A sailing ship at sea is one of God's most patient, yet most steadfast and courageous creatures. So those who live with her, who watch her day by day, running bravely, lying becalmed for weeks or yielding with grace to the slope of the wind, such people learn from her in time...'

Well, I didn't have months as they did. I had only ten days. But whether in a race or a passage, whether in seas of dolphin-haunted blue or ragged grey, the fact is that using your body's weight and strength and having a common purpose night and day to keep a big beautiful ship safe, is better than any therapy. You are never too old or too wobbly to know that magic thing that happens when you come up from the cabin, tired and shaking, and suddenly see the stars. And perhaps take the wheel, and feel the drive and the power of the ship under your own hands. As Louis MacNeice wrote: 'Our end is Life. Put out to sea.' ●

WHEN TO GO

Races take place in summer but remember this is not the only time these ships sail – there are opportunities all year round. Jubilee Sailing Trust (www.jst.org.uk) sails November to May.

GETTING THERE

In spring and autumn, there are many week-long trips out and back to the same UK port, which works out cheaper.

ORGANISING YOUR TRIP

For Tall Ships races 2009 and information, see www.sailtraininginternational.org. Adults can join sailings with Jubilee Sailing Trust, Ocean Youth Trust South (www.oytsouth.org) and Classic Sailing (www.classic-sailing.co.uk). The Tall Ships People (www.tallshipspeople.com) provides a booking service for a number of organisations and vessels.

COST

Berth costs vary considerably, and don't include flights to start and finish points. By way of example, OYTS's non-race voyage from Kiel (Germany) to Gdynia (Poland) costs £750; JST's 13-day Tall Ships race (July) from St Petersburg to Turku (Finland) £950; and Classic Sailing's seven-day Tall Ship Island-hopping taster in the Canaries £449.

AM I UP TO IT?

Top fitness isn't essential but it helps (note: going aloft is not compulsory). Seasickness medication is useful and should be tried out (on land) in advance.

MORE LIKE THIS

All the companies mentioned above organise adult, non-race and, in the case of Ocean Youth Trust and Jubilee, day-sailing trips. Not all the fleet are square-riggers; there are big yachts run by various organisations around the UK, such as Ocean Youth Trust.

FOR REFERENCE

Tall Ships on the Tyne, by Dick Keys and Ken Smith, details the history of Tyne shipbuilding.

From tip to top

Simon Richmond takes the long way up Table Mountain and discovers the comforts and joys of 'slackpacking'.

WHAT	HOW LONG
Hoerikwaggo Trail in Table Mountain National Park	6 days, 5 nights

WHERE	THRILL FACTOR
Cape Town, South Africa	● ● ● ● ●

'Look around,' said my guide Louis, 'enjoy the view.' Dangling on a rope off the edge of Table Mountain, 1,000 metres above sea level, I twisted my body, exchanging the vista of the 669-metre-high pimple of Lion's Head for the panorama of the craggy buttresses known as the Twelve Apostles. Far in the distance, I could just make out the lighthouse at Slangkop where I had camped at the start of my hike. For four days, I had worked my way across the mountainous Cape Peninsula, from its southernmost point to the flat top of Table Mountain, and now I was more than happy to hang, breathing in the view.

Since there's a perfectly good cableway up Table Mountain, some might wonder why I had just hiked 38 miles up the Cape, over several lofty peaks, to get to this point. But the journey had been its own reward. The spectacular walk had taken me from the edge of the rugged Cape of Good Hope across moors scattered with wild flowers, down icing-sugar-soft beaches and along rocky ledges and ridge lines with views out to both the Atlantic and Indian Oceans to the precipice of Table Mountain. And while It had been physically demanding, an innovative new scheme means that you don't have to be a hardened mountaineer to tackle it. Walkers following the 'Hoerikwaggo Tented Classic' trail are required to travel in the company of a guide, have their bags portered for them and stay in comfortable tent lodges – all of which makes the Table Mountain climb relatively accessible.

INCREDIBLE HULK

Add up the sum total geological ages of the Alps, Andes, Himalayas and Rockies, and you still won't get near Table Mountain's 250 million years. This level-topped 1,087-metre hulk is one of the oldest mountains in the world and the star attraction of Table Mountain National Park, a diverse reserve covering nearly three-quarters of the Cape Peninsula. The park is crossed by over 500 trails, but the authorities have been working since 2003 to link several of them up into a six-day, five-night route running the entire length of the peninsula – around 53 miles in total. Built by

a previously unemployed workforce, according to the mantra 'touch the earth lightly', the Hoerikwaggo Tented Classic is expected to be complete by the time this book comes out.

The tents at the overnight stops are roomy and robust, sleeping up to 12 on proper beds, and there are hot showers and kitchens. Each camp has been designed to match its natural environment; the one at Slangkop, for example, blends imaginatively with the milkwood and wild olive covered dunes and incorporates the bones of a southern right whale that washed up dead on the beach in 2006. Its 35-tonne spine, inset with lights, hangs above the kitchen while parts of its ribcage have been used as tent arches.

The quality of the facilities doesn't, however, diminish the physical challenge at hand – even

'THE JOURNEY IS THE THING – ACROSS MOORS SCATTERED WITH WILD FLOWERS, DOWN ICING-SUGAR-SOFT BEACHES AND ALONG ROCKY LEDGES ABOVE THE ATLANTIC.'

without a heavy backpack and tent pitching, the Hoerikwaggo is no easy stroll, taking in several strenuous ascents, and the erratic weather of the Cape can turn treacherous at a moment's notice.

More people have died through misadventure on Table Mountain than on Mount Everest, so being given a guide who knows the way and what to do if anything goes wrong is very reassuring.

PARK LIFE

In order to meet the deadlines for this book, we walked the Hoerikwaggo before it was fully completed. Ultimately, it will start right at the tip of the Cape and head northwards. The first, demanding day will take you over three peaks to Smitswinkel Bay at the entrance to the Cape of Good Hope Nature Reserve, the second to Signal School near the naval base above Simon's Town. We picked the path up near here and spent our first day following it across the peninsula. This is a relatively

easy stage, passing under the 391-metre summit of Grootkop through pristine fynbos, the hardy bushland unique to the Cape.

'Look, a springbok', said our guide Mixolisi (meaning 'peacemaker'), pointing ahead. We all squinted, but the well-camouflaged gazelle was quickly gone. It was a rare sighting: over 350 years of European colonisation haven't been kind to the peninsula's fauna. The big game – elephants, lions and leopards – that once roamed the land have long since been hunted to extinction. If you're lucky, you might spot ostriches, Cape Mountain zebras and troupes of Chacma baboons south of here on the Cape of Good Hope Nature Reserve.

But the traditional African safari thrill of watching lions feasting on their kill was almost matched by the close-up I had of the carnage being inflicted on a clump of Watsonia bushes by a ravenous posse of citrus swallowtail caterpillars. Our guide Babalwa (meaning 'blessed one' in Xhosa, the Bantu language spoken in southern Africa) was expert at pointing out small but riveting natural details, such as a tiny dung beetle I could easily have squished with my boot or the seemingly innocuous 'cat's claws', a parasite flower that sucks nutrients from the surrounding foliage. This is no mean feat given that the park contains 2,285 different plant species, more than in the whole of the British Isles.

'WE SAW SPRINGTIME PINK GERANIUMS, YELLOW PINCUSHIONS AND BLUE ARISTEAS, AND WHITE EVERLASTINGS CARPETED OUR WAY.'

Thankfully, the area's remarkable floral biodiversity remains intact – and the vividly coloured plant life is a highlight of any trek. We saw springtime pink geraniums, yellow pincushions and blue aristeas, and white everlastings carpeted our way. The gale force winds that whip across the Cape, combined with centuries of deforestation, mean that most of the landscape is pretty open but the trek also goes through pockets of Afromontane forest.

DOWN NOORDHOEK BEACH

Tobisa (meaning 'happiness') couldn't have been more appropriately named. Her infectious laughter greeted us at the entrance to Slangkop camp, next

to the tallest lighthouse in South Africa. She had prepared the camp and had been watching over our overnight bags, which had arrived before us.

The 'slackpacking' aspect of the trail was particularly appreciated the next day, when the 11-mile hike took us up and over both 593-metre Chapman's Peak and the 754-metre Noordhoek Peak. This came after a morning following the coast around the surfers' paradise of Kommetjie to Noordhoek Beach, a long, dreamy sweep of white sand popular with horse-riders and kiteboarders. Here we got a close-quarters sighting of a pod of whales just offshore. In the middle of the beach, like a contemporary sculpture, is the rusted shell of the steamship *Kakapo* that in 1900, on its maiden voyage from Britain to Australia, ran aground. It's said that the embarrassed captain refused to leave the ship for three years.

Later on, while lunching atop Chapman's Peak, we could still see the whales frolicking in Chapman's Bay, a couple of kite-surfers riding the waves around them.

AFROMONTANE FOREST

The next camp, Silvermine, is beautifully crafted from oak, poplar, pine and gum tree timber – alien trees that are being removed from the delicate environment of the park. It's a treat to sleep in such peaceful, natural surroundings, as it is also at the forest haven of Orange Kloof, the final camp. That both lodges are within a ten-minute drive of Cape Town's scattered suburbs is hard to credit.

The route between the two is particularly dramatic – after passing below the 926-metre summit of Constantiaberg, we were treated to a grand-circle view down Blackburn Kloof towards the dazzlingly blue Hout Bay. We paid for it with a knee-wobbling walk along a narrow path that hugged the mountainside before turning away from the coast and progressing through vine-clad slopes and forest trails to Orange Kloof.

Sheltered from the savage winds that blast the peninsula, this valley is a rare patch of Afromontane forest on the Cape. Boekenhout, yellowwoods, rooiels and asagai trees provided shade and the

rushing waters of the Disa River refreshment as we climbed the back of Table Mountain. Compared to the summits we had already conquered, this was a gratifyingly easy ascent.

With barely an hour of the hike left, we paused to eat lunch under a rock ledge. From our eyrie we could see back over the entire peninsula, from False Bay to the east to the Atlantic Ocean to the west. Centuries earlier, this had been the sole province of the Khoe-San peoples who had called Table Mountain Hoerikwaggo – Mountain in the Sea. It was moving to realise how little, essentially, had changed.

The feeling of achievement at having walked from tip to top and the elation of communing with nature were soon replaced by the anti-climax of mingling with the tourist crowds who had taken the no-sweat cableway route up the mountain. I peeled off to meet the guys from Abseil Africa who were to provide my personalised climax to the Hoerikwaggo Trail. ●

WHEN TO GO
October to early December is the best time for seeing flowers and avoiding the summer heat. Likewise the autumn months of March to May see more pleasant temperatures for hiking.

GETTING THERE
Cape Town International Airport is served by direct flights from Europe. From there, it's around 30 miles to the start of the trail.

ORGANISING YOUR TRIP
Book the 'Hoerikwaggo Tented Classic' at www.hoerikwaggotrails.co.za. For Abseil Africa, see www.abseilafrica.co.za.

COST
Each night on the Hoerikwaggo Trail costs R420 (£37), so for the entire trail (five nights) you'll pay R2,100 (£185). If you don't have a sleeping bag, it's R75 per night extra for the provision of bedding. The abseil costs R495.

AM I UP TO IT?
There's a lot of up and down so you'll need to be fit and in good health to complete the hike. Don't do the abseil if you have a heart condition.

FOR REFERENCE
Mountains in the Sea: Table Mountain To Cape Point, by John Yeld and Martine Barker, is an excellent interpretive guide to the national park.

MORE LIKE THIS
Other great treks in South African national parks (www.sanparks.co.za) include the Otter and Tsitsikamma Trails in the Eastern Cape or the Giant's Cup Trail in the Drakensberg mountains of Kwazulu-Natal (www.kznwildlife.com).

The big wheel

Ruth Jarvis takes to the Lincoln Highway – with 15,000 other cyclists.

WHAT	HOW LONG
'RAGBRAI' mass bike ride	One week

WHERE	THRILL FACTOR
Across Iowa, USA	● ● ● ● ●

Tuesday. 8am. Somewhere in Iowa. I pulled off the road at the top of a hill, red-faced and jelly-legged after a 600-metre climb before breakfast. Ahead of me, the road spooled onward, waves of identical hills ·forming a boundless sea of green slashed only by a single ribbon of tarmac.

This was the Lincoln Highway, America's first cross-country road, and for most of the year an ordinary motoring route. But instead of speeding cars it was plied by a neverending stream of cyclists, stretching like a column of ants to the horizon. I turned around and the view was identical: hill, corn, water tower, grain store; hill, corn, water tower, grain store. Bikes. And more of the same, for the rest of the day, and the next, and the next, unless a tornado intervened. Iowa is pretty, but it's not known for its variety, nor – contrary to popular belief – for its flat terrain. What was I doing here?

The answer is RAGBRAI, an acronym for the Register's Annual Bike Ride Across Iowa, *The Des Moines Register* being the biggest daily newspaper in the state. More than 35 years ago,

Don Kaul and John Karras, *Register* feature writers, decided to get to know their beat by cycling all the way across the state, inviting readers to join them and writing about it every day. People liked the idea: 300 started and 500 took part in the most popular stage. In year two, nearly 3,000 started and 1,700 completed the course. Since then, RAGBRAI has expanded into a mass ride of serious proportions, attracting around 15,000 cyclists each day; around half do the entire week-long trip. It still crosses the Tall Corn State, west to east, on a route that varies every year but always totals close to 500 miles, from the Missouri to the Missisippi, and includes a 100-mile 'century' day.

Other than getting a place – some riders miss out on the lottery every year – there are no entry requirements except having a bike. Or, for the masochistic, a unicycle. The bikes in question vary tremendously, from state-of-the art road bikes via home-made recumbents pulling solar-powered stereos, to trikes, trailer bikes and tandems. So do the riders, from the unfit and unprepared pushing their mounts up hills to the semi-pros swooshing past to finish before lunch.

'FOR MANY OF THE SMALL TOWNS ALONG THE ROUTE (AND THERE ARE PLENTY OF THEM IN IOWA), YOUR ARRIVAL IS AN EXCUSE FOR A CARNIVAL. THE HOSPITALITY IS ASTONISHING.'

500 MILES IN A WEEK

You don't need to be a fitness fanatic or an experienced long-distance cyclist to do a ride of this length, but unless you're Chris Hoy or Lance Armstrong (and Armstrong has been known to ride RAGBRAI, with his Livestrong cancer survivor team), you're going to need to do some sort of training to cover 500 rolling miles in a week. Three months of regular rides, increasing in length and average speed, at least one of them over more than one day, and another that covers the maximum RAGBRAI day distance should do it. Put in some leg-strength and cardio work, and you'll actively enjoy driving up your average speed and pushing hard uphill. This is categorically not

strong that a blade of grass could pierce your eyeball, and hailstones can be the size of golfballs. The next day we cycled past the devastation of uprooted trees and demolished barns, so when they say 'evacuate', you move.

PUSHING OFF

We started with a big bike fair on a Saturday afternoon in the little apple-pie town of Missouri Valley, just over the border from Nebraska. As riders gathered and tents mushroomed in the high-school grounds, we grasped the scale of the event. It felt like a friendly invasion: riders outnumbered locals by about five to one, but they welcomed us, out of natural Midwestern hospitality, curiosity and economic pragmatism. Every school sports field and private lawn was dotted with team tents as residents opened their doors; bars called in extra staff; local churches and schools held fundraising suppers to feed and propel the masses (hearty, carb-rich pasta bakes and chilli-laden baked potatoes are favourites).

The next morning, one of clear blue skies, started at 5am when it became impossible to ignore the sound of other people breaking camp. We did the same: filled bottles, checked cables and minimally packed shirt pockets and a small bag – spare tube, cash, sun cream, energy bar, phone. We left camp in a fast-flowing stream of cyclists; swooping down a car-free road there was a feeling of exhilaration, pedal power and nerves. What were the gradients going to be like? Had I trained enough? How could we find our own pace on a crowded road? And just how saddle sore can one get in 500 miles?

Experienced RAGBRAI-ers shouted out hazards: 'Rider up!' 'On your left!' The first hill was long but at a comfortably achievable gradient and I realised that the roads in a state comprised almost entirely of cornfields were going to be graded to the climbing abilities of combine harvesters. Fear of embarrassment receded. The hill also quickly rearranged the riders, spreading them out, and it became easy to go at my own

a race, but there is fun to be had indulging in private battles with cyclists just ahead of you.

But that's about as far as antisocial urges go. RAGBRAI is as much a week-long rolling party as a ride. Lots of groups cycle in teams and dress up, down to ridiculous helmet-top headgear (my favourite was Team Pie, with Team Beer a close second – no prizes for guessing what was in their water bottles) and even themed support buses. There's plenty of supportive banter and pace-making, and an enormous feeling of fellowship, as for once in car-centric USA the bicycle becomes king of the road. Teams work out their own accommodation, but everyone else camps in arranged sites en route (luggage is carried for you) and shares in the rigours of variable showers and the occasional night-time storm evacuation. The storms out here are *Wizard of Oz*-style – for three days the clouds gathered above us and when the storm finally broke and the sirens wailed, the entire town climbed down into their cellars or simply left town. The winds here are so

speed safely. The next time we bunched up again was off the bikes in the queue for the pancake breakfast laid on in a barn ten miles out of town.

CRUISIN'

It was 59 miles and 1,157 metres to handsome, leafy Harlan in Shelby County where several thousand cyclists cooled off at the Aquatic Centre, shorts and all. A hundred miles and 1,597 metres to endearing Jefferson with its landmark bell tower and doughnut shop (Randy Bunkers, owner of the downtown bakery, reckoned he would be preparing 7,200 glazed doughnuts for when RAGBRAI cycled into town). Waves of corn, heat haze, getting in the zone. Drafting at speed in the slipstream of a speeding peloton, then slowing down to chat or match your cadence to the music pounding out of solar-powered boom-boxes. Fifty-seven miles to the college town of Ames, 78 more to Tama and Toledo. A routine of long, grinding hills followed by head-down descents at more than 30 miles an hour. Spotting the next town miles ahead from its water tower. Waiting for trains at railroads. Another 76 miles to up-and-coming North Liberty, where the locals dressed as pirates to greet us.

'THE LINCOLN HIGHWAY MIGHT BE OUTDATED AS A CROSS-COUNTRY AUTO ROUTE, BUT AS A BIKE ROUTE IT'S PERFECT.'

The weather was dangerously, dehydratingly hot at first (hence the early storms) but cycling acts as natural air-conditioning. We needed to take on a lot of water and electrolytes and put loads of sun lotion on (there was the odd nasty lip blister for lack of SPF). It rained around day five and then the weather started to get greyer.

The wind changed, and the going got hard, and aches and pains slowed down the unprepared. I knew I was going to be able to finish, but it wasn't always fun any more. The interminable rolling summits seemed like a baleful joke. But the distances decreased as the ride progressed: 65 hard miles to pretty Tipton, where a bluegrass band lifted the sprits, and then the last day: 53 miles to LeClaire, on the Illinois

border, and we could happily have had more. Speeding along in the sun, the end came too quickly, and a little anticlimactically, with a queue for the ritual front-wheel dip in the Missisippi and self-congratulatory civic speeches.

EATING ALL THE PIES

Such formality is atypical. For many of the small towns along the route (and there are plenty in Iowa), your arrival is an excuse for a carnival. The hospitality is astonishing: banners are hung out, bars opened at 6am, burgers flipped, corn grilled and pies baked – cherry, peach, raisin, apple – in their thousands. Fatted calves (and pigs) are slaughtered. Temporary stages put on acts from Elvis impersonators to clarinet-tooting farmers; cheerleaders welcome you in; lawn sprinklers are set up roadside to cool you down. Tractors and fire engines are displayed for your pleasure, local attractions opened, water pipes set up for bottle-filling. A fleet of first aiders, portapotties, traffic cops and bike mechanics ghost your route and appear, as if by magic, when needed.

More esoteric attractions pop up: motorised toilets, steam-driven ice-cream makers, piglet-hugs and, in a town called Coon Rapids, a human-size raccoon pretending to be roadkill.

The Lincoln Highway might be outdated as a cross-country auto route, but as a bike route it's perfect. Gentle gradients, sweet towns, an accompanying railroad and roadside attractions aplenty: the world's largest walnut rocking chair (Amana Colonies); a traffic light in the middle of the road (Shelby); a historic Coke mural (Toledo); a sign for No Name Street; and many more. The largest pass-through was the college town of Ames (pop. 50,731), the smallest Chelsea (pop. 250). We rarely passed a chainstore, but found locally run doughnut shops, the best pork sandwiches in the Midwest, a restored pioneer-era drugstore, boom towns and a moving civic pride. RAGBRAI avoids major roads so its adventure is as much in discovering small-town life and history as the personal challenge of making the distance. Though that small success is something that you'll cherish. ●

WHEN TO GO
RAGBRAI runs in mid-July every year; check the website for exact dates.

GETTING THERE
The route varies each year but Chicago is likely to be the nearest international airport.

ORGANISING YOUR TRIP
www.ragbrai.org to enter (usually in November).

COST
Around $150 for registration, including camping and luggage transfer.

AM I UP TO IT?
This is a 500-mile cycle ride and, although the terrain is in general gentle and cycle-friendly,

some training is going to necessary if you're going to complete the course.

MORE LIKE THIS
There's nothing else quite on the scale of RAGBRAI, but various US states have their own version, for example Nebraska (www.bran-inc.org) and Georgia (www.brag.org). Alternatively, try riding a stage of the Tour de France in the company of 7,500 others: www.letapedutour.com. New York, London and Montreal organise memorable day-long traffic-free bike takeover rides.

FOR REFERENCE
RAGBRAI: Everyone Pronounces It Wrong by John and Ann Karras, which is written by RAGBRAI's co-founder.

A walk in the clouds

Damian Hall wends his way along the Overland Track,
Australia's most spectacular walking trail.

WHAT	HOW LONG
The Overland Track	5-8 days
WHERE	THRILL FACTOR
Cradle Mountain-Lake St Clair National Park, Tasmania, Australia	● ● ● ● ●

'No need for one of those,' I coolly told my girlfriend while making preparations to trek Tasmania's legendary Overland Track. 'Sleeping mats are for girls.' My comment would come back to haunt me on the very first night; indeed, my macho swagger would be severely tested throughout my five-day hike. Not that you have to be a He-Man to do the Overland Track; you don't. But sometimes your ego can lead you astray – and a walk in the park becomes an epic journey.

WALK ON THE WILD SIDE

Tasmania's Overland Track is Australia's most famous walking trail, taking trampers through an Arcadian landscape of dolerite mountains, glacier-carved valleys, deep lakes and wild rivers. Stretching for 45 miles through Cradle Mountain-Lake St Clair National Park, it follows a north –south path that links the park's two namesakes: the curious, double-headed mountain, a state icon, and the continent's deepest lake.

Both landmarks are a big draw: every year, 8,000 people muddy their boots along the route. The national park is part of the Tasmanian Wilderness World Heritage Area, which covers 5,328 square miles – more than 20 per cent of the island – of temperate wilderness. It became protected in 1983, after the government tried, and failed, to dam the Franklin River.

Despite its loveliness, most visitors to Australia skip Tasmania. And Australians don't show it much respect either: mainlanders joke that Tasmanians have two heads, and charmingly use the expression 'map of Tassie' as a euphemism for the female genitalia.

I had not overlooked Tasmania. But I had overlooked the small matter of a sleeping mat –

and I would have ample time to regret my decision. On our first night, I tossed and turned on my hard wooden 'bed', while my girlfriend dozed contentedly on a mat. I had imagined soft, spongey grass for camping; in this park, however, the designated accommodation is in huts on raised wooden platforms, a practice that protects native bush land (park authorities stipulate that you carry a tent, in case of overbooking or emergency). So I was lugging around a three-man tent I never used. And sleeping on wood.

WHERE ARE THE SHOPS?

If you don't plan and pack carefully, you'll face more privations than just a sore back. No food supplies are available along the Overland Track, so you need to pack in enough to fuel your whole trip, allowing a good margin for error or emergency. Stock up in Launceston, Hobart or Devonport en route to your start point.

'TASMANIA'S OVERLAND TRACK IS AUSTRALIA'S MOST FAMOUS WALKING TRAIL, TAKING TRAMPERS THROUGH AN ARCADIAN LANDSCAPE OF DOLERITE MOUNTAINS, GLACIER-CARVED VALLEYS, DEEP LAKES AND WILD RIVERS.'

Each end of the track has a visitors' centre where you can buy maps, water bottles and souvenirs. You'll need a fuel stove, as campfires are not permitted and huts don't offer cooking facilities. Bear in mind that neither the ferry nor most airlines allow the carry-on of gas canisters, so you'll need to stock up in Tasmania.

Even in midsummer, conditions in the park can quickly become cold, wet and windy,

so pack worst-case clothing and equipment. Recommended basics include waterproofs, warm sleeping bag, sleeping mat, sufficient food, thermal inner and outer layers, warm hat, map and sun protection (necessary even on grey days).

HARD GOING

The lack of a mattress wasn't the only thing causing me to feel sorry for myself that first night. It had been a tough day, with little reward for our slog. We had climbed from the Ronny Creek car park up the grassy hill into a sea of mist; pausing to photograph Lake Lilla, which laps at the ankles of the foreboding Cradle Mountain, we were body-checked by strong winds and aggressive rain. Then, as we mounted the steep, rocky path, the weather gods began to fling sleet, snow and hail at us.

When we finally glimpsed Cradle Mountain's teeth-like summit ridge (the peak has four named summits in total) through gaps in the murk, the journey started to feel rewarding. But the worst wasn't over. Snowdrifts started to block our path, the white stuff stung our faces. After eight tough miles, the Waterfall Valley Hut – sleeping mat or no sleeping mat – was a very welcome sight.

After a night of fitful sleep, we woke to the kind of sunny morning that makes you want to burst into song. Setting off, we had a feeling that everything was going to go our way; and if it hadn't been for my foolhardy side once again getting the better of me, it probably would have. Most people who do the trail take eight or even ten days – this makes for a leisurely, manageable pace and allows time for side trips, of which there are many. We, on the other hand, had only allowed ourselves five. Since the following leg, to Lake Windermere, was estimated to take a mere three hours, I thought we should take advantage of the good weather and do two legs in one day. It was a cunning plan to my mind.

Thirteen painful miles later I was cursing my boneheadedness. By the end of the day my feet

hated me, and the feeling was mutual. I spent the walk daydreaming of hot baths, foot massages and comfortable beds. Fortunately, the scenery provided generous compensation: steep green valleys on either side framed the grassy, boggy plateaux, and lonesome lakes and snow-capped mountains stretched into the distance. It is a dramatic landscape whose contours and crags have been shaped and then reshaped over aeons by glaciers and lava flows.

It was 8pm and the light was fading when we arrived, shattered, at Pelion Hut. Not even the hard wood bed could keep me awake: lying exhausted on an ad hoc mattress of T-shirts, towels and jumpers, I slept like a sloth on Valium.

CLIMBING THE MOUNT

On day three, my macho instincts kicked in again. This time, I was glad I listened. As the trail passed Mount Ossa – at 1,614 metres, Tasmania's highest peak – I couldn't resist the urge to climb it. For the next two hours I waged war with the dolerite monster. I charged at it relentlessly, wading through deep snow. With my naked legs a disturbingly bright pink,

'AS WE MOUNTED THE STEEP, ROCKY PATH, THE WEATHER GODS STARTED FLINGING SLEET, SNOW AND HAIL AT US.'

I finally stood on the summit, pride restored. I stayed up there for a while, on a high, trying to memorise the fantasy panorama of secret valleys, craggy peaks, mossy plateaux and growling clouds. Then I sat on my coat and slid back down.

LAKESIDE FINALE

After a final tired trudge, we reached Lake St Clair. Serene and shimmering, the lake is a great reward – worthy of the pilgrimage. We sat on its shores and ate the remainder of our chocolate rations as the sun set.

From Narcissus Hut, you can catch a water ferry across to the finishing point of the trail at

Cynthia Bay. Or you can, like us, walk the last ten-and-a-half miles around the lake for maximum self-satisfaction.

WILD THINGS

You'll see critters as well as crags on the Overland Track. Day by day, as the weather improved, we chanced upon an increasing number of wallabies and wombats; when caught unawares, they dashed into the undergrowth. And we saw the creature often cited as evidence that God has a sense of humour: the duckbilled platypus, basking in a small stream.

Many pests that were introduced to Australia haven't made it across the Bass Strait, so native wildlife is more abundant here than on the mainland. This is mostly a good thing. But as we walked through enchanting woods, my girlfriend stopped dead in her tracks. There, on the path, lay a long, shiny and very black tiger snake – a streak of death that anybody could mistake for a stick. We nervously stepped over it and tiptoed on our way feeling lucky and freshly alert.

For the first time on the trip, my inner gorilla was mute. And he was equally low-key a few days later, when I entered a camping shop to enquire about sleeping mats... ●

WHEN TO GO

December to March is peak season, and huts get full, so the best time to walk is October to November, when there's still some snow about. From June to September, the weather is unpredictable, so experienced hikers only.

GETTING THERE

Launceston is the best base for the walk; flights to the state's second city go regularly from major Australian cities. Alternatively, you could fly to Hobart and do the Track from south to north. The *Spirit of Tasmania* ferry (www.spiritoftasmania.com.au) to Devonport, near Launceston, leaves nightly from Melbourne.

ORGANISING YOUR TRIP

The best starting point is Tasmania Parks & Wildlife Service (www.parks.tas.gov.au). Or go straight to its Overland-dedicated site www.overlandtrack.com.au. The state government tourism site is also helpful: www.discovertasmania.com. If you can't do without hot showers and want someone to carry your bags, visit www.overlandtrack.com.au/doing_guidedtours.html for guided tours.

COST

From 1 November to 30 April advance bookings are required, and a fee of AUD$150 (AUD$120 for reductions) charged. You'll be required to walk from north to south during this period. There's also a year-round National Parks Pass fee of AUD$11 per day, or AUD$28 for up to eight weeks.

AM I UP TO IT?

It's a decent slog, but a person of average fitness could accomplish this walk without much drama. Pack carefully to minimise backpack weight, allow a sensible amount of time – and remember a sleeping mat.

MORE LIKE THIS

If the Overland is too crowded for you, try the less-developed (ie no huts) South Coast Track, a 53-mile route in Tasmania's Southwest National Park (for more information visit www.parks.tas.gov.au).

FOR REFERENCE

http://bushwalk-tasmania.com/forum is a good place for chatting and exchanging tips with fellow hikers.

'IT IS ALWAYS THE ADVENTURERS
WHO DO GREAT THINGS, NOT THE
SOVEREIGNS OF GREAT EMPIRES.'

CHARLES DE MONTESQUIEU

All-time classics

Slow boat

Chris Moss goes native on Brazil's great river.

WHAT	HOW LONG
Amazon riverboat voyage	Two weeks

WHERE	THRILL FACTOR
Brazil	● ● ● ● ●

Amazonia is fixed in the collective unconscious. Even without reading conquistadors' accounts, watching *Fitzcarraldo* or listening to music by the Kayapó Indians, we all harbour some notion of the mighty region and its snaking brown river. Boarding the *M/N Santarem* in Belém, the gateway to the Amazon on Brazil's east coast, I took with me a fair amount of mental baggage. I imagined I was embarking on a tranquil, meditative and romantic passage through the dark heart of the rainforest. I wondered if, away from the areas destroyed by loggers and ranchers, there wasn't something like the legendary 'lost world' – perhaps deep inside the jungle, or up some forgotten branch of a minor tributary.

Then someone turned on the PA system and the throb of Música Popular Brasileira turned the small poop deck into a fiesta venue. Cans of cold Skol were cracked open, groups formed, couples smooched. As darkness fell, and the decibels increased, it barely registered when we set sail.

There were about 200 passengers on board. Four of us were gringos; there were half a dozen Brazilian tourists; the rest were going home, going to find work, setting off for college or to see their families. Less than a tenth of us had cabins, and most people strung up a hammock on the two lower decks.

Amazon river people are hyper-social, so there was a lot of chat and laughter as we chugged at five knots up the main stream. But there were still long stretches of empty time to gaze out at the river and its low, densely forested banks. It was July when I visited, the end of the rainy season, so the flood plains were full to brimming, and the *palafitos* (houses on stilts) were only a foot above the gently lapping water.

THE RHYTHM OF THE RIVER

Sometimes the banks are half a mile away from the central channel adopted by the cautious Amazon captains, so you spend many hours staring down at the chocolate-brown river with its eddies, sluggish deep areas, and the fast currents that appear on steep bends. In the narrower sections, children paddled alongside in their long canoes and climbed aboard to sell freshwater prawns, palm hearts and home-made chilli-pepper vinaigrettes.

Some of our own number quietly slipped into their vocations too, selling jewellery made from native beans and seeds, sun-hats and popcorn. Busiest of all was the bar, reliable purveyor of ice-cold beers and tins of guaraná.

The daytime temperature was a constant 35°C, and cloud-free skies meant competition for a shady space for your deck chair in the stifling afternoons. Three times a day we were summoned to the middle deck for meals: fresh fruit and eggs for breakfast, simple lunches of

'AT THE END OF THE RAINY SEASON, THE FLOOD PLAINS WERE FULL TO BRIMMING, AND THE STILT HOUSES ON THE RIVERBANK WERE ONLY A FOOT ABOVE THE GENTLY LAPPING WATER.'

roast chicken, rice, manioc flour, and the same for dinner, always followed by a dessert of guava jelly and cream.

This wasn't luxury, in the usual sense, but it was truly pleasurable to be offline and away from a mobile phone signal, with time to think, drink, dance, chatter, and, in the evening, sit down to watch a football match or a corny *telenovela*.

Six nights is enough to get used to the gentle rhythm of life on deck; you plan, vaguely, when to take a stroll, when to have a cool siesta, when to have your first beer. Along the way there were a few small towns – Almerin, Prainha, Monte Alegre, and even a proper city, Santarém. Arriving in these places was a major event, whether you were disembarking or not.

Each conurbation boasted the same basic elements: a sand-dusted, asphalted main boulevard, a *feira dos produtores locais* (a sort of farmers' market), a big church and, most importantly, an ice factory. All the towns were low-slung and, if less than lovely, they were at least compact and convivial. Most were a mere quarter of a mile of human habitation, concrete extensions of the untidy jungle all around.

ARCHIPELAGOGO

Then, on the morning of the seventh day, we sailed across the famous Meeting of the Waters – the confluence of the chocolate-coloured Amazon and the black Negro rivers – and the city of Manaus appeared, sprawling behind a long

line of busy cargo and passenger ports, and you could see, amid the grimy high-rises and hotels, an aspiration to grandeur.

Just north up the Rio Negro – one of the Amazon's many major tributaries – are the Anavilhanas: elongated islands that make up a 400-square-mile archipelago, the largest freshwater island group in the world. The forest here isn't strictly rainforest, but *várzea*, seasonally flooded forest close to the riverbank.

I sailed up the Negro on the *Amazon Clipper*, a relatively luxurious riverboat I shared with 20 other Europeans, Americans, Brazilians and Argentinians (we slept in cabins; this was not a dorm-and-hammock affair).

The Anavilhanas are the main attraction. My first foray into the network of narrow channels between the islands – known as *igarapés* – was during the late afternoon. Away from the busy, wide Amazon, I was suddenly plunged into a cacophony of screaming cicadas, groaning caimans calling to each other across the islands and a waterworld unsuited to human habitation – but a mecca for birds.

THE SECRET LIFE OF BIRDS

During a four-hour morning excursion, we saw a blue macaw, sloths, parrots, doves, hawks and falcons. Another morning we watched the sun rise, and then motored into the Rio Cuieras, a tributary

'THE MOST STRIKING BIRDS WERE A TRIO OF CITRON-THROATED TOUCANS, PREENING THEMSELVES IN THE HIGHEST BRANCHES.'

of the Negro. (This is how the Amazon works: you are always searching for a tributary of a tributary of a tributary until you find 'the real thing'.) The most striking birds were a trio of citron-throated toucans, preening themselves in the highest branches. Then there were shiny black cuckoo-like ani, a tiny bat falcon, a yellow-headed vulture – big and spooky, perched on its own bare stump – and assorted hawks and flycatchers.

A gang of yellow-rumped caciques mimicked the other birds, whooping and boinging and screeching. 'The cacique is an Indian chief,' explained our guide. 'All he does all day is play the part of the male. He does nothing else.' But the screaming piha, with his three ear-splitting notes – 'peeeee-heeeee-haaaaarrh' – was the king of the aural jungle. We didn't see any, but they talked to each other across the canopy.

JUNGLE FLORA AND FAUNA

It's not all ornithology. We saw delicate passion flowers, a cactus fruit (pitaya) and lots of epiphytes. Then there were the huge discs of Victoria amazonica lilies, space-rocket-shaped ceiba trees and dendê palms. Filling any gaps, knotted lianas and vines strangled and dangled everywhere. Once you have boated about a bit you ache to get back on land and smell all the flowers and plants that you catch glimpses of from the water.

'WHEN WE TURNED ROUND IT WAS NIGHTTIME AGAIN. THE BLACKWATER RIVER IS INVISIBLE AFTER DARK. IT MERGES WITH THE SKY ABOVE.'

During a jungle trek, we focused on biting small creatures. Many of the jungle species are dormant or disguised in the leaf litter but, with an expert guide, you can find them. First came giant carnivorous ants ('one bite, pain; two bites, lots of pain; three bites, 24 hours of pain'). Then small carnivorous ants, then a massive bird-eating tarantula that reared up on its legs, in attacking position, when prompted by a machete.

Back on the water, I was surprised when the pilot pulled over into a dark, dank dead end and our guide took out a dozen bamboo fishing rods. It was time to catch piranha. 'They're aggressive,' he warned, 'and like to fight, so you have to do this…' He thrashed away at the water with his rod, causing great commotion. We all cast, dropping our hooks baited with rancid chicken into the stagnant waters – and waited. All of ten seconds. Soon half of the lines began to bob and we began to pull in piranha after piranha. On extracting the hook, the guide showed us how the piranha's teeth could devour a large leaf. 'Imagine that was your skin,' he said, grinning. We could have got our revenge by eating these maneaters, but instead we threw ours back.

To cool off, we headed back to the Rio Negro for a dip. The tea-coloured waters were surprisingly refreshing and here, away from the

igarapés, there were no caiman, piranha, anaconda, electric eel or stingray to spoil the fun. Similarly, the much mythologised urine-drinking, penis-invading catfish – the vandellia – failed to materialise. The river is warm, shallow and sluggish, and harbours only 400-odd species of fish. This is ten times the number of fish types in British fresh waters, but far short of the 4,000 species that are known to swim in the Amazon.

When we turned round to head for Manaus it was nighttime again. The blackwater river is invisible after dark. It merges with the sky above. On the top deck of the *Clipper*, I breathed and let the jungle gather around my senses. I tried to make out the horizon, but it was no use. Only the red eyes of the caimans gave me any bearings, and when these dipped below the water's surface, the lights went out. ●

WHEN TO GO
There are boat services all year. The rainy season is October to April; the period after this is the flood season, when the author travelled. As the floods recede it's easier to see wildlife as they eat, compete and fight in the shallows.

GETTING THERE
Fly to Rio de Janeiro, Brazil, then take a side-flight to Manaus.

ORGANISING YOUR TRIP
Last Frontiers (01296 653000, www.last frontiers.com) arranges two-week cruises up the Amazon on passenger boats – from Belém to Anavilhanas. If you don't travel with an organised trip, you can take the following boats: Belém to Manaus (*Santarem Amazon Star*, Rua Henrique Gurjão, +91 3212 6244), the best passenger boat for trips to Manaus; or Manaus to Anavilhanas (Amazon Clipper Premium Office, Rua Sucupira 249, Manaus, +92 3656 7338), a luxury passenger boat offering trips into the Anavilhanas from the jetty of the Hotel Tropical. Visit the Latin American Travel Association website (www.lata.org) for a full list of tour operators in the region.

COST
Last Frontiers' trip from Belém to Anavilhanas costs £1,600 per person for 13 nights, including five nights of stopovers costs (full board on the boat and lodges, breakfast only for stays in Manaus; flights not included). Six days from Belém to Manaus on the Santarem Amazon Star costs from £250 for a double with bunk beds (www.brazilnuts.com).

AM I UP TO IT?
Anyone can cruise up a river on a boat – but be prepared for heat and lots of bugs (though not mosquitoes, as they don't fly to the centre of the river). A yellow fever inoculation is highly recommended for a river cruise and obligatory for some areas in Brazilian Amazonia.

MORE LIKE THIS
The Brazilian main stream is unique, but the Amazon watershed cuts through Bolivia, Peru, Ecuador, Colombia, Venezuela and Guyana. Iquitos in Peru is a popular base for river trips. The national parks and reserves close to the headwaters of the Amazon in the Andes harbour great diversity and have not been developed as thoroughly as the Brazilian lowlands. The further west you go, the greater the biodiversity and the varieties of forest.

FOR REFERENCE
Tree of Rivers, by John Hemming (Thames & Hudson, 2008), is the long-time Amazonia ambassador's latest and most populist book to date, exploring the history of the river from pre-Columbian times to post-deforestation.

Wonder wall

Away from the crowds, **Dominic Fitzsimmons** works up a sweat in search of the real Great Wall.

WHAT	**HOW LONG**
Walk the Great Wall of China	About 4 hours
WHERE	**THRILL FACTOR**
Huairou to Simatai, Beijing	● ● ● ● ○

As with rock stars or good bars, great travel destinations can easily be ruined by too much fame – a cultural icon often loses its cachet and descends into a tacky imitation of its former self. Go to the Acropolis, Angkor Wat, the Taj Mahal or the Pyramids and you'll be fending off sleeve-tugging beggars and hawkers, while fighting to take a photograph that doesn't include somebody else also trying to frame a picture without you in it. To paraphrase Sartre, hell is other tourists.

Since 1984, when Communist Party leader Deng Xiaoping declared, 'Let us love our country and restore our Great Wall', there has been much rebuilding and modifying of the ancient but crumbling Great Wall of China: too much, some critics would argue. While the renovated sections, with their handrails and chairlifts, make for easy treks and great photo opportunities, the rougher, run-down sections are by far the most evocative and peaceful. And, on a crisp, clear day, the sight of the Wall against the parched mountains remains extraordinary.

LEGENDS OF THE WALL

From the fifth century BC, northern China had defensive walls. Between the third century BC and the 17th century AD, a succession of dynasties joined up huge sections to create a structure that has as much symbolic as military value. If you flew over the length of it – over 4,000 miles in total – you would see that there is, contrary to common belief, no continuous Great Wall but rather a series of sections. From the west, it snakes its way spectacularly over the hilltops of the Lop Nor desert, now the remote site of the Chinese nuclear testing facility, and finishes on the east coast, near the port of Tianjin.

One of the Seven Great Modern Clichés has to be that the Great Wall is visible from space. Yang Liwei, China's first astronaut, shattered the myth after a voyage in 2003; it turned out that a river had been mistaken for the Wall.

A VIEW TO A THRILL

It might not be visible in orbit but that doesn't stop this man-made wonder thoroughly deserving its title. The sheer size of the Great Wall

'IT'S NOT JUST THE VIEWS THAT OVERWHELM, BUT ALSO THE FEELING OF SPLENDID ISOLATION AND SENSE OF TIMELESSNESS. THE ONLY SIGN OF CIVILISATION WAS THE ANCIENT WALL.'

appeals endlessly to adventurers: its length would suggest that the wall can be visited anywhere in the northern part of the country, no matter how remote. But there are practical considerations: some intrepid travellers spend hours schlepping to some obscure section only to discover remains that have been reduced to rubble – not to mention angry farmers whose land you are pottering through.

Opting for a middle ground between accessibility and solitude, my four-hour hike started off the beaten track in Jingshanling, with a finale at Simatai, an atmospheric and moderately visited section of the Wall about 70 miles from Beijing.

After a packed bus journey from Beijing to the market town of Huairou and a hair-raising hurtle through country lanes, I arrived at Jingshanling to find a scene of perfect desertion. 'Why on earth did you come here?' the driver asked, as I hopped out of his battered minivan. 'Foreigners go to Mutianyu – there are restaurants and a market there.' As I teetered up the tiny brick steps of the Wall, prone to crumbling underfoot after centuries of exposure to the elements, I found my answer: there wasn't a soul to interrupt the view of the ancient battlements, silhouetted against the bright blue autumn sky.

For once, the postcards didn't lie: the Wall is one of those memorable experiences, like Venice or the Iguazu Falls, that can still catch you unawares, no matter how many pictures and documentaries you've seen beforehand. And it's not just the views that overwhelm, but also the feeling of splendid isolation and sense of timelessness. With the exception of a few roofs in the distance, the only sign of civilisation was the ancient wall beneath my feet.

Though some parts of the Great Wall date back 2,000 years, this section is virtually brand new in Chinese terms. It was built during the late 1300s by the Han-Chinese Ming Dynasty. It had just ousted the Mongol-led Yuan Dynasty, and wanted to ensure its enemy stayed in the north. But history has a way of repeating itself: a couple of centuries later, Manchurians conquered China from the northeast to form the Qing Dynasty, China's last set of Emperors.

RETURN TO REALITY

After many hours of solitary hill walking, it was almost a relief to see another human being, even if she was intent on selling me one of the

souvenirs she was peddling hopefully in the middle of nowhere. Not long after this rude awakening, I arrived jelly-legged at Simatai, with its beacon towers and rugged ramparts. Here you can dismount in style with a Flying Fox wire ride across a reservoir, or take a breather in the cable car ride down the hill.

In noisy contrast to the peaceful desolation prevailing in Jingshanling, Simatai offers a taste of the bazaar that is commonplace at other sections of the Wall. Remember to haggle hard for your very own 'I climbed the Great Wall' T-shirt, not just because it's overpriced, but because you've earned it. ●

WHEN TO GO
Open year-round but best between September and the end of October. The temperatures are comfortable in the day and cool in the evening.

GETTING THERE
This section of the Wall is about 68 miles from Beijing. Take the bus (60mins) to Huairou and then catch a passing minibus (they are frequent) for the 30min drive to Jingshanling, or get a Chengde-bound bus, alight at Jingshanling and take a taxi to the entrance.

ORGANISING YOUR TRIP
This walk can be completed independently but all the hotels and hostels in Beijing offer Great Wall packages. However, check first where they go – avoid Badaling.

COST
Entry to Wall RMB40, to be paid at both ends.

AM I UP TO IT?
Thanks to steeply inclined steps, this walk isn't for anyone with bad knees or heart problems.

Hit the road, Jack

Will Fulford-Jones motors across America.

WHAT	**HOW LONG**
Road trip across the USA	Three weeks
WHERE	**THRILL FACTOR**
New York to Los Angeles	● ● ● ● ●

'What is the feeling when you're driving away from people and they recede on the plain till you see their specks dispersing? – it's the too-huge world vaulting us, and it's good-by. But we lean forward to the next crazy venture beneath the skies'

– Jack Kerouac, from On the Road

Hammered out over three weeks and grounded entirely in the author's own experiences (the character names in the first draft were all real people), Jack Kerouac's novel *On the Road* inspired a generation of young Americans to hit the highways in search of adventure. Arriving at the same time as rock 'n' roll, which the jazz-loving Kerouac detested, the book became a clarion call, mythologising escape for escape's sake and establishing the American road as a destination in its own right. (Against such a background, it's a surprise to discover that the writer himself was a lifelong mommy's boy who never learned to drive.)

On the Road wasn't the story of one road trip but of many, stirred together by Kerouac with a gallon of poetic licence. Still, while the book is a composite, it hangs together as one epic journey. And it's what had brought us one afternoon to an ugly corner of a New York airport, where we were queueing to collect a thankfully reliable but defiantly uncharismatic rental car with the vague aim of following in the writer's tyre-tracks. Little remains of the United States that Kerouac traversed in the 1950s, and we were not aiming to trace the routes he described. Still, we were hopeful, like countless travellers before us, of finding similar inspiration in the open road and whatever lies alongside it.

All the traditional road-trip icons – the open highway, stereo cranked up to 11, riding with the top down under brilliant blue skies – have long since passed into cliché, rolled out in a million movies, books, songs and lazy TV travelogues. But for all that, they retain an indelible appeal, one that's apparent from the moment you hit the highway and ease away from the city traffic. There's a real freedom in the knowledge that, in this age of air travel and organised tours, you'll be making your own way: slave to no one's timetable but your own, in a land where the car

'THE HEART OF AMERICA'S APPEAL REMAINS WHERE IT'S ALWAYS BEEN: IN ITS BIG CITIES AND SMALL TOWNS, ALWAYS AND FOREVER ALONG MAIN STREET.'

is still king and the landscape morphs dramatically in front of your eyes from coast to coast. It's not the destination but the journey.

We had decided to cross the continent by following a circuitous route between New York and Los Angeles, but it's far from the only way to go. Today's road tripper has the choice of countless pieces of published fact and fiction to galvanise and guide, plus a universe of websites.

Still, it's best to use them as inspirations rather than prescriptions, instead finding your own way from A to B. As Kerouac wondered in *The Subterraneans*, 'What's in store for me in the direction I don't take?'

CITY TO COUNTRY

The inspiration we were hoping to find proves hard to draw from the irascible New York traffic that greeted us as we left the car-rental lot, and it was slow to strike further down the road. The early stages of an odyssey such as this offer as many urban thrills as you choose to allow: in New York City, of course, but also in toughened-up Philadelphia, battered Baltimore and regal Washington, DC. However, on the road itself, I-95 and the dreaded New Jersey Turnpike between New York and Richmond, Virginia offer the kind of dreary driving only a local could love.

Edging further inland from Richmond, though, the travel becomes less of a chore. On Highway 60, the cities soon melted into memory. Small town followed small town, with some

smaller than others – the oddly named and oddly beautiful Forks of Buffalo seemed entirely deserted. This was the road less travelled, the destination a wonderful irrelevance.

The scenic Blue Ridge Parkway, which crosses Highway 60 and runs on a north-east to south-west arc through Virginia and North Carolina, is said to be the most visited sight in the US National Park System. Still, in balmy late summer, even its busiest stretches offered little traffic to derail us. Winding for nearly 500 miles through the Appalachian Mountains, the Parkway was a product of Roosevelt's New Deal, introduced in the 1930s to alleviate hardships caused by the Great Depression. It's hard – absurd, even – to imagine anything so worthwhile emerging as a direct result of today's economic crisis, but no matter. Cresting and dipping over hills and through valleys, a story in every town and a picture-postcard view around every corner, it's a wonderful drive.

SOUND ADVICE

The south-eastern states are the cradle of much American traditional music, one of the reasons to choose this particular route. Having served as the location for the earliest recordings of the Carter Family, the small town of Bristol in Tennessee claims to be the birthplace of country music. The town celebrates at the annual Rhythm & Roots Reunion weekend in September, and we joined them. South of here, in the homely North Carolina college town of Asheville, we spent the following evening sweatily learning the arcane traditions of contra dancing at a bar on the outskirts of town.

MEMPHIS, TENNESSEE

From here, it was back into Tennessee and on to Nashville, where the none-more-basic Arnold's Country Kitchen provided hearty food to sustain us around the excellent Country Music Hall of Fame & Museum. Some 200 miles west took us to earthier Memphis, where the best music is

found away from the tourist-friendly joints on Beale Street. And then we headed due south to the Gulf Coast and New Orleans, still attempting to rebuild itself after Hurricane Katrina but pleased to welcome visitors who pass its way.

The section of fabled Highway 61 that links Memphis and New Orleans is a curious stretch, aware of its place in history but reluctant to exploit it. Take Clarksdale, for instance, a scruffy town about 70 miles south of Memphis. WC Handy lived here, Bessie Smith died here and, according to legend, Robert Johnson sold his soul to the devil at the junction of Highways 61 and 49. But it's only in recent years that Clarksdale has attempted to capitalise on its infamy, and visitors are still both unusual and unexpected in this part of the world.

'ALL THE TRADITIONAL ROAD-TRIP ICONS – THE OPEN HIGHWAY, STEREO CRANKED UP TO 11 – HAVE PASSED INTO CLICHE. BUT FOR ALL THAT THEY RETAIN AN INDELIBLE APPEAL.'

Onwards. First across the astonishing Pontchartrain Causeway, then west past Baton Rouge, over the southern swamps and across to Lafayette on I-10. Along Highway 90 to the unbecoming town of Jennings, Louisiana, with a stop for some awesome sausages at a tiny food stop called Boudin King (throughout the journey, aided by a great book called *Roadfood*, we sought out roadside pit stops). And then west along a series of rural roads to 222 Malone Street in Houston, roughly the halfway point of our journey, where John Milkovisch spent his last two decades drinking beers, crushing the cans and attaching an estimated 50,000 of them to the outside of his home. The Beer Can House, as it's inevitably known, is a folk art monument of the most American kind.

HIGHWAYS AND BYWAYS

Kerouac wrote *On the Road* in 1951, typing it as a single paragraph on to a 120-foot-long roll of paper. However, by the time of the book's publication six years later, the roads he'd deified were soon to be usurped by the Federal-Aid Highway Act of 1956. The brainchild of President Eisenhower, the act authorised the construction of a 40,000-mile long network of interstate highways, carving eight-lane valleys of asphalt and concrete across the country and adding a previously unimagined world of convenience to American road travel.

There's a Ballardian thrill to be found in the arrow-straight relentlessness of often-vast freeways such as I-10, which we took from Houston to San Antonio. Still, for the wide-eyed vacationer, the choice between interstate and surface-road is too often the choice between utility and romance. By design, most interstates take you around or over towns and cities, clear of the delays that civilisation inevitably provides. But without these diversions and digressions, you might as well take the plane. The heart of America's appeal remains where it's always been: in its big cities and small towns, always and forever along Main Street.

SMALL-TOWN AMERICA

West of San Antonio, deep in the heart of Texas, the variety of the American landscape and the glory of a cross-country road trip both started to reveal themselves. We forewent I-10 in favour of Highway 90, which soon opened out into endless acres of nothing much. Towns fall 20, 30, even 40 miles apart; when they arrive, they're not worth the wait. But in the railroad town of Alpine, an exhausting 350 miles from San Antonio, a warm welcome awaited. After a day-long detour through Big Bend National Park, a magically isolated sprawl separated from Mexico by the Rio Grande, and the beautiful little town of Marfa, we continued west. This is the American desert: a world away from the soaring Appalachians, but possessed of an eerie, elemental beauty all its own.

After a night at the Shady Dell in Bisbee, Arizona, where the lodgings are all in vintage trailers, we pushed on to the hazy south-Arizona town of Tucson, wide-eyed at the uncountable saguaro cacti that stood to attention as far as the eye could see. Unfortunately, though, not even judicious freeway use could take us swiftly past the city of Phoenix, which carries all of the Los Angeles area's ugly characteristics (unremitting sprawl, mediocre architecture, car-choked roads) but none of its cultural advantages. We left as quickly as we arrived.

66 TO THE COAST

The final part of our journey, though, was as satisfying a drive as any portion before it. We crossed I-40 for the first time since Memphis at Kingman, riding the ever-lonesome Highway 93 north-west towards Nevada beneath vast desert skies. Around 100 miles later, past the awe-inspiring Hoover Dam, we arrived on the Strip in Las Vegas, a dazzling parade of lights and construction and excess. And then, the morning after the night before, it was the surprisingly skinny I-15 south-west through the Mojave Desert, past Baker (home, as we saw from some distance away, to the world's tallest thermometer) and towards the coast.

We broke the journey at Barstow, a once-thriving California town that's struggled to adjust since the railroad network faded into irrelevance. Before Kerouac and rock 'n' roll, travellers

'SLAVE TO NO ONE'S TIMETABLE BUT YOUR OWN, IN A LAND WHERE THE CAR IS STILL KING AND THE LANDSCAPE MORPHS DRAMATICALLY IN FRONT OF YOUR EYES.'

passing through here were full of hope, headed west on Route 66 in search of a new life in Southern California. Today, such optimism is conspicuous by its absence. And so, to most travellers, is Route 66 itself, which ran from Chicago to LA before it was superceded by Eisenhower's interstates. But you'll still find the old Mother Road here, unheralded and largely unused yet still just about alive. And with a little initiative, you can follow it from Barstow more or less uninterrupted all the way to the coast.

West of San Bernardino, old Route 66 is lined by a slew of blink-and-you'll-miss-them roadside businesses. They've seen far better days, of course, but they offer a glimpse of what life must have been like for the '30s and '40s adventurer. Take the daft Wigwam Motel in Rialto, for instance, or the orange-coloured, orange-shaped orange stand in nearby Fontana.

By now, though, we were nearly in LA, and the end of the road. After all that's come before it – from the beauty of the autumnal Appalachians to the mile-wide skies of the Mojave – Sunset and Santa Monica Boulevards were a curious anticlimax, but we perked up when we caught our first glimpse of the glistening Pacific. 'The road is life,' reckoned Kerouac. Hokum, of course. But just for a moment, with three weeks and more than 4,000 miles in the rear-view mirror, we could kind of see what he meant. ●

WHEN TO GO
Any time, but the best month is September, after Labor Day, when the weather is still good but prices are cheaper.

GETTING THERE
The author drove from New York to LA – via the Blue Ridge Parkway, Nashville, Memphis, New Orleans, Houston, Tucson and Las Vegas – but you can start and finish wherever you please.

ORGANISING YOUR TRIP
Book hotels in big cities, and at either end of your trip. But otherwise, be flexible.

COST
On top of flights, UK travellers can expect to spend £750-£1,250 on a three-week, coast-to-coast rental; you can do the trip in two weeks if you take a simpler route. Book online to save money. (US travellers with their own car insurance should pay less.) Gas should cost $300-$400. You can often find a room in a budget motel outside town for $50 a night, with prices rising to $100-$200 for small-town hotels; the sky's the limit for big-city lodgings.

AM I UP TO IT?
If you can drive, yes.

MORE LIKE THIS
Other great North American road trips include the coastal road from the Mexican border to the Canadian border; Highway 93 from Canada to Arizona; and old Route 66 from Chicago to LA.

FOR REFERENCE
On the Road, by Jack Kerouac, the motherlode of road-trip fantasias, is essential reading. Consult Roadfood by Jane & Michael Stern for small-town diners, barbecue shacks and other off-the-beaten-path eateries.

Roads by Larry McMurtry, in which the Lonesome Dove author glories in the interstate network.

The Lost Continent by Bill Bryson. Small-town America through an expat's eyes.

Blue Highways by William Least Heat-Moon. A beautiful evocation of the landscape.

www.roadsideamerica.com and www.roadsidepeek.com revel in arcane Americana: vintage neon, bizarre tourist attractions and much more.

Breaking England's backbone

Chris Moss does the Pennines *his* way.

WHAT	**HOW LONG**
Walk the Pennine Way	Two to four weeks
WHERE	**THRILL FACTOR**
Derbyshire to Scotland	● ● ● ● ●

Some Pennine Ways end in Scotland, with a free pint of beer at the pub in Kirk Yetholm – or so the myth goes. Others end in Derbyshire, with a deep sense of satisfaction. Mine ended in the middle of a godforsaken heath nowhere in particular, with my best mate, Mike, grumbling about 'this bloody tedious trudge'.

It was my fault – because it was entirely my idea that we should walk down England's backbone in late May with a tent for shelter. The snows had receded, but not the cold and, while some days were blue and sparkling, many were deep grey and overcast – and overcast in north-central England means there are clouds a few inches above the bobble on your woolly hat.

THE NORTH–SOUTH DIVIDE

But the attractions of the great Pennine Way walk are obvious. At 268 miles, it isn't Britain's longest national trail (that badge goes to the 630-mile South West Coast path), but it is the oldest and best-known. It cuts the northern half of England and a tiny bit of the Scottish Borders in half, following the east–west watershed along the ridge of hills that divides Lancashire (my homeland and a county of honest working men) from Yorkshire (*Emmerdale Farm* and pub bores). It passes through some of England's prettiest rural towns and villages, and some of the most quintessentially northern landscapes – and, well, every man likes a conquest and little Britain offers only a handful of serious epic trails.

We were taking on the Pennines from south to north, so we started at the official point in Edale, Derbyshire. The night before, Mike and I had had a few pints of Gray's at the Old Nags Head but now we walked right past the pub at a jaunty pace and headed off into the Dark Peak – the evocative name of the moorland plateau in the north-eastern reaches of the Peak District. Straight away we were into a classic Pennine

topography of sloping pastures of dank, dark-green grassland, drystone walls containing Gritstone sheep, and farm cottages that look idyllic from outside but which probably feel like draughty mountain refuges in deep winter.

The first stage of the climb seemed welcoming enough, as the land rises at first very steadily to the foot of Jacob's Ladder, a steep, rocky stairway that takes you up to Kinder Scout – famed as the location of the mass trespass in 1932 that forced Ramsay MacDonald's government to review public access to farmland. Quite abruptly, civilisation fell away and the wind cooled and hastened us as we found ourselves on an exposed moor. Mike and I stopped chatting and bowed our heads into the wind. And rain. And then sleet.

'QUITE ABRUPTLY CIVILISATION FELL AWAY AND THE WIND COOLED AND HASTENED US AS WE FOUND OURSELVES ON AN EXPOSED MOOR. WE STOPPED CHATTING AND BOWED OUR HEADS INTO THE WIND. AND RAIN. AND THEN SLEET.'

An army man stopped and recommended we get off the hill. It was with a mixture of defeat and exaltation that we decided to jack it in and skip the first stage of the Pennine Way.

BRONTË COUNTRY

We started – again – from a natural second stage of the Way, at Hebden Bridge. We slept in a B&B and after a hurried breakfast went up to Heptonstall, the quite beautiful stone walled town where Sylvia Plath is buried, and, rejoining the Way proper, went across its namesake moor and into Brontë country. We crossed Haworth Moor, passing close by Top Withins, the ruin thought to be the inspiration for *Wuthering Heights*, and then put our tent up on the south side of the Worth Valley.

The next morning there were ice windows on the tent that cracked as we unzipped the doors, but the sky was huge and blue.

The land changed from bog and marsh to heath and limestone pavement, and soon we were passing through quaint Dales villages – Ickornshaw, Lothersdale, Thornton-in-Craven – and the abundance of B&Bs kept us out of the tent for a couple of nights. We breakfasted on full Englishes, lunched on Mars bars and sarnies, and evenings were pints of Theakston, Timothy Taylor or Black Sheep ('Two Sheep, please love'),

THE MOOR THE MERRIER

There were a few people around, but many looked like Territorial Army teams. A mountain biker came down one sharp brew as we were going up. Now there was a mist and a sort of hail mixed in with the sleet. 'The things you do,' the cyclist quipped as he bounced past.

Still, we persevered and found ourselves on another exposed, blasted moor. Everyone seemed to be going in the opposite direction, including a group of men in army fatigues. By the time we got to the southern section of Bleaklow – an aptly named high-altitude range of peaty moorland – we were soaked through, freezing (I had snow round my lips like an Antarctic explorer) and somewhat dazed by the initiation.

'THE PENNINE WAY IS HIGH AND LONELY AND ONE OF ITS CHIEF ATTRACTIONS, ON THIS CROWDED, BUSY LITTLE NATION IS THE DEARTH OF HUMANITY.'

and steak pies and chips. The après-walk blowout is no mean reward, but we deserved it, as blisters began to appear and joints inflamed and became sore.

FOLLOW THE ACORNS

Because of the relentless nature of this kind of long walk, you never have a chance to rest your limbs. It becomes a sort of paradoxical relief to get up and out in the morning to keep muscles moving. Each day had several moods of walking: marching, tramping, strolling, ambling, skipping, running (when some big hairy cows got fed up of us), and pausing now and again to check the map, take a bearing on the compass, take in the view.

An acorn symbol appears on all the Pennine Way waymarkers, but the trail is sometimes diverted to allow damaged stretches to recover and there are other parts where there are very few signposts – locals are always a great help, and it's very difficult to get truly lost. The watershed, after all, is always nearby and you cross many major roads and rivers, all of which are clearly visible on all maps.

There were many lonely hours, but some sections of the Way are favourites all year round. Who would not love Pen y Ghent mountain? Even sardonic fell-lover Alfred Wainwright proclaimed, on arriving here, 'A real mountain, at last'. Mike and I spent a night at Malham, a tiny hamlet but the regional trekking capital and home to a decent youth hostel where we collapsed for the night.

The next day was a long, remote path, taking us past pretty Malham Tarn, past 668-metre-high Fountains Fell and, finally, into the quaint market town of Hawes.

HIGH ON A HILL

The Pennine Way is high and lonely, and one of its chief attractions is the dearth of humanity. Britain is a crowded, busy little nation, and yet up here you escape faces, commerce, traffic, shops, modernity, and your mind rediscovers older rhythms for long periods. We met some eccentrics on the way, though. John from Dover was celebrating his retirement by breaking Britain's backbone with his old boots; a former merchant seaman, he was going from Land's End to John O'Groats.

Hawes was the last familiar stop for me. From here on in it was just me, Mike, the sodden grass, the sodding sheep, hill after hill after hill, and those ever lowering clouds. The human imprint was there in the shape of the bridges of the Settle–Carlisle railway, and barns, byres, reservoirs and spires. But there were very few humans indeed as we walked into Wensleydale's higher reaches; nearby was a waterfall called Hardraw Force on Hardraw Beck in Hardraw Scar. That gritty language again.

It was at Great Shunner Fell that Mike uttered the words that open this narrative, and I have to admit that I too was shattered and nearly beaten by this stage. We'd been walking for 16 days and were beginning to consider a way out of the Way. I won't lie – we never made it to Kirk Yetholm, for the pat on the back and the mythic pint. But we forged on a few more days beyond Bowes and into the more rugged wastes of the North Pennines. But Mike's moan had marked a drying-up of spirit, and we'd have to come back some day to finish the job in hand. ●

WHEN TO GO
Spring to early autumn; rain is always likely.

GETTING THERE
The Edale starting point is on the Hope Valley railway line between Manchester and Sheffield.

ORGANISING YOUR TRIP
Ramblers Holidays (www.ramblerscountry wide.co.uk) and HF Holidays (www.hfholidays. co.uk) can help arrange self-guide trips along sections of the Pennine Way. If you want to organise accommodation yourself, see www.nationaltrail.co.uk/pennineway; Sherpa Van (www.sherpavan.com) can arrange baggage transfer between points.

COST
Food and accommodation for 14-20 days, depending on whether you camp or use B&Bs. There is no charge for using the trail footpath.

AM I UP TO IT?
Well, what do *you* think? It's a tough walk and you'll need good strong legs, decent lungs, stamina and a bloody good jacket.

MORE LIKE THIS…
There are 15 major national trails in England and Wales (www.nationaltrail.co.uk) and 24 in Scotland, where they are called 'long-distance routes'. The 630-mile South West Coast Path is a worthy rival to the Pennine Way, taking an average of 56 days to complete.

FOR REFERENCE
Alfred Wainwright's *The Pennine Way Companion* is full of lovely sketches and personal anecdotes, but isn't a practical guidebook. Tony Hopkins's *Pennine Way North* and *Pennine Way South* handbooks contain useful background material, and have maps as well as directions.

The big one

Chris Pierre scales Africa's highest peak.

WHAT	**HOW LONG**
Climb Kilimanjaro	10 days
WHERE	**THRILL FACTOR**
North-eastern Tanzania	● ● ● ● ●

From the pool of the Kilimanjaro Mountain Resort Hotel, in the village of Marangu, it was hard to grasp the enormity of climbing Africa's highest mountain. And too hot to believe that soon I would be very, very cold (temperatures can drop as low as minus 30°C on the mountain) – and quite possibly suffering from altitude sickness. Around 20,000 people attempt the summit of Mount Kilimanjaro each year and, infamously, almost half have to turn back – usually hampered by the debilitating effects of high altitude.

Kilimanjaro is the tallest stand-alone mountain in the world and the most accessible of the world's 'seven summits' (the highest mountain in each continent): you can walk up without recourse to specialist climbing skills or crampons. A long-dormant volcano standing a smidgen south of the equator, near Tanzania's border with Kenya, it rises in solitary splendour out of the vast African savannah.

Technically speaking, 'Kili', as it is known, is a triple stratovolcano: it might look like one hulking mass from afar, but it is in fact made up of three volcanic peaks, each comprising complex layers of ancient ash, rock and lava from the various phases of its eruption. Of its three cones – Kibo, Mawensi and Shira – Kibo is the highest, with its Uhuru peak, at 5,895 metres, the ultimate target for the tens of thousands of hikers who walk up its slopes each year.

UNDER THE VOLCANO

A number of paths lead to the summit; my group would be climbing the Rongai route, the one with the gentlest gradient and least crowds. The trip started gently enough, with a tame (by African standards) drive in 4x4s along red-dirt roads through the plains to the gate of Kilimanjaro National Park. Then it was a pleasant half-hour walk to a cool forest, where we ate lunch while watching colobus monkeys darting about. We reached the first campsite a few hours later. Our porters had arrived well ahead of us and set up camp (there were 42 staff on the trip – cooks, guides and porters, who carry not only luggage but also tents, cooking equipment and the chemical loo – all for 12 hikers).

This was designated an 'easy' day, but some of the group were sunburned, and none of us had drunk enough water. It was hard getting through the daily four to five litres recommended, but crucial for the days ahead – that and moving 'pole pole', Swahili for 'slowly slowly', something the guides reiterated constantly. We had already gained some altitude but, to acclimatise properly, we needed to ascend a little further and then drop back down to sleep at a lower level – we slowly climbed a steep path, got our breath and then returned to camp.

As dinner was served, the skies opened (despite December being the 'dry season') and the rain hammered all night. Fortunately, the camping equipment supplied was high-spec, and most of us woke dry to a good walking breakfast of porridge, eggs, bacon, bread and fruit.

A very different day's hike took us through cloud forest, where the trees were draped with old man's beard lichen – and gradually we began to get an impression of how high we'd climbed, with glimpses out through the trees of the plains that stretched out below. The vegetation soon thinned, and the scenery became rugged and rocky: arriving at Mawensi tarn after a steep but straightforward bit of climbing, we found the peak of Mawensi (5,149 metres) shrouded in

cloud except for a few tantalising glimpses of its jagged pinnacles.

In the evening, the skies cleared to reveal astonishing views up its shattered flank and across the saddle between the two volcanoes to Kibo. Early risers the next day caught the sunrise turning Mawensi's rock golden and making the plains below glow.

TOUGH AT THE TOP

The day before 'summit day' was cold, the ground was rock hard, and a few of us had started to get headaches and nausea. I fainted before breakfast. It was easy to forget how oxygen-depleted the air is even at this altitude, but the attentive guides kept a close eye on their charges. (I was declared 'old man but strong'!)

We had an exhilarating day's walk up to and over the ridge, and down to the saddle. This was an empty, lifeless place, with a small, recently crashed light aeroplane adding to the eeriness, and thousands of lava bombs, some as big as cars, scattered around. These were violently ejected during the eruptions of Mawensi and Kibo, 350,000 and 500,000 years ago respectively. Kibo (a less attractive mountain, not unlike a giant slag heap) loomed ahead all day, building trepidation about the approach to the summit.

'THIS WAS AN EMPTY, LIFELESS PLACE, WITH A SMALL RECENTLY CRASHED LIGHT AEROPLANE ADDING TO THE EERINESS, AND THOUSANDS OF LAVA BOMBS SCATTERED AROUND.'

Because of the lack of oxygen at this altitude, sleep wasn't easy and many of us were tired – the insomnia was exacerbated by the frequent night visits we had to make to the 'long drop' or chemical loos to process the daytime water intake. The silver lining to this particular cloud was the fabulous starry sky.

THE FINAL PUSH

We left camp at midnight in order to reach the crater rim at sunrise. In a confusing day, we'd had supper at 4.30pm, then slept, only to be woken for breakfast at 11.30pm. We registered for the summit climb, which is the most dangerous section of the route, giving our names, professions and ages. I was 52, but when I signed

back in the next day I would be 53, and I silently hoped to make the summit on my birthday.

As we left camp the full moon lent the already spooky landscape a silver-grey caste; it wasn't as cold as we'd expected and soon jackets were shed and anoraks removed as we zigzagged very slowly up a switchback through the scree. It was very quiet, with just the occasional cow bell-like sound of a trekking pole hitting a metal water bottle. We walked in single file, slowly and with extinguished head torches as the full moon lit our way.

I thought about Hans Meyer (a cave is named for him on the way up), the first white man to climb Kilimanjaro, and of Otto Ehlers who described 'the wall of ice which encircles the entire summit'. Much of the ice has gone – global warming has seen to that – but the crater wall is still a formidable barrier.

As we walked 'pole pole' ever upwards, none of us needed to be reminded to drink water, and we didn't notice the bad taste of the boiled purified liquid any more. We stopped frequently to get our breath and to eat energy bars, but we were flagging – the air contained just half the oxygen we were used to. Spirits were still high, but many were suffering the more unpleasant effects of altitude: extreme nausea, vomiting, migraine-like headaches, exhaustion and disorientation.

The mood darkened when we passed Jamaica Rock and in the last of the moonlight we saw the jumbled wall of boulders and scree that pushes up to the crater rim – not the ice that early climbers had to contend with but even so a seemingly insurmountable obstacle to reaching the top. The full moon disappeared behind Kibo and the mountain plunged into darkness. The temperature was minus 10°C and falling.

NEW HEIGHTS

Gillman's Point, at the crater's edge, came suddenly; our guides broke out thermos flasks of hot, sweet black tea. Although euphoric, some of us were disoriented, and others so cold that foil blankets were pressed into service. We couldn't properly appreciate the curved line of pink and orange that was the sunrise on the horizon, the splendour of the crater or the view across the plains and the Great Rift Valley. Still, the guides decided that we were all fit enough to attempt the true summit, the highest point on the crater rim, Uhuru ('freedom' in Swahili).

Encouraging one another, we headed towards the summit, revelling in the crater scenery: ash cones, fumaroles, glaciers, lava towers and, of course, the formidable ice sheet – tens of feet thick in vivid blues, with soaring cliffs. I had climbed higher than this, but there is nowhere on earth that gives the feeling of being above everything else like Kilimanjaro, standing solo in the savannah.

Thanks to the support of our guides (in some cases physical), we all made the summit. Mount Meru, some 40 miles west and visible in the forming clouds below us, provided a spectacular backdrop for group photos. But we couldn't linger – it's dangerous to dawdle at this altitude.

On jelly legs we descended (one of the party had to be carried) and, though it was much faster going down, it was still hours before we signed back in and fell into our tents. It was mid-morning; we had been walking all night and soon we had to set off again across the lava-bomb-strewn saddle to the next campsite. This was the most beautiful site so far, but it went unappreciated – all anyone was interested in was sleep.

On the final day we awoke as if from comas and wearily walked past acres of giant senecio plants into a quietly beautiful cloud forest. Arriving at Marangu Gate, the exit from the national park, we waited for our certificates, savouring the thought that we'd climbed three miles into the sky to stand at the highest point in the continent – but mainly dreaming of hot showers and the hotel pool. Kili might be the most accessible of the 'seven summits' but, crampons or no crampons, I didn't hear anyone saying it was easy. ●

WHEN TO GO
Either late December to mid March, or late June to October. These are the 'dry seasons', but don't expect to escape bad weather entirely. Avoid the long rainy season from March to May, and a shorter one in November.

GETTING THERE
Fly to Kilimanjaro International airport.

ORGANISING YOUR TRIP
Exodus (0845 863 9601/www.exodus.co.uk).

COST
The 10-day Kilimanjaro Rongai Route itinerary is priced from £1,824 per person including flights, accommodation, the park fee and most meals.

AM I UP TO IT?
No technical skills are required and any reasonably fit person can tackle this route. The walking is no more difficult than a strenuous hike in the Peak District – it's the altitude that's the real challenge. It is vital to allow ample time for acclimatisation and, even being cautious, the oxygen-starved air near the summit may give you some unpleasant symptoms.

MORE LIKE THIS
Iran's Mount Damavand (see page 48), standing at 5,610 metres, is another demanding but non-technical volcano climb. Cotopaxi in Ecuador is a snow-capped still-active volcano in the Andes, at 5,897 metres.

'IF YOU'RE NOT LIVING ON THE EDGE,
YOU'RE TAKING UP TOO MUCH SPACE.'

ANONYMOUS

Natural highs

Flight of fantasy

Anna Norman goes up, up and away in Cappadocia.

WHAT	**HOW LONG**
Hot-air balloon flight	One and a half hours
WHERE	**THRILL FACTOR**
Cappadocia, Turkey	● ● ● ● ●

I watched with apprehension, as the huge butter-yellow and cornflower-blue patterned fabric was unpacked, laid on the ground, connected to the wicker baskets and burners, and then gently inflated to form a huge, recognisable balloon – firstly through the use of fans, and then using the burner flame. In the distance, other brightly coloured globes began to creep quietly up from behind the peaks of the still dawn-lit Cappadocian landscape – an entrancing expanse of weather-sculpted volcanic rock formations, canyons and valleys.

It took about 15 minutes for our balloon to inflate fully to an upright position. After a short briefing, our group of eight was instructed by the pilots to clamber into the basket and, as more hot air was blown into the balloon, it began to rise, and the requisite chase vehicles started up.

Put any dramatic thoughts relating to vertigo, turbulence or the traumatic hot-air balloon scene in the opening pages of Ian McEwan's *Enduring Love* out of your head: this is adventure of a serene (and actually very safe) sort. Although there was very little sensation of movement, the constantly changing plateau, rotating slowly beneath us, and the gentle rise and fall of the balloon (pilots can't steer, but rather climb or

'WE GOT A TRUE BIRD'S-EYE VIEW OF THE GENTLY UNDULATING LANDSCAPE, WITH ITS DISTINCTIVE "FAIRY CHIMNEYS", SOFT PEAKS AND FOLDS, AND PALE PINK, YELLOW AND WHITE TONES RESEMBLING A BLANKET OF FLAVOURED WHIPPED CREAM.'

descend into wind currents) created a feeling of invigorating tranquillity; even the sporadic roar of the propane burners sounded enchantingly traditional and organic.

DAWN FLIGHT

Rising before dawn, when the air is normally at its calmest, and travelling in twilight fostered a sense of expectancy from the outset. From the headquarters of Kapadokya Balloons – the company that put hot-air ballooning on the map

here – we were taken by bus to the take-off site, which varies according to the wind direction (balloon flights don't go out at all in the event of strong winds or heavy rain).

Standing in a wicker basket in the sky may not be an everyday event, but it felt entirely natural in this context. In fact, a fear of flying is no barrier to enjoying this experience – which is actually very different to an aeroplane flight – allowing even pronounced aviophobics to take to the air without the usual sweaty palms and fast breathing. Cappadocia (an ancient appellation meaning 'land of beautiful horses'), in central Anatolia, is an extraordinary sight, a great plateau of surreal rock formations and gorgeous colours

– and there is no better way to see it than from the air. Most of the flight takes place at fairly low levels (somewhere between 15 and 150 metres), so you get a true bird's-eye view of the gently undulating landscape, which, with its distinctive 'fairy chimneys', soft peaks and folds, and pale pink, yellow and white tones, resembles a blanket of flavoured whipped cream.

Now-empty cave-dwellings (sometimes containing visible tombs), cave-churches and 'pigeon houses' (man-made pigeon roosts) from the Byzantine era and later reveal the unique human influence on the landscape, while apricot and walnut trees, along with untied vines, pepper the ground (flights are so gentle that fruit can be

picked from the trees in season). I spotted a grey fox nestling on a ledge, staring up at us as we drifted past, while a shepherd with his small flock also took a cursory interest in our presence; but other than this, it was just us and the weird and wonderful rock formations.

HEAVEN'S ABOVE

The most exhilarating part of the flight – and the only time at which I felt any genuine trepidation – was when our pilot decided to take us up above the clouds, to a height of around 460 to 600 metres. Travelling through the clouds was an unforgettable experience, the all-encompassing pure white mist provoking a disconcerting feeling of nothingness. But once above, or seemingly on top of, the clouds, the sensation was like no other.

Standing in the open air at such a height evoked a feeling of surreal disbelief. Thoughts of heaven were inevitable, made more palpable by the peace and quiet; that, and the fact that I was standing with an international group of strangers, as though this basket of people had all died simultaneously and we were on our way up to meet our maker. And if that sounds dark, it's not meant to: the experience was almost euphoric, akin to a 'peak experience', in all its possible meanings.

As the balloon drifted down below the clouds once again, the descent to earth began. The chase vehicles that had been monitoring the flight were contacted by radio as the balloon gently returned to lower levels. Our pilot's comment about 'just helping the autumn do its work' as the basket skimmed over the tree tops, shaking a few leaves to the ground, was entirely apt. As we slowly approached the ground, a crew was ready to grab the basket for a steady touchdown. If it hadn't have been for a chill in the October air, I would have happily prolonged the experience. Then, with the balloon safely deflated, we were treated to the traditional post-ballooning champagne toast. ●

WHEN TO GO
Hot-air balloon flights can be taken year-round, but March till the end of November is the best time in Cappadocia. Flights are always taken at dawn, avoiding the heat in summer; wrap up in winter.

GETTING THERE
There are no direct flights to the region from outside Turkey; fly to Istanbul and then take a connecting flight to Kayseri or Nevsehir.

ORGANISING YOUR TRIP
Kapadokya Balloons (www.kapadokya balloons.com) is the most reputable hot-air ballooning company operating in the region (March to November only). Goreme Balloons (www.goremeballoons.com) flies off-season. Book directly, or through Argeus Tourism & Travel (www.argeus.com.tr). Staying in an authentic cave-hotel is an integral part of a trip to Cappadocia; Serinn House (www.serinnhouse.com) in Ürgüp is one of the most stylish, with a spectacular location.

COST
A balloon flight with Kapadokya Balloons costs €250 per person.

AM I UP TO IT?
There are no age or training restrictions but you must be able to stand for an hour and a half.

MORE LIKE THIS
Other famous ballooning sites include the Dubai desert; over the Nile in Luxur, Egypt; and above the rolling Somerset countryside in Bath.

FOR REFERENCE
Louis de Bernières' novel *Birds Without Wings* is set during the collapse of the Ottoman Empire, throwing light on Anatolian history.

Taking the plunge

Julie Davidson swims close, very close, to the edge.

WHAT Swimming at the edge of Victoria Falls	**HOW LONG** One and a half hours
WHERE Victoria Falls, Zambia	**THRILL FACTOR** ● ● ● ● ○

Some call it the Devil's Pool, others the Devil's Armchair; but on a day when the mercury hit 40°C, for me it was the Devil's Coolbox. Once the nerves had subsided, it was possible to lean back and cool off against the narrow barrier of rock (the 'armchair'), which was all that prevented me from tipping over the edge of Victoria Falls with the rest of the Zambezi river's flotsam. On the opposite rim of this death-defying natural 'swimming pool' stood Prince, truly a prince among Zambian guides, who gave me a confident grin as he dived into the water. 'Quite safe!' he called as he surfaced.

THAT'S A LOT OF WATER

The words registered in my brain but hadn't reached as far as my fibrillating heart. At the height of the flood season, 19,280 million cubic feet of water crash down over the edge of the Victoria Falls every minute. Even summoning up the courage to turn around, lean over and look down into the boiling pot of water 100 metres below – as we'd watched others do from the Zimbabwean side of the falls – seemed too dangerous. Not aware that their adventure was more controlled than it looked, we had stared, transfixed, as we watched them pick their way across Livingstone Island, which lies mid-river on the lip of the falls, and disappear into a hole on top of the precipice. When they reappeared we could see that they were swimming, while two or three leaned on the ledge that overhung the void.

So how do you swim on the brim of the world's widest curtain of falling water without being swept into the gorge below? Seasonally, that's how. Between August and December or January, depending on water levels, the Devil's Pool is calm enough to swim in.

When the Zambezi is in full flood (around Easter), you see towering columns of spray and boiling cascades at the falls: 'Mosi-oa-Tunya' or 'the smoke that thunders' is how the locals

> 'EVERY SO OFTEN THE WIND PUSHED THE CURRENT OF THE WATER, AND HINTED THAT IT COULD, EVER SO GENTLY, PUSH ME OVER THE EDGE.'

described them before David Livingstone gave them their European name in 1855. But in the dry season the river level drops, the spray dwindles and the mighty curtain of water magically parts between the main cataracts to expose the cliffs.

ROCKY ROAD

Livingstone Island, in the middle of the Zambezi, is a World Heritage Site – accessible only from the Zambian side. Visitors to the island are picked up from the colonial Royal Livingstone Hotel, on the edge of Livingstone town. From the hotel jetty it's a short boat ride to the island but, to protect its unique status, only 16 people are allowed there at any one time, so it's best to prebook one of five daily outings offered by Tongabezi Lodge (who manage the island). Its team of guides know every eddy in the river and you won't be allowed to swim unless one of them is around.

We visited in November, when the water was unusually low, and the expanse of cliff revealed was such that the local wits renamed the falls 'the Victoria Walls'. Even so, there was still plenty of Zambezi tumbling into the gorge when Prince conducted our foursome into the river for the short swim from Livingstone Island to the neighbouring islet and its swimming hole.

You don't just swim in the Devil's Pool, you swim to it, across a channel near the edge of the falls. The channel is only a few metres wide and the modest current was easily tackled but we still kept our eyes firmly fixed on Prince, following his every stroke. The next stage was actually more difficult – a barefoot totter across sharp rocks (you're advised to wear rafting shoes or old trainers) to the pool, which is deep enough to accommodate the guide's spectacular dives.

SMOKE AND THUNDER

Diving seemed a little over confident so I slid in slowly, and made my way cautiously to the rim of rock, our safety barrier. Backing up against it did make me feel safer, but every so often the wind pushed the current of the water, and hinted that it could, ever so gently, push me over the edge; but it's an illusion – in the right conditions it's impossible to fall unless you climb up on to the ledge and do your own kamikaze dive over the edge. That realised, I managed to peek over the edge into the abyss. The feeling was extraordinary: the noise was deafening, the water falling so fast that it created clouds of spray. It was so exhilirating being inches from death and destruction (and yet so wonderfully safe), that I hardly noticed that my foot was hurting.

I had forgotten to bring the right footwear and gashed my foot on the scramble across the rocks. The cut was quite deep and the scar remains, but I am proud to show it – it's my badge of honour. ●

WHEN TO GO
It is only possible to swim the Devil's Pool between August and December or January, depending on water levels.

GETTING THERE
Flights (British Airways and South African Airways) operate daily between South Africa's Johannesburg Airport and Zambia's Livingstone Airport. Livingstone Airport is 20 minutes from the Falls Resort.

ORGANISING YOUR TRIP
Swimming outings are organised by the Tongabezi Lodge (www.tongabezi.com).

COST
Tongabezi's 'Breezer' visits cost around £40.

AM I UP TO IT?
Contrary to appearances, swimming the Devil's Pool isn't dangerous, but you will need a strong head.

Running on ice

Alf Anderson gets high on speed trying out
the world's fastest winter sport.

WHAT	HOW LONG
Bobsleighing on an Olympic track	About 60 seconds

WHERE	THRILL FACTOR
Park City, Utah, USA	● ● ● ● ●

The last thing I heard before setting off down the Olympic bobsleigh course at Park City was 'Don't worry, it'll all be over in a minute'. These words of encouragement came from beneath the helmet of the guy in front of me, squeezed between my legs rather too tightly for comfort. The intimacy of our positions – along with that of the unknown girl sitting behind me – was quickly forgotten as we got moving, led by a professional bobsleigh driver up front in charge of the Heath Robinson-esque array of handles and wires that controlled – we assumed – our sled.

Bobsleighs got their name from the fact that in the early days riders would 'bob' back and forth on their sleigh at the top of a run to get the thing moving; none of that for us – we were given a push-off by a team of track-side assistants wearing spiked boots. All was quite genteel at first; the sled's runners glided smoothly across the hard blue ice, a breeze started to whisk past my helmet and, very briefly, there was time to think, 'Hey, this isn't *too* bad…'

And then we hit the first real slope, and it began to sink in: I was separated by nothing more than a few thin slivers of highly polished metal from the most friction-free natural surface on the planet, and we were heading steeply downhill for the next mile.

MISSILE IMPOSSIBLE

The first bend was fun as the sleigh gained acceleration and slid up and around to careen back on to the following straight. Our speed continued to increase, the air whistling past became a roar, and the whole machine began to shake and rattle as 40, 50, 60 and then 70mph was reached.

By the second bend I was under no illusion that the next 50 seconds or so were going to be frighteningly fast – and then time suddenly became suspended. By the time we reached a top speed of 80mph-plus, we were hitting bends like a missile, hammering into the arc of the curve and thrashing our way violently around it at almost 90 degrees from the horizontal.

You're advised to keep your head down for the entire length of the run; you're pulling up to five Gs on the bends, the kind of G-force you'd experience in a fighter jet, and trying to lift or turn

> 'WE WERE HITTING BENDS LIKE A MISSILE, HAMMERING INTO THE CURVE AND THRASHING OUR WAY VIOLENTLY AROUND IT AT ALMOST 90 DEGREES FROM THE HORIZONTAL.'

your head is almost impossible. No wonder the sleigh driver has a neck like a bull.

FASTER, FASTER!

By this point, I was somewhere between shrieking 'Faster, faster!' and 'Slow down, slow down!' but since only one of those two options was possible I sat back and revelled in the adrenaline rush of it all. The thrill of the speed, the noise, the rushing and clattering was like nothing I'd ever felt. As we hurtled past each curve, we were blatted around inside the sleigh like pinballs, and every sense was on overload.

When my extended minute finally drew to a close, when the gradient lessened and the sled's brakes slammed into the ice, the feeling was a curious mix of relief that we'd survived and disappointment that it was over – a desire to never, ever do it again, mixed with an urge to do it all over again right away.

A bobsleigh ride is not actually as death-defying an adventure as it seems to either participant and onlooker, but it's still one of the biggest sub-zero buzzes you're ever likely to experience. And, best of all, all you need to do is sit back and enjoy it. ●

WHEN TO GO
October to the end of February.

GETTING THERE
Park City Ski Resort (www.parkcitymountain. com) is a half-hour drive from Salt Lake City International Airport; there are shuttle buses between city and airport, and the resort.

ORGANISING YOUR TRIP
Contact Utah Olympic Park (www.utah olympicpark.com) for more information; be sure to reserve your ride in advance.

COST
$200 per person; includes a safety talk before the ride and use of a helmet.

AM I UP TO IT?
Bobsleigh rides are not for people with chronic neck, back, heart or kidney problems, anyone recovering from surgery or suffering from high blood pressure, or pregnant women.

MORE LIKE THIS
The bobsleigh track at Olympiaworld (www.olympiaworld.at) in Innsbruck, Austria, and the Olympic run at La Plagne (www.la-plagne.com), in the French Alps, are both open to the public in season.

FOR REFERENCE
The feel-good movie *Cool Runnings* (1993) – tag line 'One Dream. Four Jamaicans. Twenty Below Zero' – is rather loosely based on the true story of the first Jamaican bobsleigh team, which competed in the 1988 Olympic Games.

The International Bobsleigh Federation (www.fibt.com) is the official home of bobsleigh and skeleton sports (skeleton is like the luge but with head, rather than feet, first).

Kite kicks

Cyrus Shahrad gets board in the Red Sea.

WHAT	HOW LONG
Kiteboarding	One week

WHERE	THRILL FACTOR
Abu Soma, Red Sea	● ● ● ● ●

It was somehow right that our kiteboarding instructor's nickname was 'Goose'. It wasn't just the facial resemblance, though the beady eyes and broom moustache were certainly reminiscent of Maverick's dapper but ultimately doomed wingman in *Top Gun*; no, there was something about the tongue-in-cheek way he ran his watersports centre (like a military boot camp) that attracted comparisons.

Within moments of arriving at the beach huts in the Red Sea resort of Abu Soma, Goose was barking orders into his walkie talkie and chucking waterproof bags of equipment to the boys and girls under his command – perma-tanned youths with the buffness and lazy bravado of *Shipwrecked* contestants. They, in turn, guided us through the process of preparing kites like the ones we could see on the horizon – colourful canopies effortlessly carrying their board-riders at scary speeds over the turquoise sea.

RISING HIGH

The stratospheric rise of kiteboarding has made such scenes commonplace on coastlines the world over. Its popularity isn't hard to fathom: wind permitting, kiteboarders can plot their own courses over seas, rivers or lakes (something unthinkable for waterskiers or wakeboarders, at the mercy of whoever is driving the boat). This is done by means of a finely tuned system linking the rider's harness to a seven- to 12-metre kite hovering up to 27 metres above them – the slightest tug on the control bar sends the canopy soaring one way or the other, and the rider with it.

The equipment doesn't come cheap – kite and board starts at £750 – but that hasn't stopped kiteboarding becoming the world's fastest-growing watersport (the first kiteboard only came on the market in 1998). The environmental demands of the sport mean that it can't be performed everywhere – consistent cross-shore winds are required, as well as uninterrupted expanses of water – but those places that do fit the bill are becoming meccas for a new breed of sporting pilgrim.

SAIL PATH

The graceful spectacle of the kiteboarders belied the exhausting effort of rigging a kite, especially for a green-gilled first timer like myself. I was

paired with an enthusiastic American auditor called David and given the task of inflating the struts of its 12-metre wingspan – with the thing flapping and snarling like a wounded pterodactyl the whole time – while he walked the 20-metre lines along the beach and checked for frays and tangles. It was then carefully wound and wrapped into a single bag for a fuss-free water launch, a process that takes seasoned boarders ten minutes, but which David and I managed to stretch out into an hour.

'Lock and load,' shouted Goose, and his platoon began stacking kites, boards, and bags filled with sandwiches and sun cream, into the outboard motor dinghy bobbing in the harbour. The rest of us lined up by the water's edge, resisting the urge to salute as Goose walked down the line handing out helmets, safety leashes and lifejackets; moments later we were sitting on board and skipping over the ocean, conversation curtailed by the roar of the engine as the hotel retreated behind us.

We sped through the windsurf area first, carefully avoiding the paths of sails zipping across the water like upright insect wings. The sea was

'NOTHING COULD HAVE PREPARED ME FOR THE POWER OF THE KITE. WHEN I SWUNG IT TOO HARD, I FLEW SEVERAL FEET OUT OF WATER.'

deepening beneath us but still bright and clear enough to make out clusters of rock and coral, and fleeting schools of colourful fish. From here, we entered kiteboarding territory, our mouths hanging open in a mix of awe and horror at how aggressively the riders seemed to be thrown around by their canopies, occasionally launching into aerial spins and flips so high that I kept thinking: 'They're going to get sucked into the sky like the guy on You Tube who gets caught in an air pocket.'

Our driver killed the engine as we approached the pontoon, passengers disembarking directly into water no more than waist deep and warm as bath water despite it being late November. 'We call this the Oakley Graveyard,' Goose remarked as he walked the lines of the first kite backwards from the pontoon, 'because of how many pairs of sunglasses end up lost at the bottom of the sea.'

With the rush of what sounded like a plane taking off, the first kite swung into the air – all 12 metres of its bright green awning rippling high overhead – as though it were the most natural thing on earth; which it was, I suppose, although looking down I couldn't help feeling there was something less than natural about the elaborate harness that was about to connect me to it, or the twin-tipped fibreglass boards that were being unpacked on the pontoon.

BACK TO BASICS

'Don't panic,' Goose was saying, not even looking at the kite as he unclipped it from his harness and prepared to attach it to mine. 'Just remember what Carrie taught you.'

Ah yes, Carrie. How simple it had all seemed on that first afternoon in Abu Soma, when I'd stood on the desert's edge and been taught the basics of kite handling, with the sun setting behind the crimson Sinai mountains and lending the scene the air of a flashback long before it was one.

'THE KITE WAS FLAPPING AND SNARLING LIKE A WOUNDED PTERODACTYL.'

Carrie had explained to me the three-dimensional wind window and how the kite operates within it – sitting naturally at 12 o'clock (directly overhead) and picking up speed as it swoops back up from nine or three o'clock (ground level on the port or starboard sides respectively). She showed me how to manipulate the lines for launching and landing, how to swing the kite through figures of eight to maintain a constant speed, and how to bring myself from a seated to a standing position with one mighty swoop across the window – something that left me scrambling over the sand before collapsing to my knees, the kite crashing to earth with a thud. How we laughed.

THE THEORY BEFORE THE PRACTICE

Later, sitting down in a café, we'd carefully gone through the British Kite Surfing Association (BKSA) guidelines – a long-winded legal requirement outlining the laws of both man (starboard has right of way over port) and nature (warm and cold weather fronts, high and low pressure areas, how

and why the wind works). All of which seemed to imply that messing around with kites in the middle of the ocean was a dangerous pursuit, and one that shouldn't be undertaken without a thorough understanding of the risks involved.

As a result, there's a certain amount of friction between kiteboarders and windsurfers, who keep to their own area in Abu Soma and tend to view the likes of Goose and Carrie with the same snorting disdain that skiers once reserved for snowboarders. It's not surprising, given that kiteboarding has many of the same attributes – the baggy clothes, the soul brother lingo and the swelling litany of aerial tricks and rotations.

And daredevil behaviour is the main bone of contention: even if most accidents involve lines rather than kites, and happen on land rather than in the water, kiteboarders have a tendency to hurl themselves recklessly into the air (occasionally crashing into buildings or landing on other people) – making them, and their recreation, look very dangerous indeed.

All of which weighed heavily on my mind as I lowered myself into a seated position in the

water, one hand on the bar to keep the kite at 12 o'clock as the other fumbled with the board. Feet finally secured in the straps, I looked back at the kite and found myself blinking away sunlight – Oakley Graveyard or not, a pair of sunglasses wouldn't have gone amiss at this point.

RUSH HOUR

I listened for the wind whistling in both ears, a good sign that I was facing directly downwind, and pointed my leading foot slightly forward. Then a deep breath before bringing the kite down to around ten o'clock and, with a pull on the side of the bar, swinging it across the wind window to two. Goose's shouts of encouragement competed against the roar of the kite and the high-pitched rush of water that peeled away from my board as it jolted suddenly to life, lines tightening and lifting me

to my feet, my shadow rippling over the surface of the sea as I sped away from the pontoon. The rush was ten times more powerful than I'd ever imagined it would be: I was up and kiteboarding on my first attempt.

All right, so it wasn't exactly my first attempt. The time between Goose hooking the kite to my harness and me soaring away from the group was a morning spent learning the less-than-subtle art of body dragging (allowing the kite to tow a person across the surface of the sea, essential in escaping deep water or retrieving lost boards). Even after I was allowed to strap a board to my feet, there were still hours of false hopes and miserable failures, of lines becoming tangled and kites crashing into the ocean. But that moment, when it came, was one of unmitigated joy – a moment that, in a final tribute to *Top Gun*, really did take my breath away. ●

WHEN TO GO
Abu Soma is a year-round destination, almost constantly blessed with the cross-shore winds necessary for kite-boardin, but temperatures may be uncomfortably high in July and August.

GETTING THERE
Fly to Hurghada; there are 40-minute bus transfers to the resort.

ORGANISING YOUR TRIP
www.markwarner.co.uk/sun/egypt/abu-soma.

COST
Flights, transfers and half-board accommodation at Abu Soma cost £688 per adult per week based on two sharing; BKSA-standard kiteboarding tuition costs £240 for parts one and two (or £120 each), and covers everything from basic kite handling to board riding over the course of four three-hour sessions. Extra private tuition is £30 per hour.

AM I UP TO IT?
Almost everyone should be able to stand and surf, if not turn around, after 12 hours of tuition; that said, waterskiers or wakeboarders will reap the rewards, and any kind of board sport experience helps with balance.

MORE LIKE THIS
European kiteboarding destinations include Tarifa in Spain, where the Dragon Kite School (www.dragonkiteschool.com) runs courses, and St-Pierre-la-Mer in the south of France, where Sud Windsports (www.sudwindsports. com) operates a beginner's programme. Closer to home, Surface2Air Sports (www.s2as.com) runs courses in Folkestone, Kent and Poole, Dorset. For a list of kiteboarding schools worldwide, see www.kitesurfingschool.org.

FOR REFERENCE
The British Kite Surfing Association (www.britishkitesurfingassociation.co.uk).

Fire water

Robert Twigger takes on the world's wildest white water.

WHAT	HOW LONG
Multi-rapid white-water rafting	8 days
WHERE	**THRILL FACTOR**
Zambezi river, Zambia	● ● ● ● ●

Said Dan, our Kiwi raft guide: 'You're about to undertake the white-water equivalent of Everest, except on Everest the guides get paid an awful lot more.'

Dan was short, but broad; he had the kind of heft to height ratio that can likely only be attained by navigating rapids for a living. The six of us gathered in a ranch-style hotel in Livingstone hung on Dan's every word. He was, after all, the man who was going to help us survive the mighty Zambezi. The briefing over, Dan handed out lucky wrist charms to protect us from drowning. Had he handed out a batch of lucky spandex thongs, we would probably have donned those too.

Our jitters were easily justified: we were about to set off on a descent of the Zambezi river, via some of world's most extreme white-water rapids. Over half of the rapids below Victoria Falls are classified by the British Canoe Association as Grade 5: 'extremely difficult, long and violent rapids, steep gradients, big drops and pressure areas'. To put this into perspective, Grade 6 rapids are considered 'unrunnable'. The Zambezi has several Grade 6 rapids – one of which is nicknamed 'Commercial Suicide' – and these must be 'portaged' (walked around).

Supposedly, like Everest, the Zambezi has an 'easy' line to take; and the rapids, though huge and noisy, are not made lethal by underwater rocks lying in wait to snag a swimming body. But I couldn't help wondering how much comfort this offers when faced with a wall of falling water reminiscent of a collapsing skyscraper.

RAPID REACTION

We started just below Victoria Falls, by most criteria the world's largest waterfall. The current was whip-fast and our paddling felt as effective as the flapping wings of a baby sparrow trying to extricate itself from a storm drain in full flood.

Almost instantly, it seemed, we were at the first rapid. I failed to follow Dan's bellowed instructions and we hit a wall: a huge rock wall – precisely the kind of wall you don't want to smash into in a raft. Luckily, we merely got bounced about a little – and very wet.

Earlier, Dan had told us: 'My first season here I lost my bag, so all I had was shorts and a T-shirt

'JUST AS MY PULSE RATE WAS THREATENING TO DROP BACK INTO DOUBLE FIGURES, A GIANT WAVE CRASHED OVER US FOR WHAT FELT LIKE SEVERAL MINUTES – IT WAS ACTUALLY MORE LIKE EIGHT SECONDS.'

and that was enough.' 'Well, yes,' I thought, 'perhaps it would have been enough if you'd been sitting at the back.' Up front, as I was, you are a sponge for every errant wave. The canyon of the Zambezi just below Vic Falls is sunless and deep, and soon I was shivering in my shorts and short-sleeved shirt – wimps like me are better off in a thin paddling jacket or even a cagoule with rolled-up sleeves.

The rapids kept on coming, and we kept on shooting them. Then, just as my pulse rate was

threatening to drop back into double figures, a giant wave crashed over us for what felt like several minutes. (It was actually more like eight seconds, but if you've ever wiped out in a big wave while surfing, you'll appreciate that eight seconds can be a very long time under a tsunami of white water.)

When the spray cleared I saw that we were a couple of oars short: two of my fellow paddlers had been sucked into the foaming torrent. Nice to have known you, I thought.

A second later, I spotted them, bobbing along with the current like seals, and we soon dragged them aboard.

PLAY MISTY FOR ME

At night, the camp routine revolved around food and drink: curry with popadoms, beef and Yorkshire pudding – not an instant-noodle hash in sight. Then there was the beer and the beatbox, turning the camp into a beach party. It summed up the strangeness of rafting in foreign climes, stripping the location of its uniqueness and turning it into a Platonically ideal rafting trip; one endless river where only the rapids change, and the thrills are interspersed with barbies and booze round the campfire.

Back on the river we portaged Upper Moemba rapid: a stark, wide waterfall that drowned out our voices and (even though it was hundreds of feet below us) buffeted our faces with fine mist.

Eagles had been our overhead companions since the beginning, but as we descended we began to see more wildlife. There were crocodiles, black and lazy, sunbathing on the

rocks and slithering into the water as we advanced. As I leaped out of the boat to tie up, a tiny croc slid off not three feet away. I would have felt brave were it not for the fact that, had I seen it, I never would have stepped out of the boat. On the bank, great packs of baboons kept pace with us and, at night, monkeys jumped from tree to tree around the camp.

Most of the rapids have vivid, often darkly suggestive, nicknames such as Devil's Toilet Hole, Oblivion and Stairway to Heaven. Round about the fifth day, we approached Ghost Rider. This is the longest, most sustained dragon's back of a wave train on the river. It is a long sequence of high waves that you aim to ride up before plunging down into the watery tumult. And then up again… and down again.

With ordinary rapids there may be one or two points of interest – massive waves or scary holes – but on Ghost Rider you mount the aquatic equivalent of a Disneyland rollercoaster. It was almost too much fun, too easily; we didn't even have to queue up. I had begun to keep my eyes open and read the way the stream went, digging my paddle in so it made a difference instead of just biting air. I was also learning to predict lifts and dips and bracing myself against them, which gave me extra confidence that I wouldn't be thrown out.

The river widened and slowed, and our adrenaline levels plunged accordingly. A pod of hippos (the Zambezi resident most feared by the local population) regaled us with toothy yawns, as if to confirm that the fun was over. At journey's end there was a chopper waiting for us: more luxury of the kind that's too delicious to wriggle away from. Our pilot had once flown the Queen, he told us. Twenty minutes later we were back where we started, hovering over the spectacular width of Victoria Falls and its arc of crashing water.

Next time, I mused, there'll be no softness, no luxury. I'll do it in a Michelin man suit; just hurl myself in and take everything the river can throw at me. Dan, the raft guide, heard me out and said, 'Might work,' before turning back to the list in front of him. The next group of people he'd been charged with keeping alive were due the next day. ●

WHEN TO GO
Trips run in the dry season, October to May.

GETTING THERE
Fly via Johannesburg to Livingstone, Zambia. Try Ebookers (www.ebookers.com) for cheap flights.

ORGANISING YOUR TRIP
Either ask about raft trips at Jollyboys hostel, Livingstone (www.backpackzambia.com) or check out Water by Nature (www.waterby nature.com), the outfit we travelled with.

COST
The cost with Water by Nature is £1,295 including hotels and a helicopter ride.

AM I UP TO IT?
Water by Nature accommodates clients at all levels of fitness, but the stronger you are the more fun you'll have. You also need to be mentally tough: rapids this extreme can be terrifying – and potentially dangerous.

MORE LIKE THIS
Go to the Water by Nature site for similar trips in Nepal, Turkey and the USA.

FOR REFERENCE
For a rafting film with whitewater sequences, try The River Wild; for an IMAX spectacular, watch Mystery of the Nile, about a descent of the dangerous Blue Nile. The book of the same is by Richard Bangs.

Tour operators

USEFUL ORGANISATIONS & SCHEMES

Several tourism bodies and web-based firms group together small, specialist firms, including adventure travel operators. The not-for-profit **Association of Independent Tour Operators** (AITO; www.aito.com) has an easily searchable website and an accent on financial protection and responsible tourism. The website of the mainstream **Association of British Travel Agents** (ABTA; www.abta.org) is also worth a look – not least because members include the two megafirms that handle most UK travel: Tui and Thomas Cook Group own dozens of sub-companies that offer adventure trips. A third trade organisation worth noting is the **Travel Trust Association** (www.traveltrust.co.uk).

Air Travel Organisers' Licensing (ATOL) is a Civil Aviation Authority protection scheme for air holidays and flights. It protects travellers from losing money or being stranded if their operator goes bust.

If you book online, paying by credit card ensures you get your money back if your company goes out of business – debit cards offer no equivalent protection.

Websites such as www.responsibletravel.com and www.gapyear.com are useful portals for exploring travel ideas, but note that they are commercial enterprises. Year Out Group (www.yearoutgroup.org), is a not-for-profit organisation.

Dealing directly with local tour firms is often a way of spending money where it is most needed.

Independent-minded travellers can easily book flights to, say, Kenya or Argentina, then contract local services from mountain guides to 4WD expeditions. However, as there is little international accreditation, there is an element of risk in this. Ask around the traveller community and at national park offices and official visitor organisations, and consult well-reputed guidebooks for recommendations. Always check local guides' training and qualifications, particularly for mountain explorations. All scuba guides should have professional PADI certification.

Local firms may have limited or no insurance (see page 249) and you risk being left out of pocket if the company you have booked with goes bankrupt.

Some of our trips include wildlife watching. Animals can be unpredictable and dangerous so always go with an organised group and/or accredited guide.

ALL-ROUNDERS

Activities Abroad Adventure holidays worldwide, including snowmobiling, canyoning and skydiving trips. 01670 789 991, www.activities abroad.com

Audley Travel Offers journeys around the world, from snorkelling in Madagascar to dune-boarding in Auckland via horseriding and safaris. 01993 838600, www.audleytravel.com

Black Tomato Runs a variety of trips for adrenalin junkies and other intrepid travellers. 020 7426 9888, www.blacktomato.co.uk

Cox & Kings Having begun sorting out the logistics for the Foot Guards back in 1758, Cox & Kings now arranges tours and adventures across the world, from India and the Far East to Latin America and Europe. 020 7873 5000, www.coxandkings.co.uk.

Discover Adventure Activity, adventure and fundraising trips all over the world. 01722 718444, www.discoveradventure.com.

Distinctive Americas Specialist concentrating on the Americas, Caribbean and Polar Regions. 01844 347005, www.distinctive americas.com

Dragoman Overland operator specialising in global adventures and journeys. 01728 861133, www.dragoman.com

Exodus Specialists in walking, cycling, winter and wildlife holidays. 020 8675 5550, www.exodus.co.uk

Explore Small group adventure holiday operator selling tours worldwide, including astronomy and eclipse tours, as well as European cycling and a new brochure of rail journeys. 0844 499 0901, www.explore.co.uk

1st Class Holidays Trains, mountains, horseriding, whales, polar bears and more in America, Canada, New Zealand and the South Pacific. 0161 877 0433, www.1stclassholidays.com

High Places Expeditions all around the world. 0845 257 7500, www.highplaces.co.uk

Journey Latin America Latin America specialist offering group and tailor-made holidays, and flights-only trips. 020 8747 8315, www.journeylatinamerica.co.uk

Last Frontiers Latin America
Tailor-made travel to South America. 01296 653000, www.lastfrontiers.com

On the Go Tours Cruises around the Galapagos, tours to South America (including to Machu Picchu and the Amazon) and China (including Tibet), as well as Trans-Siberian journeys. 020 7371 1113, www.onthegotours.com

Ramblers Worldwide Holidays Walking holidays that include railways, cruises, skiing and special interests. 01707 331133, www.ramblersholidays.co.uk

Wild about Africa Guided trips to Namibia and beyond. 020 8758 4717, www.wildaboutafrica.com

Wilderness Journeys Worldwide adventure holidays, including specialist trips for families. 0131 625 6635, www.wilderness journeys.com

Wild Frontiers Small tours and tailor-made adventure holidays: trekking, horseriding, skiing (in Iran, Kashmir and the Georgian Caucasus). 020 7736 3968, www.wildfrontiers.co.uk

CYCLING/MOUNTAIN BIKING
See also **Explore** (p246).

ATG Footloose & ATG Freewheeling Walking and cycling routes through Europe. 01865 315678, www.atg-oxford.com

Bents Bicycle & Walking Tours Cycling and walking holidays in Europe. 01568 780800, www.bentstours.com

Inntravel Cycling & More Independent cycling trips in Europe. 01653 617906, www.inntravel.co.uk

HORSERIDING
See also **Audley Travel** (p246), **Discover Adventure** (p246),

Discover the World (p248), **Journey Latin America** (p246), **Last Frontiers Latin America** (above) and **Wild Frontiers** (above).

American Round-Up A specialist for ranch-riding holidays in the United States and Canada, white-water rafting and other adventures. 01404 881777, www.americanroundup.com

Archipelago Azores Tailor-made holidays on the Azores, with options that include horseriding, whale-watching, swimming with dolphins, cycling, walks. 01768 775672, www.azoreschoice.com.

Bushbaby Travel Horseriding holidays and safaris to South Africa and the Indian Ocean. 0870 850 9103, www.bush baby.travel

Equine Adventures Riding holidays to Africa, America, Asia, Europe and the Middle East. 0845 130 6981, www.equineadventures.co.uk

In the Saddle Organises a wide range of riding holidays across the globe. 01299 272 997, www.inthesaddle.com

Inntravel Riding Holidays for All Trails and centre-based riding for all abilities in the most unspoiled corners of Europe. 01653 617930, www.inntravel.co.uk

KE Adventure Trekking, climbing, biking and exploring Europe, Africa and the Americas. 01768 773966, www.keadventure.com

Ride World Wide Riding holidays and horse safaris in locations all around the world. 01837 82544, www.rideworldwide.com

MOUNTAINEERING
Collett's Mountain Holidays Summer and winter holidays in the Italian Dolomites, and the French and Spanish Pyrenees. 01763 289660, www.colletts.co.uk

RAIL
See also **Audley Travel** (p246), **Explore** (p246), **On the Go Tours** (above) and **Ramblers Worldwide Holidays** (above).

Ffestiniog Travel Escorted or unescorted rail travel in 30 countries – specialists with over 30 years in the business. 01766 772030, www.festtravel.co.uk

Great Rail Journeys 22 fully escorted holidays by rail all over the world. 01904 521950, www.greatrail.com

Railselect Design your own rail journey and get help with hotels, transfers and itineraries. 01904 521921, www.railselect.com

The Russia Experience The Trans-Siberian Express. 020 8566 8846, www.trans-siberian.co.uk

Treyn Holidays Affordable rail trips around Europe. 01904 734939, www.treynholidays.co.uk

SAFARI
See also **Audley Travel** (p246), **1st Class Holidays** (p246), **Journey Latin America** (p246) and **Last Frontiers Latin America** (above).

Bales Worldwide Africa specialist in tailor-made and escorted journeys to over 50 countries worldwide. 08456 345112, www.balesworldwide.com

Frontier Wildlife Fly-driving and touring, wildlife and nature safaris in Canada, sub-Saharan Africa and the Polar Regions. 020 8776 8709, www.frontier-wildlife.co.uk

Naturetrek – Sub-Saharan Africa Expertly guided natural history tours and safaris to the best wildlife areas in Sub-Saharan Africa. 01962 733051, www.naturetrek.co.uk

Okavango Tours & Safaris – Africa Our Way Tailor-made itineraries. 020 8347 4030, www.okavango.com

Rainbow Tours Small-group trips, nature, bird and wildlife safaris, and honeymoons in destinations across southern and East Africa, and the Indian Ocean. 020 7226 1004, www.rainbowtours.co.uk

Somak Worldwide Award-winning experts on travelling to Africa. 020 8423 3000, www.somak.co.uk

Tribes – Gorilla Safaris Two specialist departures a year to trek gorillas, plus tailor-made itineraries. 01728 685971, www.tribes.co.uk

Volcanoes Safaris Specialists in mountain gorilla safaris in Uganda and Rwanda. 0870 870 8480, www.volcanoessafaris.com

SAILING & BOATING

See also **Audley Travel** (p246), **1st Class Holidays** (p246), **Journey Latin America** (p246), **Last Frontiers Latin America** (p247), **Rainbow Tours** (above) and **Ramblers Worldwide Holidays** (p247).

Arblaster & Clarke Wine Cruises Cruise on your own private yacht in the company of a small party of like-minded wine and culture enthusiasts. 01730 263111, www.winetours.co.uk

Archipelago Azores The Azores specialist offers tailor-made holidays to the islands. 01768 775672, www.azoreschoice.com

Collette Worldwide Holidays River cruises in China, Russia or around the glaciers of Antarctica. 0800 804 8701, www.collette worldwide.com

Flotilla Sailing Holidays Flotilla-sailing holiday specialist giving ordinary people the opportunity to have a go at sailing in the sun. 020 8459 8787, www.sailing holidays.com

Frontier Canada A range of cruises and boat trips to Quebec, Newfoundland and the Arctic. Choose from a range of vessels including a Tall Ship. 020 8776 8709, www.frontier-travel.co.uk

Polar Journeys 2008-2009 Organises polar expeditions in both the Arctic and Antarctic. 01737 218800, www.discover-the-world.co.uk/antarctica

Treyn Holidays – River Cruising Rail journeys combined with a cruise along some of Europe's finest rivers. 01904 734925, www.treynholidays.co.uk

Sunvil Sailing Holidays Learn how to sail and skipper a yacht around the Ionian Islands as part of a small flotilla of vessels. 020 8758 4780, www.sunvil.co.uk

Veloso Tours Trips around South America – including cruises through the fjords of Tierra del Fuego and Patagonia. 020 8762 0616, www.veloso.com

SKIING & WINTER SPORTS

See also **Last Frontiers Latin America** (p247), **Ramblers Worldwide Holidays** (p247) and **Wild Frontiers** (p247).

Discover the World Husky sledging, ice hotels, Northern lights, polar bears, skiing in Lapland, snow-mobiling, Arctic and Antarctic expeditions, and whale-watching. 01737 218800, www.discover-the-world.co.uk

Ski Weekend The ultimate short-break skiing specialist. 01392 878 353, www.skiweekend.com

TREKKING

See also **Audley Travel** (p246), **Discover the World** (above), **Explore** (p246), **1st Class Holidays** (p246), **Journey Latin America** (p246), **Last Frontiers Latin America** (p247) and **Ramblers Worldwide Holidays** (p247).

Archipelago Azores The Azores specialist offers tailor-made holidays to the islands, including guided and self-guided walking tours. 01768 775672, www.azoreschoice.com

Discover Adventure Including Sahara camel trek, Patagonia, Great Wall of China, Cuba, Hadrian's Wall and a Masai volcano trek. 01722 718444, www.discoveradventure.com

Explore Family Adventures Small-group family adventures worldwide. 0844 499 0901, www.explore.co.uk

KE Adventure Travel Treks, climbs and mountain biking for all levels. 017687 73966, www.keadventure.com

Ramblers Countrywide Walking holidays in Britain and Ireland. 01707 386800, www.ramblerscountrywide.co.uk

Robin Pope Safaris A family-run business that organises safaris in Zambia's national parks. http://robinpopesafaris.net

Walks Worldwide Walking tours for all ages, group sizes and fitness levels. 01524 242000, www.walks worldwide.com

WATERSPORTS

See also **Audley Travel** (p246) and **Discover the World** (above).

Dive Worldwide Tailor-made scuba-diving holidays around the world. 0845 130 6980, www.diveworldwide.com

Regaldive Worldwide Learn to dive and diving holidays in the Red Sea and worldwide. 01353 659999, www.regaldive.co.uk

Wilderness Scotland Specialists in small group sea-kayaking and canoeing holidays in Scotland. Some international trips are also offered. 0131 625 6635, www.wildernessscotland.com

Travel checklist

IS MY DESTINATION SAFE?

It's important to research your destination thoroughly before you book your trip. No matter how adventurous you are, entering a war zone isn't a great idea, for example. The Foreign & Commonwealth Office website (www.fco.gov.uk) has up-to-date information on political situations, health issues and crime scenes worldwide; travellers from the US should go to www.travel.state.gov. It is also wise to buy a good guidebook to help you with your planning and to inform you about local laws and customs.

Some of our featured trips are safe only at certain times of year. Consult our 'When to go' information for general guidelines and check with your tour operator or local authorities for planning specific trips.

DO I NEED A VISA?

The website of the British Foreign & Commonwealth Office (www.fco.gov.uk) is constantly being updated with information about the latest visa and entry requirements; it is searchable by country. Some countries stipulate that you must obtain your visa before arrival – these include China, India and the United States. Issues that might possibly affect entry into a country are certain medical conditions and/or reliance on particular types of medication, prior criminal convictions and stamps from previous visits abroad. Contact the relevant foreign embassy before you travel. Some visas are exorbitantly expensive (those for travel in Russia, Mongolia and Zambia, for example), so you should make sure you've factored this into your overall budget.

DO I HAVE A VALID PASSPORT?

Some countries require a specific number of months' validity on your passport when you travel, which means you might need to order a new passport in advance of your trip. Some also require a minimum number of blank pages in your passport so they can stamp it – check with the relevant foreign embassy well before you travel. It's always a good idea to carry a photocopy of your passport while abroad, and to keep the copy separate from all your other valuables.

DO I NEED TRAVEL INSURANCE?

It's absolutely vital to ensure you have adequate travel insurance before you set off. Tour companies may require you to take out their insurance, and include it in the price; if, not, or if you are travelling independently, you will need a personal travel-specific policy. In either case, it is essential to check in advance that the policy covers all the specific activities that you plan to undertake, for the whole time you are away. Standard policies often exclude adventure and winter sports so you may need to upgrade your cover or change insurers.

Ensure that benefits include: health care for injury or sudden illness; 24-hour emergency service and assistance; personal liability in case you're sued for causing injury or damaging property; cancellation or cutting your trip short; and lost and stolen possessions.

Some insurance policies also offer financial protection should your travel company or airline go bankrupt before your trip. However, if your travel company is protected by ATOL (Air Travel Organisers' Licensing; www.atol.org.uk), the company is obliged to find you an alternative holiday or flight should your airline close down before you travel. If your travel company goes under due to the financial troubles of an airline, ATOL will refund the price of your holiday.

ARE MY ROUTINE IMMUNISATIONS UP-TO-DATE?

Many diseases that have been eradicated in your home country may not have been eradicated where you're going. Visit your GP and check that your routine immunisations are all up-to-date well in advance of your trip.

DO I NEED ANY SPECIAL IMMUNISATIONS?

As soon as possible before you travel, preferably two months, visit your GP and find out which extra immunisations you need. Some courses of medication (for instance, anti-malarials) will need to be started before you travel. The World Health Organisation (www.who.int) and the Centre for Disease Control & Prevention (wwwn.cdc.gov/travel) have excellent websites packed with information on worldwide health issues.

At the moment, you will need to have a vaccination against yellow fever if you visit Brazil and are planning to visit the Amazon region or the north or centre-west of the country. Anti-malaria tablets are recommended for travel in many tropical regions, with the exact medication differing according to country. It is also worthwhile being immunised against hepatitis and typhoid. Take a good mosquito repellent and anti-histamine cream.

The NHS and NHS Scotland websites (www.nhs.uk/Conditions/Travel-health and www.fitfortravel.scot.nhs.uk respectively) contain useful maps and information, as does the National Travel Health Network (www.nathnac.org).

WHAT SHOULD I DO ABOUT MY MEDICATION?

Obtain all necessary prescription medicines before you leave. In case of strict border control, it is wise to keep prescription medication in its original packaging and to carry a copy of the prescription signed by your GP.

WHAT EQUIPMENT DO I NEED?

If you are taking part in an organised trip a checklist of equipment will be supplied – make sure you read this carefully. Some equipment will be supplied by your travel company, but some items – notably specialist clothing or bedding – may well not be included (and can hike up the price if you forget to bring them).

Good boots, a strong rucksack and a daypack are useful for most trips; sandals to change into, a torch for nocturnal trips to the loo,

and breathable clothing are also recommended. If you're heading for cold climates, get a serious hat, gloves, socks and thermal base layers. Good outlets for adventure travel equipment are Blacks, Cotswold, Millets and YHA shops; online retailers are very competitive.

If you are travelling independently be sure to research what specialist technical and safety equipment you need for your chosen activity.

When packing, plan for the worst conditions you are likely to encounter, having consulted park staff or other local authorities. Never skimp on food or water.

WHAT SHOULD BE INCLUDED IN MY FIRST-AID KIT?

A good first-aid kit should include: adhesive tape, antiseptic wound cleanser, bandages, emollient eye drops, insect repellent, insect bite treatment, nasal decongestant, oral rehydration salts, paracetamol, scissors, safety pins, sterile dressing and a thermometer. Depending on your specific destination and individual needs you may also want to carry: anti-diarrhoeal medication, antifungal powder, anti-malarial medication, condoms, prescription medication, sedatives, sterile syringes and needles, and water disinfectant.

HOW MUCH MONEY WILL I NEED?

Before your trip, buy some local currency (you may need to order less common currencies a week or so in advance). If you're taking travellers' cheques, write down the cheque numbers and keep them separately. It's also wise to check that your credit card is valid in your country of travel, and to note down the expiry date and credit card number and leave them safely at

home. Make sure you take enough money to cover your trip and emergencies. If you are taking part in an organised trip, many costs will be covered by your original fee, but some things might not be included – for instance, tips for staff, entrance fees to parks, even meals and accommodation – check all your holiday details carefully before you travel.

IS MY TRIP RESPONSIBLE?

Unlike, say, the food industry, the tourism sector has no recognised, non-commercial body controlling its environmental policies. The reason for this is two-fold: one, travel is the most global of industries and therefore almost impossible to govern, or to encourage to self-govern, in any seriously sustainable fashion; two, it is not in the interest of countries, airlines, tour operators or travel agencies to introduce regulations that will damage profitability. In general, terms such as 'green' and 'eco' pegged to hotels, tours and modes of transport should be treated with suspicion.

That said, you can encourage good practice by looking closely at the environmental policies of tour operators and, of course, the political and environmental policies of governments. As a rule of thumb, travel experiences that use local people, local food, small hotels with green house-rules, non-motorised transport and as few air miles as possible (and all these offset) are better than those that do not.

On the positive side, a lot of adventure tourism is about using your energy to explore wild, off-the-beaten-track destinations, so the chances are you're being greener than beach bums, spa-users, golfers and luxury cruisers.

Index

BEST FOR…

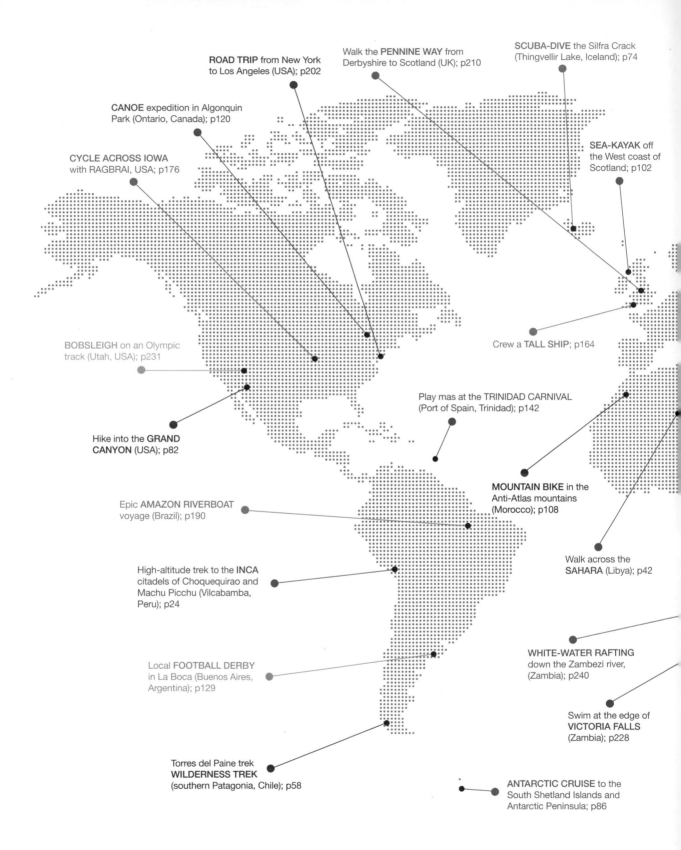

ROAD TRIP from New York to Los Angeles (USA); p202

Walk the **PENNINE WAY** from Derbyshire to Scotland (UK); p210

SCUBA-DIVE the Silfra Crack (Thingvellir Lake, Iceland); p74

CANOE expedition in Algonquin Park (Ontario, Canada); p120

SEA-KAYAK off the West coast of Scotland; p102

CYCLE ACROSS IOWA with RAGBRAI, USA; p176

BOBSLEIGH on an Olympic track (Utah, USA); p231

Crew a **TALL SHIP**; p164

Play mas at the TRINIDAD CARNIVAL (Port of Spain, Trinidad); p142

Hike into the **GRAND CANYON** (USA); p82

MOUNTAIN BIKE in the Anti-Atlas mountains (Morocco); p108

Epic **AMAZON RIVERBOAT** voyage (Brazil); p190

Walk across the **SAHARA** (Libya); p42

High-altitude trek to the **INCA** citadels of Choquequirao and Machu Picchu (Vilcabamba, Peru); p24

Local FOOTBALL DERBY in La Boca (Buenos Aires, Argentina); p129

WHITE-WATER RAFTING down the Zambezi river, (Zambia); p240

Swim at the edge of **VICTORIA FALLS** (Zambia); p228

Torres del Paine trek **WILDERNESS TREK** (southern Patagonia, Chile); p58

ANTARCTIC CRUISE to the South Shetland Islands and Antarctic Peninsula; p86

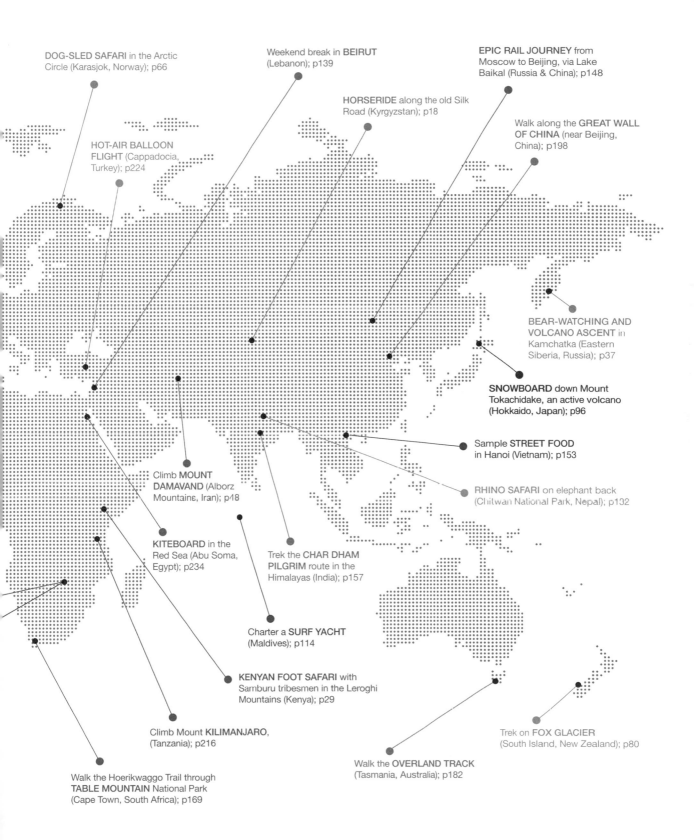

DOG-SLED SAFARI in the Arctic Circle (Karasjok, Norway); p66

Weekend break in BEIRUT (Lebanon); p139

EPIC RAIL JOURNEY from Moscow to Beijing, via Lake Baikal (Russia & China); p148

HORSERIDE along the old Silk Road (Kyrgyzstan); p18

Walk along the GREAT WALL OF CHINA (near Beijing, China); p198

HOT-AIR BALLOON FLIGHT (Cappadocia, Turkey); p224

BEAR-WATCHING AND VOLCANO ASCENT in Kamchatka (Eastern Siberia, Russia); p37

SNOWBOARD down Mount Tokachidake, an active volcano (Hokkaido, Japan); p96

Climb MOUNT DAMAVAND (Alborz Mountains, Iran); p18

Sample STREET FOOD in Hanoi (Vietnam); p153

RHINO SAFARI on elephant back (Chitwan National Park, Nepal); p132

KITEBOARD in the Red Sea (Abu Soma, Egypt); p234

Trek the CHAR DHAM PILGRIM route in the Himalayas (India); p157

Charter a SURF YACHT (Maldives); p114

KENYAN FOOT SAFARI with Samburu tribesmen in the Leroghi Mountains (Kenya); p29

Climb Mount KILIMANJARO, (Tanzania); p216

Trek on FOX GLACIER (South Island, New Zealand); p80

Walk the OVERLAND TRACK (Tasmania, Australia); p182

Walk the Hoerikwaggo Trail through TABLE MOUNTAIN National Park (Cape Town, South Africa); p169

Notes